Eric Rohmer: Interviews
Conversations with Filmmakers Series
Gerald Peary, General Editor

Eric Rohmer
INTERVIEWS

Edited by Fiona Handyside

University Press of Mississippi / Jackson

www.upress.state.ms.us

The University Press of Mississippi is a member
of the Association of American University Presses.

Copyright © 2013 by University Press of Mississippi
All rights reserved
Manufactured in the United States of America

First printing 2013

∞

Library of Congress Cataloging-in-Publication Data

Rohmer, Éric, 1920–2010.
 Eric Rohmer: interviews / edited by Fiona Handyside.
    p. cm. — (Conversations with filmmakers series)
 Includes index.
 ISBN 978-1-61703-688-0 (cloth: alk. paper) — ISBN 978-1-61703-689-7 (ebook) 1. Rohmer, Éric, 1920–2010—Interviews. 2. Motion picture producers and directors—France—Interviews. I. Handyside, Fiona, 1974– II. Title.
 PN1998.3.R64A3 2013
 791.4302'33092—dc23   2012035308

British Library Cataloging-in-Publication Data available

Contents

Introduction   vii

Chronology   xv

Filmography   xix

Eric Rohmer: An Interview   3
   Graham Petrie / 1971

Eric Rohmer: Choice and Chance   15
   Rui Nogueira / 1971

Moral Tales: Eric Rohmer Reviewed and Interviewed   28
   Beverly Walker / 1973

Rohmer's Perceval   41
   Gilbert Adair / 1978

Comedies and Proverbs: An Interview with Eric Rohmer   50
   Fabrice Ziolkowski / 1981

Eric Rohmer on Film Scripts and Film Plans   58
   Robert Hammond and Jean-Pierre Pagliano / 1982

Interview: *Pauline at the Beach*   67
   Serge Daney and Louella Interim / 1983

Celluloid and Stone   72
   Claude Beylie and Alain Carbonnier / 1984

Interview with Eric Rohmer   82
    Gérard Legrand, Hubert Niogret, and François Ramasse / 1986

Interview with Eric Rohmer   101
    Gérard Legrand and François Thomas / 1990

Eric Rohmer: Coincidences   111
    Olivier Curchod / 1992

The Amateur: An Interview with Eric Rohmer   124
    Antoine de Baecque and Thierry Jousse / 1993

Interview with Eric Rohmer   140
    Aurélien Ferenzi / 2001

Interview with Eric Rohmer: Does Cinematography Have an Artistic Function?   146
    Priska Morrissey / 2004

Interview with Eric Rohmer: Video Is Becoming Increasingly Significant   165
    Noël Herpe and Cyril Neyrat / 2004

I'm a Filmmaker, Not a Historian   170
    Philippe Fauvel and Noël Herpe / 2007

Eric Rohmer: Father of the New Wave   182
    Kaleem Aftab / 2008

Interview with Eric Rohmer: The Memory of the Figurative   185
    Philippe Fauvel and Noël Herpe / 2010

Major Interviews Given by Eric Rohmer   191

Index   197

Introduction

Despite a reputation for shyness, Eric Rohmer (1920–2010) gave many excellent, insightful, and engaging interviews over his film career in a wide variety of publications and also on television. As Gilbert Adair writes in 1978, Rohmer cut rather a solitary figure in the world of French cinema: when his New Wave contemporaries were riffing on Hollywood genres in their films, he was planning his *Contes moraux/ Moral Tales*, more indebted to the French literary tradition of libertinage than the influences of American cinema. He avoided becoming involved in the Marxist/Leninist politics of the later 1960s, holding onto his own vision of the function of cinema and society, and describing himself as a "theological" filmmaker in a landmark interview/interrogation published in 1970 in the *Cahiers du cinéma*, in which they claim to "disagree with Rohmer on every point." The fundamental disagreement concerns the very nature of cinema itself, with *Cahiers* keen to underscore their view of cinema as a form of ideological *production* of reality, and Rohmer defending a position in which cinema is understood as mechanically *reproducing* that which is outside of it. This bruising encounter, not reproduced in this collection but available to read in English in issue 54 of *Senses of Cinema*, left its mark on both sides and Rohmer never gave another interview to *Cahiers* for all of the 1970s. Ironically, however, the 1980s, 1990s, and 2000s saw Rohmer routinely interviewed by both the major French cinema journals, *Cahiers du cinéma* and *Positif*, and several of his interviews with these journals are available here for the first time in English. It was not Rohmer who changed, but the intellectual, political, and cinematic climate around him, seeming to demonstrate his point that art's progression is not teleological, but rather circular, and that modernity can sometimes appear classical and old-fashioned at certain points. He never seems to consider himself anything other than a modernist, for all that his films are constructed with dense plots, complex characterization, and a desire for transparent realist presentation. Rohmer declares to Gilbert Adair that non-narrative cinema seems passé and his films tell stories. At the same time, he emphasizes the structural nature of his cinema, so that when Carbonnier and Beylie attempt to summarize his films with an invented proverb, he returns to the geometric, claiming his films should be read as the conflict between the stable and the unstable, immobility and change. In his rendering of *Perceval* Rohmer emphasized the medieval construction of space, creating a tension between a highly stylized flat décor and the three dimensions desired by cinematic photography. This love of form endures, to the extent that in 2007 Rohmer discusses the mathematical pattern in *L'Astrée* and attributes his admiration of Murnau, Lang, and Hitchcock to their ability to invent new forms (and that he also attributes to Picasso and Cézanne in the realm of painting). These interviews allow Rohmer and his interviewers to explore the structural tension of his films as they pull between the psychological interests of detailed stories and expressive acting and the geometric abstraction of behavior, gesture, and décor, ranging as they do over his scriptwriting techniques, his interest in the presentation of space and time, his use of innovative technologies, his opinion on music, architecture, and painting, and relationships with his collaborators.

What is particularly striking about these interviews, alongside his intellectual coherence and impressive breadth of knowledge, is a twinkly-eyed charm: Rohmer is able to laugh at the ironies of fate (for example, that by the time a 1993 interview takes place, *Cahiers du cinéma* will happily discuss the influence of Balzac and realism, against structuralism) and interviewers attest to his vitality and youthful demeanor well into his eighties, an insight into the reasons why Rohmer would have commanded such loyalty from his small group of actors and crew, discussed particularly in two interviews taken from the landmark 2007 publication *Rohmer et les Autres* which examined Rohmer's world through the lens of influences and intertexts. As befits a man who proclaimed the virtues of modesty and economy in filmmaking, his interviews are not about the creation of a personal myth, or an indulgence in the cult of director as celebrity (Rohmer refuses to discuss his personal life, dismissing it as banal and irrelevant, and is vague and contradictory about such details as his date of birth). When Rohmer proclaims himself an auteur, as he does, it is not a claim based on an assertion of individual "genius," but attributed to the body of work he has created, a body of work that has been carefully elaborated and that defends his thesis that cinema is a tool that allows one to discover the beauty of the world. He privileges the cinema over art forms, he tells us, because cinema leads us back to nature itself. His philosophy of cinema is infused with a theological and ecological view, in which the role of the filmmaker is to record (and conserve) the ordered beauty of the world, rather than attempting its transformation (as an architect or a painter may). Given this view of cinema, Rohmer films almost entirely on location, and in several interviews discusses the complexities of location shooting, from the need to respect people's property when they loan it out to you for a shoot, to the need to be constantly aware of the weather—he describes his films as "slaves to the weather." Discussions of the weather, both in terms of its practical challenges for the filmmaker and its symbolic and narratological possibilities, occur frequently (on one occasion for example, Rohmer muses that Carné's decision to abandon filming due to mist would not have occurred to him, and he welcomes the way weather forces his films to accommodate themselves to chance). Of course, once it is placed onto celluloid and captured, what was contingent becomes fixed and absolute, a paradox captured in the title of Rui Nogueira's *Sight and Sound* interview which he called "Choice and Chance."

This interest in cinema's ability to preserve the constantly mutating landscape takes different directions in differing interviews, illustrating the differing perspectives interviewers open up onto Rohmer and his filmmaking techniques and philosophy. For example, in the 1986 interview in *Positif*, this interest in preservation leads to a discussion of the fragility of film stock, and Rohmer's interest in film archives. In the 1993 interview with *Cahiers du cinéma*, the interview concentrates on questions of ecology and politics, given that it focuses on *The Tree, the Mayor and the Mediatheque*, a film in which the environment as a political as well as aesthetic issue comes to the fore. In a 1985 interview, Rohmer's interest in the landscape is linked to his critical engagement with issues of architecture and urban planning. Rohmer is delighted to be asked the question, glad that his interest in urban planning is visible in his films. Rohmer argues that given the thematic similarity he imposes on his films through placing them into series, variety will come through showcasing a multitude of locations and seasons, and his films deliberately examine different milieus.

Certain themes predominate in the interviews: an interest in the relationship between cinema and the other arts (literature, theatre, and especially architecture and painting); the use of technology and the desire to keep abreast of new developments (in terms of color, sound, and digital recording); an interest in the ontology of the cinema and an indebtedness to André Bazin's view of the cinema (although he considers him rather hidebound in his fetish for the sequence shot and depth-of-field);

a desire to educate and inform, which, for Rohmer, can be part of entertainment; and, finally, a resounding defense of his stylistic principles of privileging dialogue and thought over action. This leads us to second strand in Rohmer's philosophy of filmmaking that may appear in contradistinction to his interest in external questions of season, weather, environment, space, and setting. Rohmer is also interested in interior questions: why people make the (amorous) choices they do; how they justify their choices to themselves; the complexity of negotiating new relationships alongside friendships, families, and our own romantic pasts. Rohmer's films have to find a way to make visible and audible the interior thought processes of his characters, which they do through a combination of appearance, gesture, and speech. On the one hand, this leads to an interest in the choice of actors, and their ways of behaving, particularly their gestures. A 1983 interview with *Libération* and a 1990 interview with *Positif* testify to Rohmer's interest in bringing together different modes of acting, combining actors who behave in different ways and express themselves corporeally in different manners. Above all, however, this takes us back to the vexed question of the written word that subtends the cinematic image, and the relationship between the shooting script and the finished film. Rohmer's shooting scripts for the *Moral Tales* were practically short stories (to the extent they were later published in this format), and he adapted Heinrich von Kleist, Chrétien de Troyes, Grace Elliott, and Honoré d'Urfé. Rohmer rejects the idea that the process of adaptation is so very different from that of working from an original screenplay—for Rohmer, both processes involve a kind of adaptation as the relationship between the film and its screenplay is one in which the written word provides the basis for the film, and yet is not the entire film—a film cannot be resurrected from its screenplay, whereas a theatrical play can exist as text alone independent of any one individual performance. Here, he rejects to a certain extent his declaration of the primacy of the cinema as mechanical reproduction, and proclaims that he sees adaptation as "a means to an end. A means of serving literature. Why not, after all?" This 1978 defense of adaptation as a means of resurrecting forgotten texts (and possibly an arena in which cinema serves literature, rather than competing with painting) resurfaces in 2007, when Rohmer declares that his interest in adapting Honoré d'Urfé's *Les Amours d'Astrée et de Céladon* is to give it new life and appeal to a new audience who may not have heard of it. Rohmer recounts that "my idea was to try and enable people to feel the charm that *L'Astrée* had for the generations that loved it, without modernizing it. I asked the sound engineer if he thought the characters' speeches were comprehensible for a modern audience, and he said yes, that it was more comprehensible hearing it spoken than seeing it written. That's what interested me: saying and performing this text in the cinema is to make it more accessible to today's spectators": here cinema is as much a tool of rejuvenation as of preservation.

The importance of dialogue in Rohmer's scripts and films is referred to frequently—Rohmer considers dialogue exciting and cinematic, and says that writing dialogue comes more easily than finding initial ideas for scripts. A tightly written script provides complex dialogue which carries the plot, enables deep characterization, and allows for philosophical debate in the films. The theme of the position of thought, and how we choose to represent it, itself develops through Rohmer's films, as he explains in a 1990 interview in *Positif*: "In *La Femme de l'aviateur/ The Aviator's Wife*, I expressed it naively, through people who weren't really intellectuals, and now I've taken up this theme [in *Conte de printemps/ A Tale of Springtime*]. As my films advance, certain themes are reconsidered, developed, and I think that's normal. We carry our baggage with us."

In terms of carrying baggage, Rohmer's background as a critic for and then editor of the *Cahiers du cinéma* can be strongly felt. Rohmer's interviews are peppered with references to other filmmakers: Renoir, Murnau, Hitchcock, Carné, Griffith, Godard, Rossellini. Rohmer both discusses his films in relation to their work and offers valuable insights into their films. Rohmer also happily discusses the technical organization of his shooting schedules, his (usually) small, restrained crews, and a working practice that he identifies from very early on as uniquely suited to the French cinema, which culminates in a 1993 interview where he identifies himself as an "amateur." In this remarkable consistency of vision in the interviews, which echoes the carefully constructed harmony of Rohmer's film work, we nevertheless sense both Rohmer's shifting sense of the role of cinema as it responds to wider social change, and of course, the changing approaches of his interviewers. In 1973, for example, Rohmer's films are put under a fascinating feminist microscope, in an interview which concentrates particularly on his tendency to depict "free" or "independent" women. Indeed, Rohmer's sympathy for women and an understanding of the impact of gender difference surfaces frequently, as in 1978 when he argues that women of earlier periods were subject to a much stricter etiquette governing behavior than men, or in 1971 when he tells Nogueira he shouldn't be considered an apologist for his complacent male characters. Intriguingly he seems to hint in the 1990 interview with *Positif* when he discusses *A Tale of Springtime* that the *Tales of the Four Seasons* are more interested in questions of female friendship than relations between men and women (an interpretation that could certainly be applied to both *A Tale of Springtime* and *An Autumn Tale*), but equally he is rather reluctant to comment on whether his decision to film with predominantly female crews impacts on his films. In 2001, however, his interviewer Aurélien Ferenzi ignores the "feminist" implications of Rohmer's decision to film the French Revolution from the point of view of an unmarried woman. Rohmer is asked rather whether his film would encourage an audience to sympathize with the monarch (indeed, Rohmer's depiction of the French Revolution from a broadly monarchist perspective was still considered shocking enough to have the film banned from entry at the Cannes Film festival). When a similar accusation was put to him in a *Cahiers du cinéma* interview on the same film we are unable to include for reasons of space, Rohmer's reply that while the French Revolution may be celebrated in France, we should not forget the Terror which may well be of greater political relevance to contemporary society, points to yet another Rohmerian paradox. He has an almost uncannily brilliant grasp of the contemporary (the film was released just ten days prior to 9/11), yet he rejects the label sociologist and constructs a highly personal vision of the world and his preoccupations, concerns, and pleasures.

In the range of interviews selected for this book, the entirety of Rohmer's filmmaking career is covered. Major interviews on his three main series (*The Moral Tales*; *The Comedies and Proverbs*; *The Tales of the Four Seasons*) are included, as are discussions of his "history" films and some of his "out of series" productions. Adhering to the traditional practice for University Press of Mississippi's Conversations with Filmmakers Series, the interviews selected for inclusion have not been modified at all from their original publications. As a result, there is a certain amount of repetition, but the very presence of such repetition serves only to highlight the remarkable consistency of Rohmer's vision over more than forty years of filmmaking. In all of these interviews, Rohmer ranges with ease over a variety of topics—from in-depth discussion of how the crew were organized and how casting decisions were made, to discussion of the nature of the cinema's audience, to discussion of music, painting, philosophy, and literature. There are also interviews where Rohmer discusses painting and architecture, two arts that interest him greatly in their complex relation to the cinematic. The interviews have been selected to try and bring new insights to an Anglophone public, and included are ten interviews that have previously only been available in French, all translated by myself. The aim of the book is to offer a good overview of the range and depth of Rohmer's interviews, and interviews are included from a wide range of sources, including newspapers, journals with very limited circulations, and some of the most influential film journals in the world. A summary of all major interviews in French and English is provided, along with information concerning availability of translations into English of French interviews. Not only do these interviews offer great insight into one of the most remarkable bodies of film work produced in twenty- and twenty-first-century France, they also provide us with a range of theoretical and critical insights into the cinema and its possibilities.

I would like to thank the late Peter Brunette, who was general editor of this series, for having given me the opportunity to undertake this book project. While I have long been an admirer of Rohmer's brilliant filmmaking, it has been an additional pleasure to get to know him through his interviews and to appreciate the considerable insight he brings to both his own films and film's place within French cultural life. Thanks also to Leila Salisbury at the University Press of Mississippi for her help with this process, and to the University of Exeter for granting me study leave to provide the time to finish the book. Finally, my niece Amelia Nancy Kerr Markham was born during the time this book was in preparation and it is to her that this book is dedicated with love.

FH

Chronology

1920	4 April [sometimes given as 21 March 1920], Tulle, France [location sometimes given as Nancy, France], Eric Rohmer born, né Jean-Marie Maurice Schérer, the son of Mathilde and Lucien Schérer. He has one younger brother, René Schérer, born 1922, who becomes a philosopher.
1942–50	Teaches literature in school in Nancy, France.
1946	Publishes novel *Elisabeth* under the pseudonym Gilles Cordier (Paris: Gallimard, 1946).
1948	Begins to publish articles in *La Révue du Cinéma, Les Temps Modernes, Combat,* and *Opéra*.
1949	Makes first short, *Journal d'un scelérat*.
1950	Moves to Paris and becomes founding editor of *La Gazette du Cinéma* with Jacques Rivette and Jean-Luc Godard.
1951	Begins to write articles and reviews for *Les Cahiers du Cinéma*.
1951	*Charlotte et son steak*.
1952	Begins filming *Les Petites Filles modèles*; the film remains unfinished.
1954	*Bérénice*.
1956	*Sonate à Kreutzer*.
1957–63	Editor-in-chief of the *Cahiers du Cinéma*.
1957	Publishes *Hitchcock*, a study of the filmmaker, with Claude Chabrol (Paris: Editions Universitaires, 1957) [republished 1980 and 1986: translated as *Hitchcock: The First 44 Films* by Stanley Hochman (Ungar, 1979)].
1957	Marries Thérèse Barbet—they go on to have two sons.
1958	*Véronique et son cancre*.
1959	Films *Le Signe du Lion/ The Sign of Leo* although the film is not released until 1962.
1962	*Moral Tales 1: La Boulangère de Monceau/ The Girl at the Monceau Bakery*.

1963	*Moral Tales 2: La Carrière de Suzanne/ Suzanne's Career.*
1964	*Nadja à Paris* and *Place de l'Etoile.*
1964–70	Makes educational films for schoolchildren under the auspices of *Institut Pédagogique Nationale.*
1965	Two films for television series *Cinéastes de notre temps*: *Carl Th. Dreyer* and *Le Celluloïd et le Marbre.*
1966	*Une étudiante d'aujourd'hui.*
1967	*Moral Tales 4: La Collectionneuse.* Wins Silver Bear Jury Extraordinary Prize at the Berlin Film Festival 1967.
1968	*Fermière à Montfaucon.*
1969	*Moral Tales 3: Ma Nuit Chez Maud/ My Night at Maud's.* Nominated for Best Foreign Film at the Academy Awards and Palme d'Or at the Cannes Film Festival and wins Le Prix Méliès. Wins Best Screenplay at New York Film Critics Circle Awards and at National Society of Film Critics Awards (USA).
1970	*Moral Tales 5: Le Genou de Claire/ Claire's Knee.* Wins Le Prix Louis-Delluc, Le Prix Méliès, and the San Sebastián Film Festival.
1972	*Moral Tales 6: L'Amour l'après-midi/ Love in the Afternoon.* Publication of postface to *Charlie Chaplin* by André Bazin (Paris: Cerf, 1972).
1974	Publication of short stories *Six Contes moraux* (Paris: L'Herne, 1974).
1975	Four-part television series *Ville Nouvelle* transmitted 10 August–22 September.
1976	*Die Marquise von O.* Wins Grand Prix Spécial du Jury at the Cannes Film Festival.
1977	Publication of *L'Organisation de l'espace dans le Faust de Murnau* [doctoral thesis], (Paris: UGE, 1977).
1979	*Perceval le Gallois/ Perceval.* Wins Le Prix Méliès. Directs a stage production of Kleist's *Catherine de Heilbronnn* at the Théâtre des Amandiers in Nanterre at the Festival d'Automne starring Pascale Ogier and Pascal Greggory. Recorded and transmitted on television 6 August 1980.
1981	*Comedies and Proverbs: La Femme de l'Aviateur/ The Aviator's Wife.*
1982	*Comedies and Proverbs: Le Beau Mariage/ A Good Marriage.* Nominated for César for Best Original Screenplay.
1983	*Comedies and Proverbs: Pauline à la plage/ Pauline at the*

	Beach. Wins FIPRESCI Prize and Silver Berlin Bear for Best Director at the Berlin Film Festival 1983. Wins Best Screenplay at the Boston Society of Film Critics Awards. Wins Le Prix Méliès.
1984	*Comedies and Proverbs: Les Nuits de la pleine lune/ Full Moon in Paris.* Nominated for César for Best Director, Best Film, Best Original Screenplay. Wins Le Prix Méliès. Publication of a collection of his articles on cinema: *Le Goût de la Beauté* (Paris: Editions de l'Etoile, 1984) [English translation by Carol Volk, *The Taste for Beauty*, published 1990 by Cambridge University Press].
1986	*Comedies and Proverbs: Le Rayon vert/ The Green Ray/ Summer.* Wins FIPRESCI Prize and the Golden Lion at the Venice Film Festival. Directs pop music video with Rosette and Pascal Greggory for Jean-Louis Valéro's *Bois ton café.*
1987	*4 Aventures de Reinette et Mirabelle/ 4 Adventures of Reinette and Mirabelle. Comedies and Proverbs: L'Ami de mon amie/ My Girlfriend's Boyfriend/ Girlfriends and Boyfriends.* Nominated for César for Best Screenplay, Original or Adaptation. Awarded Prix Special du Festival at the Montréal Film Festival for the Comedies and Proverbs cycle, on the occasion of the presentation of *L'Ami de mon amie* in competition. Rohmer directs his own play *Le trio en mi bémol: comédie brève en sept tableaux* with Pascal Greggory and Jessica Forde at Théâtre Renaud-Barrault. The play is recorded in a studio in Toulouse and transmitted on television 11 May 1988.
1988	Publication of his play *Le trio en mi bémol: comédie brève en sept tableaux* (Arles: Actes Sud, 1988).
1990	*Tales of the Four Seasons: Conte de printemps/ A Tale of Springtime.*
1992	*Tales of the Four Seasons: Conte d'hiver/ A Winter's Tale.* Wins FIPRESCI Prize and Prize of the Ecumenical Jury—Special Mention at the Berlin Film Festival 1992. Nominated for Berlin Golden Bear. Writes preface to new edition of Balzac's *La Rabouilleuse* [*The Black Sheep*] (Paris: POL, 1992).
1993	*L'Arbre, le Maire et la Médiathèque/ The Tree, the Mayor and the Mediatheque.* Wins FIPRESCI Prize Special Distinction [presented out of competition] at the Montréal Film Festival.

1995	*Les Rendez-vous de Paris/ Rendezvous in Paris.*
1996	*Tales of the Four Seasons: Conte d'été/ A Summer's Tale.* Publication of *De Mozart en Beethoven: essai sur la notion du profondeur en musique* (Arles/Paris: Actes Sud, 1996).
1996–98	Makes several television programs in the series *Anniversaires*.
1998	*Tales of the Four Seasons: Conte d'automne/ An Autumn Tale.* Nominated for Best Foreign Language Film at Chicago Film Critics Association Awards. Wins Best Foreign Language Film at National Society of Film Critics Awards (USA). Nominated for Golden Lion at the Venice Film Festival. Wins Golden Osella for Best Original Screenplay and Sergio Trasatti Award Special Mention at the Venice Film Festival. Publication of screenplays *Contes des quatre saisons* (Paris: Editions de l'Etoile, 1998).
1999	Publication of screenplays *Comédies et Proverbes*, vols. 1 and 2 (Paris: Editions de l'Etoile, 1999).
1998–2004	Makes several television programs in the series *Le modèle*.
2001	*L'Anglaise et le Duc/ The Lady and the Duke.* Nominated for Best Director at the European Film Awards. Awarded Career Golden Lion at the Venice Film Festival. Writes preface to Grace Elliott's *Journal de ma vie durant la Révolution française* (Paris: Editions de Paris, 2001).
2004	*Triple Agent.* Nominated for Golden Bear at the Berlin Film Festival. Publication of screenplay to *Triple Agent* (Paris: Editions de l'Etoile, 2004). Full retrospective of all his films held at the Cinémathèque française.
2007	*Les Amours d'Astrée et de Céladon/ The Romance of Astrea and Celadon.* Nominated for Golden Lion at the Venice Film Festival.
2010	11 January, Rohmer dies in Paris and is buried in Montparnasse cemetery. 8 February, "soirée hommage" held at the Cinémathèque française, including a screening of *Claire's Knee* and a short film made in his memory by Jean-Luc Godard.

Filmography

This filmography separates feature films and shorts (including an episode from a multi-director film). This has led for example to the splitting of the *Moral Tales*, of which the first two are shorts. Television programs Rohmer worked on are not included. *The Green Ray* is legally classified as a telefilm as it was released on a paying television channel three days before its cinematic release, but I have nevertheless included it as a feature-length film. English language titles are given where a film has been released in the UK or the USA. If UK and US titles differ, both are given, with the UK title leading. Dates given are dates of first cinematic release, where relevant, rather than those of production.

A detailed crew list is given for the films, which emphasizes the difference between the tiny crews associated with the films made by the Compagnie Eric Rohmer, the production company founded in the mid-1980s, and the much larger crew required for productions such as *The Lady and the Duke* and *Triple Agent*. This filmography has been constructed from information given in *Cahiers du cinéma*, *Sight and Sound*, and Philippe Fauvel's excellent work in Noël Herpe, *Rohmer et les Autres* (Presses Universitaires de Rennes, 2007). A word should also be added on terminology: Rohmer preferred the term *image* to that of *cinematography* (see his discussion of this in "Does Cinematography Have an Artistic Function?" with Priska Morrissey in 2004), and I have followed his preferred style.

Feature films

LES PETITES FILLES MODÈLES (1952)
Director: **Eric Rohmer**
Script: **Eric Rohmer**, based on the novel by la Comtesse de Ségur
Technical Advisor: Pierre Guilbaud.
Director of Photography: Jean-Yves Tierce, assisted by Guy Delattre and André Tixador
Continuity: Sylvette Baudrot

Sound: Bernard Clarens, assisted by André Soler
Recorder: Cancade
Editing: Jean Mitry
Production: Consortium parisien de production cinématographique, Guy de Ray (director of production), Joseph Kéké (assistant)
Cast: Marie-Hélène Mounier (Sophie Fincini), Martine Laisné (Camille de Fleurville), Anna Misonzine or Michouze or Michonze (Madeleine de Fleurville), Catherine Clément (Marguerite de Rosbourg), Josette Sinclair (Mme de Fleurville), Josée Doucet (Mme de Rosbourg), Olga Ken (Mme Fichini), Jean-Yves Tierce (Hurel, the butcher)
Length: unknown (film unfinished)
Format: 35mm, black and white, 1.33

LE SIGNE DU LION/ THE SIGN OF LEO (1962)
Director: **Eric Rohmer**, assisted by Jean-Charles Lagneau and Philippe Collin
Script: **Eric Rohmer**, with the participation for dialogue of Paul Gégauff
Director of Photography: Nicolas Hayer, assisted by Pierre Lhomme, Alain Levant, and Robert Caristan
Continuity: Helly Stérianl
On-Set Production: Jean Lavie
Set Photographer: André Dino
Sound: Jean Labussière, assisted by René Bourdier
Recorder: Christian Courmes
Editing: Anne-Marie Cotret, assisted by Monique Gaillard and Monique Teisseire
Music: Louis Saguet
Production: Claude Chabrol (Ajym films), Jean Cotet (production director), Roland Nonin (assistant), Yvonne Benezech (administrative support)
Cast: Jess Hahn (Pierre Wesselrin), Michèle Girardon (Dominique Laurent), Van Doude (Jean-François Santeuil), Paul Bisciglia (Willy), Gilbert Edard (Michel Caron), Christian Alers (Philippe), Paul Crauchet (Fred); Jill Olivier (Cathy), Sophie Perrault (Chris), Stéphane Audran (the landlady), Jean Le Poulain (the tramp), Malka Ribowska (mother of two children), Macha Méril (blonde girl on 14 July), Françoise Prévost (Hélène), Jean-Luc Godard (the music lover), Jean Domarchi, Enrico Fulchignoni, Fereydoun Hoveyda, José Varela, Uta Taeger, Daniel Crohem, Véra Valmont, Yann Groël, Jean-Marie Arnoux, Gabriel Blondé

Length: 100 minutes
Format: 35mm, black and white, 1.33

SIX MORAL TALES, 4: LA COLLECTIONNEUSE (1967)
Director: **Eric Rohmer**, assisted by Laszlo Benko and Patrice de Bailliencourt
Script: **Eric Rohmer**, with participation for dialogue by Patrick Bauchau, Haydée Politoff, and Daniel Pommereulle
Technical Advisor: François Bogard
Director of Photography: Nestor Almendros
Editing: Jacqueline Raynal, assisted by Anne Dubot
Music: Blossom Toes and Giorgio Gomeslky
Production: Barbet Schroeder (Les Films du Losange), Georges de Beauregard (Rome-Paris Films)
Cast: Patrick Bauchau (Adrien), Haydée Politoff (Haydée), Daniel Pommereulle (Daniel), Alain Jouffroy (the writer), Mijanou Bardot (Mijanou), Annick Morice (Annick), Seymour Hertzberg or Eugène Archer (Sam), Brian Belshaw (Haydée's lover), Patrice de Baillencourt and Pierre-Richard Bré (Haydée's friends in the car), Donald Cammell (the boy in St-Tropez), Alfred de Graaf (the lost tourist), Denis Barry (Charlie)
Length: 90 minutes
Format: 35 mm, color, 1.33

SIX MORAL TALES, 3: MA NUIT CHEZ MAUD/ MY NIGHT AT MAUD'S (1969)
Director and Script: **Eric Rohmer**, adapted from an original idea by Alfred de Graaf
Director of Photography: Nestor Almendros, assisted by Emmanuel Machuel
Electrical and Camera: Jean-Claude Gasché and Philippe Rousselot
Set: Nicole Rachline
Sound: Jean-Pierre Ruh, assisted by Alain Sempé
Editing: Cécile Decugis, assisted by Christine Lecouvette.
Sound Mixer: Jacques Maumont
Music: Mozart
Production: Barbet Schroeder and Pierre Cottrell (Les Films du Losange), Alfred de Graaf and Pierre Grimberg, FFP, Simar Films, Les Films du Carrosse, Les Production de la Guéville, Renn Productions, Les Films de la Pléaide, Les Films des Deux Mondes

Cast: Jean-Louis Trintignant (the narrator), Françoise Fabien (Maud), Antoine Vitez (Vidal), Marie-Christine Barrault (Françoise), Léonide Kogan (the violinist), Father Guy Léger (the priest), Anne Dubot (the blonde friend), Marie Becker (Marie), Marie-Claude Rauzier (the student), and the engineers of the Clermont-Ferrand Michelin factory
Length: 107 minutes
Format: 35 mm, black and white, 1.33

SIX MORAL TALES, 5: LE GENOU DE CLAIRE/ CLAIRE'S KNEE (1970)
Director: **Eric Rohmer**, assisted by Claude Bertrand, Claudine Guillemin, and Lorraine Santoni
Script: **Eric Rohmer**, adapted from an original idea by Alfred de Graaf
Director of Photography: Nestor Almendros, assisted by Jean-Claude Rivière and Philippe Rousselot
Electricity and Camera: Jean-Claude Gasché and Louis Balthazard
Continuity: Michel Fleury
On-Set Production: Alfred de Graaf
Set Photographer: Bernard Prim
Sound: Jean-Pierre Ruh, assisted by Michel Laurent
Editing: Cécile Decugis, assisted by Martine Kalfon
Production: Pierre Cottrell and Barbet Schroeder (Les Films du Losange)
Cast: Jean-Claude Brialy (Jérôme), Aurora Cornu (Aurora), Béatrice Romand (Laura), Laurence de Monaghan (Claire), Michèle Montel (Mme Walter), Gérard Falconetti (Gilles), Fabrice Luchini (Vincent), Sandro Franchina (the Italian at the dance), Isabelle Pons (Lucinde)
Length: 105 minuntes
Format: 35mm, color, 1.33

SIX MORAL TALES, 6: L'AMOUR, L'APRÈS-MIDI/ LOVE IN THE AFTERNOON (1972)
Director: **Eric Rohmer**, assisted by Claude Bertrand, Claudine Guillemin, and Lorraine Santoni
Script: **Eric Rohmer**
Director of Photography: Nestor Almendros, assisted by Jean-Claude Rivière and Philippe Rousselot
Electricity and Camera: Albert Vasseur and Fernand Coquet
Set: Nicole Rachline
Costumes: Daniel Hechtor-Vog
Hair and Makeup: Karl Moisant
Set Photographer: Bernard Prim

Sound: Jean-Pierre Ruh, assisted by Michel Laurent
Editing: Cécile Decugis, assisted by Martine Kalfon
Sound Mixer: Jacques Carrère
Music: Arié Dezierlakta
Production: Pierre Cottrell and Barbet Schroeder (Les Films du Losange), with Columbia
Cast: Bernard Verley (Frédéric), Zouzou (Chloé), Françoise Verley (Hélène), Daniel Ceccaldi (Gérard), Malvina Penne (Fabienne), Babette Ferrier (Martine), Frédérique Hender (Mme M.), Claude-Jean Philippe (Mr. M), Sylvaine Charlet (the landlady), Danièle Malat (the client), Suze Randall (the nanny), Tina Michelino (the traveler), Jean-Louis Livi (the friend), Pierre Nunzi (the shopkeeper), Irène Skobline (the shopkeeper), Silvia Badescu (a student), Claude Berrand (a student), Françoise Fabien, Marie-Christine Barrault, Haydée Politoff, Aurora Cornu, Laurence de Monaghan and Béatrice Romand (the women in Frédéric's dream)
Length: 98 minutes
Format: 35mm, color, 1.33

DIE MARQUISE VON O... / THE MARQUISE OF O (1976)
Director: **Eric Rohmer**
Script: **Eric Rohmer**, adapted from the novel by Heinrich von Kleist
Historical Research: Hervé Grandsart
Director of Photography: Nestor Almendros, assisted by Jean-Claude Rivière, Dominique Le Rigoleur, Bernard Auroux, and Roswitha Hecke
Electricity and camera: Jean-Claude Gasché, Georges Chrétien, Angelo Rizzi, and André Trieli
Set and Dressing: Roger von Moellendorff, Rolf Kaden, Helo Gutschwager, and Bernhard Frey
Costumes: Moidele Bickel, assisted by Dagmar Niefind
Continuity: Marion Müller
Set Photography: Roswitha Hecke
Sound: Jean-Pierre Ruh and Louis Gimel, assisted by Michel Laurent
Editing: Cécile Decugis, assisted by Annie Leconte
Sound Mixing: Alex Pront
Music: Roger Delmotte
Production: Klaus Hellwig (Janus Film Production), Barbet Schroeder (Les Films du Losange), Margaret Ménégoz (director of production), Jochen Girsch and Harald Vogel, with Artemis, HR, and Gaumont
Cast: Edith Clever (the marquise Juliette), Bruno Ganz (the count), Peter

Lühr (the marquise's father), Edda Seippel (the marquise's mother), Otto Sander (the marquise's brother), Ruth Drexel (the midwife), Hesso Huber (the porter), Bernhard Frey (Leonardo), Eduard Linkers (the doctor), Erich Schachinger (the Russian general), **Eric Rohmer** and Richard Rogner (Russian officers), Franz Pikola and Theo de Maal (citizens), Thomas Straus (the messenger), Volker Frätchel (the priest), Marion Müller and Heidi Möller (servants), Petra Meier and Manuela Mayer (the marquise's daughters)
Length: 100 minutes
Format: 35mm, color, 1.33

PERCEVAL LE GALLOIS/ PERCEVAL (1979)
Director: **Eric Rohmer**, assisted by Guy Chalaud
Script: **Eric Rohmer**, adapted from the story by Chrétien de Troyes
Director of Photography: Nestor Almendros, assisted by Jean-Claude Rivière and Florent Bazin
Electricity and Camera: Jean-Claude Gasché and Georges Chrétien
Set: Jean-Pierre Kohut-Svelko, assisted by Pierre Duquesne and Emmanuel Peduzzi
Hair: Daniel Mourgues
Master of Arms: Claude Carliez
Horse Training and Handling: François Nadal
Set Photography: Bernard Prim
Sound: Jean-Pierre Ruh, assisted by Jacques Pibarot and Louis Gimel
Editing: Cécile Decugis, assisted by Jill Reix
Sound Mixing: Dominique Hennequin
Sound Effects: Jonathan Liebling
Music: Guy Robert
Production: Barbet Schroeder (Les Films du Losange), Margaret Ménégoz (production director), with FR3, ARD, SSR, RAI TV, and Gaumont
Cast: Fabrice Luchini (Perceval), André Dussollier (Gawain), Solange Boulanger (song, guitar, a maid, a lady, etc.), Catherine Schroeder (song and rebec), Francisco Orozco (song, lute, and medieval horn), Deborah Nathan (flute), Jean-Paul Racadon (song, mediaeval recorder, knight at arms, a valet, etc.), Alain Servé (song and mediaeval recorder, the fool, the bald gentleman, a valet, a knight, etc.), Daniel Tattare (song, a woodsman, Yvonet, Garin, the Vassal, a pilgrim, etc.), Pascale Ogier (song, a maid, a lady), Nicolaï Arutene (song, a valet, a knight), Marie Rivière and Pascale Gervais de Lafond (maids, dames, and Garin's daughters), Pascale de Boysson (a widow), Clémentine

Amouroux (the maid in the tent), Jacques Le Carpentier (the prideful man), Antoine Baud (the scarlet knight), Jocelyn Boisseau (the laughing maiden), Marc Eytaud (King Arthur), Gérard Falconetti (Ké), Raoul Billerey (Gornemont de Goort), Arielle Dombasle (Blancefleur), Sylvain Levignac (Anguingueron), Claude Jaeger (Thiébaut of Tintaguel), Michel Etcheverry (the Fisher King), Frédérique Cerbonnet (Thiébaut's eldest daughter), Anne-Laure Meury (the maiden with short sleeves), Frédéric Norbert (the king of Escavalon), Christine Lietot (the King's sister), Hubert Gignoux (the hermit), Jean-Claude Brisseau, Lisa Hérédia (artisans)
Length: 138 minutes
Format: 35mm, color, 1.33

COMEDIES AND PROVERBS: LA FEMME DE L'AVIATEUR/ THE AVIATOR'S WIFE (1981)
Direction and Script: **Eric Rohmer**
Director of Photography: Bernard Lutic, assisted by Romain Winding
Sound: Georges Prat, assisted by Gérard Lecas
On-Set Production: Hervé Grandsart
Sound Mixing: Dominique Hennequin
Music: Jean-Louis Valéro
Production: Margaret Ménégoz (Les Films du Losange)
Cast: Philippe Marlaud (François), Marie Rivière (Anne), Anne-Laure Meury (Lucie), Mathieu Carrière (Christian), Philippe Caroit (a friend), Coralie Clément (a colleague), Lisa Hérédia (a friend), Haydée Caillot (the blonde woman), Mary Stephen and Neil Chan (the tourists), Rosette (the concierge), Fabrice Luchini (Mercillat)
Length: 104 minutes
Format: 16mm blown up to 35mm, color, 1.33

COMEDIES AND PROVERBS: LE BEAU MARIAGE/ A GOOD MARRIAGE (1982)
Direction and Script: **Eric Rohmer**
Director of Photography: Bernard Lutic, assisted by Romain Winding and Nicolas Brunet
Paintings: Alberto Bali
Painted Silks: Gérard Deligne
Antiques: Hélène Rossignol
On-Set Production: Marie Bouteloup and Hervé Grandsart
Sound: Georges Prat, assisted by Gérard Lecas

Editing: Cécile Decugis, assisted by Lisa Hérédia
Music: Ronan Girre, Simon des Innocentes
Production: Margaret Ménégoz (Les Films du Losange), Les Films du Carrosse
Cast: Beatrice Romand (Sabine), André Dussollier (Edouard), Arielle Dombasle (Clarisse), Féodor Atkine (Simon), Huguette Fagier (the antiques dealer), Thamila Mezbah (Sabine's mother), Sophie Renoir (Lise), Hervé Duhamel (Frédéric), Pascal Greggory (Nicolas), Virginie Thévenet (the bride), Denise Bailly (the countess), Vincent Gautier (Claude), Anne Mercier (the secretary), Catherine Réthi (the client), Patrick Lambert (man on train)
Length: 97 minutes
Format: 35mm, color, 1.33

COMEDIES AND PROVERBS: PAULINE À LA PLAGE/ PAULINE AT THE BEACH (1983)
Direction and Script: **Eric Rohmer**
Image: Nestor Almendros, assisted by Florent Bazin and Jean Coudsi
Sound: Georges Prat, assisted by Gérard Lecas
Editing: Cécile Decugis, assisted by Caroline Thivel
On-Set Production: Marie Bouteloup and Hervé Grandsart, assisted by Michel Ferry
Sound Mixing: Dominique Hennequin
Music: Jean-Louis Valéro
Production: Margaret Ménégoz (Les Films du Losange), Les Films Ariane
Cast: Amanda Langlet (Pauline), Arielle Dombasle (Marion), Pascal Greggory (Pierre), Féodor Atkine (Henri), Simon de la Brousse (Sylvain), Rosette (Louisette), Marie Bouteloup (Marie), Michel Ferry (Sylvain's brother)
Length: 94 minutes
Format: 35mm, color, 1.33

COMEDIES AND PROVERBS: LES NUITS DE LA PLEINE LUNE/ FULL MOON IN PARIS (1984)
Direction and Script: **Eric Rohmer**
Image: Renato Berra, assisted by Jean-Paul Toraille and Gilles Arnaud
Set: Pascale Ogier
Furniture: Lucas Hillen
Costumes: Dorothée bis (for Pascale Ogier), Marie Beltrami (for Virginie Thévenet), Michel Cadestin, and Michel Toraille

Makeup: Geneviève Peyrelade
On-Set Production: Jean-Marc Deschamps, assisted by Philippe Delest
Sound: Georges Prat, assisted by Gérard Lecas
Editing: Cécile Decugis, assisted by Lisa Hérédia
Sound Mixing: Dominique Hennequin
Music: Elli et Jacno, Paul Delmet, and Charles Fallot
Production: Margaret Ménégoz (Les Films du Losange), Les Films Ariane
Cast: Pascale Ogier (Louise), Tchéky Karyo (Rémi), Fabrice Luchini (Olivier), Virginie Thévenet (Camille), Christian Vadim (Bastien), Lazlo Szabo (the painter in the café), Lisa Garneri (Tina), Mathieu Schiffman (Louise's companion), Anne-Séverine Liotard (Marianne), Hervé Grandsart (Bertrand), Noël Coffman (Stanislas)
Length: 102 minutes
Format; 35mm, color, 1.33

COMEDIES AND PROVERBS: LE RAYON VERT/ THE GREEN RAY/ SUMMER (1986)
Director: **Eric Rohmer**
Script: **Eric Rohmer**, with assistance for dialogue by Marie Rivière
Image: Sophie Maintigneux
On-Set Production: Françoise Etchegaray
Sound: Claudine Nougaret
Editing: Marie Luisa Garcia (Lisa Hérédia)
Special Effects: Philippe Demard
Sound Mixing: Dominique Hennequin
Music: Jean-Louis Valéro
Production: Margaret Ménégoz (Les Films du Losange), with participation from the Ministry of Culture, the Ministry of the Post Office and Communication, Pierre Chatard, and Gérard Lomond
Cast: Marie Rivière (Delphine), and in Paris: Amira Chémakhi and Sylvie Richez (secretaries); Lisa Hérédia (Manuella), Basile Gervaise (the pensioner), Virginie Gervaise and René Hernandez (friends), Dominique Rivière (Dominique), Claude Jullien (Claude), Alaric Jullien (Alaric), Laetitia Rivière (Bibiche), Isabelle Rivière (Isabelle), Béatrice Romand (Béatrice), Rosette (Françoise), Marcello Pezzutto (guy who chats girls up), Irène Skobline (Irène); in Cherbourg: Eric Hamm (Edouard), Gérard Quéré, Julie Quéré, Brigitte Poulain, Gérard Leleu, Liliane Leleu, Vanessa Leleu and Huger Foote (Françoise's family and friends); in La Plagne: Michel Labourre (Michel), Paulo (Paulo); in Biarritz: Maria-Couto-Palas, Isa Bonnet, Yve Doyhamboure (women chatting);

Friedrich Günter Christlein (the professor), Paulette Christlein (his wife), Carita (Léna), Marc Vivas (Pierrot), Joël Comarlot (Joël), Vincent Gauthier (stranger at the station)
Length: 98 minutes
Format: 16mm blown up to 35mm, color, 1.33

4 AVENTURES DE REINETTE AND MIRABELLE/ FOUR ADVENTURES OF REINETTE AND MIRABELLE (1987)
Direction and Script: **Eric Rohmer**
Image: Sophie Maintigneux
Paintings: Joëlle Miquel
Sound: Pascal Ribier, and for section *L'Heure bleue*: Pierre Camus
Editing: Marie Luisa Garcia (Lisa Hérédia)
Sound Mixing: Paul Bértault
Music: Ronan Girre and Jean-Louis Valéro
Production: Françoise Etchegaray (CER), Margaret Ménégoz (Les Films du Losange)
Cast: Joëlle Miquel (Reinette), Jessica Forde (Mirabelle), and for *L'Heure bleue*: M and Mme Housseau (the neighbors); and for *Les Garçons du café*: Philippe Laudenbach (waiter), François-Marie Banier and Jean-Claude Brisseau (passers-by); and for *Le Mendiant, la Kleptomane et l'Arnaqueuse*: Gérard Courant and Béatrice Romand (the inspectors), Yasmine Haury (the kleptomaniac), Marie Rivière (the hustler), Haydée Caillot (the charitable lady), David Rocksavage (the English tourist), Jacques Auffray (the beggar); and for *La Vente du tableau*: Fabrice Luchini (the gallery owner), Françoise Valier and Marie Bouteloup (the visitors)
Length: 97 minutes
Format: 16mm blown up to 35mm, color, 1.33

COMEDIES AND PROVERBS: L'AMI DE MON AMIE/ MY GIRLFRIEND'S BOYFRIEND/ GIRLFRIENDS AND BOYFRIENDS (1987)
Direction and Script: **Eric Rohmer**
Image: Bernard Lutic, assisted by Sabine Lancelin and Sophie Maintigneux
On-Set Production: Françoise Etchegaray
Sound: Georges Prat, assisted by Pascal Ribier
Editing: Marie Luisa Garcia (Lisa Hérédia), assisted by Anne Moulahem and Annick Hurst
Sound Mixing: Dominique Hennequin

Music: Jean-Louis Valéro
Production: Margaret Ménégoz (Les Films du Losange), with Investimage
Cast: Emmanuelle Chaulet (Blanche), Sophie Renoir (Léa), Anne-Laure Meury (Adrienne), Eric Veillard (Fabien), François-Eric Gendron (Alexandre)
Length: 103 minutes
Format: 35mm, color, 1.33

TALES OF THE FOUR SEASONS: CONTE DE PRINTEMPS/ A TALE OF SPRINGTIME (1990)
Direction and Script: **Eric Rohmer**
Image: Luc Pagès, assisted by Philippe Renaud and Bruno Dubet
Sound: Pascal Ribier, assisted by Ludovic Hénault
Editing: Marie Luisa Garcia (Lisa Hérédia), assisted by Françoise Combes
Sound Mixing: Jean-Pierre Laforce
Dubbing: Gil Bast and Pascale Bastien-Coulon
Music: Beethoven, Schumann, Jean-Louis Valéro
Production: Margaret Ménégoz (Les Films du Losange), Françoise Etchegaray (production director), assisted by Edouard Girardet with Investimage
Cast: Anne Teyssèdre (Jeanne), Hugues Quester (Igor), Florence Darel (Natacha), Eloïse Bennett (Eve), Sophie Robin (Gaëlle), Marc Lelou, François Lamore
Length: 106 minutes
Format: 35mm, color, 1.66

TALES OF THE FOUR SEASONS: CONTE D'HIVER/ A WINTER'S TALE (1992)
Direction and Script: **Eric Rohmer**
Image: Luc Pagès, assisted by Phillipe Renaud and for the Shakespeare play Maurice Girard
Costumes for the Shakespeare Play: Pierre-Jean Larroque
Sound: Pascal Ribier, assisted by Ludovic Hénault
Editing: Mary Stephen
Sound Mixing: Jean-Pierre Laforce
Music: Sébastien Erms [**Eric Rohmer** and Mary Stephen]
Production: Margaret Ménégoz (Les Films du Losange), Françoise Etchegaray (production director), assisted by Jean-Luc Revol with Investimage-Sofiarp and Canal +
Cast: Charlotte Véry (Félicie), Frédéric van der Dreissche (Charles),

Michel Voletti (Maxence), Hervé Furic (Loïc), Ava Loraschi (Elise), Christiane Desbois (Félicie's mother), Rosette (Félicie's sister), Jean-Luc Revol (Félicie's brother-in-law), Haydée Caillot (Edwige), Jean-Claude Biette (Quentin), Marie Rivière (Dora), Claudine Paringaux (a customer), and for the Shakespeare play: Roger Dumas (Léontès), Danièle Lebrun (Paulina), Diane Lepvrier (Hermione), Edwige Navarro (Perdita), François Rauscher (Florizel), Daniel Tarrare (Polyxène), Eric Wapler and Gaston Richard (lords), Maria Coin (flutist)
Length: 112 minutes
Format: Super 16 blown up to 35mm, color, 1.66

L'ARBRE, LE MAIRE ET LA MÉDIATHÈQUE, or LES SEPT HASARDS/ THE TREE, THE MAYOR AND THE MEDIATHEQUE (1993)
Direction and Script: **Eric Rohmer**
Image: Diane Baratier
Sound: Pascal Ribier
Editing: Mary Stephen
Music: Sébastien Erms [**Eric Rohmer** and Mary Stephen]
Production: Françoise Etchegaray (CER)
Cast: Pascal Greggory (Julien Dechaumes), Arielle Dombasle (Bérénice Beaurivage), Fabrice Luchini (Marc Rossignol), Clémentine Amouroux (Blandine Lenoir), François-Marie Banier (Régis-Lebrun Blondet), Michel Jaouën (Antoine Pergola), Jean Parvulesco (Jean Walter), Galaxie Barbouth (Zoé Rossignol), Jessica Schwing (Véga Dechaumes), Raymonde Fatu (secretary), Manuella Hesse (the au pair), Françoise Etchegaray (Mme Rossignol), Solange Blanchet (the mayor's secretary), Mathé Pillaud (the shepherd), Isabelle Prévost and Michel Tisseau (the artists), Jacky Brunet (the local worthy), Martin de Courcel (the philosopher), Jean-Claude Pubert (the student), Suzanne Thony (the shop keeper), Gaby Augin (the retired woman), Michel Bernard (the farmer), Rémy Rousseau (the bellringer)
Length: 108 minutes
Format: 16mm blown up to 35mm, color, 1.33

LES RENDEZ-VOUS DE PARIS/ RENDEZVOUS IN PARIS (1995)
Direction and Script: **Eric Rohmer**
Image: Diane Baratier
Paintings: Pierre de Chevilly
Sound: Pascal Ribier
Editing: Mary Stephen

Music: Sébastien Erms [**Eric Rohmer** and Mary Stephen]
Production: Françoise Etchegaray (CER)
Cast: For *Le Rendez-vous de 7 heures*: Clara Bellat (Esther), Antoine Basler (Horace), Mathias Mégard (guy who chats girls up), Judith Chancel (Aricie), Malcolm Conrath (Félix), Cécile Parès (Hermione), Olivier Pujol (the waiter); *Les Bancs de Paris*: Aurore or Florence Rauscher (her), Serge Renko (him); *Mère et enfant, 1907*: Michaël Kraft (painter), Bénédicte Loyen (the young woman), Veronika Johansson (the Swede)
Length: 100 minutes
Format: 16mm blown up to 35mm, color, 1.33

TALES OF THE FOUR SEASONS: CONTE D'ÉTÉ/ A SUMMER'S TALE (1996)
Direction and Script: **Eric Rohmer**
Image: Diane Baratier, assisted by Xavier Tauveron
Sound: Pascal Ribier, assisted by Frédéric de Ravignan
Editing: Mary Stephen
Music: Philippe Eidel, Sébastien Erms [**Eric Rohmer** and Mary Stephen]
Production: Margaret Ménégoz (Les Films du Losange), Françoise Etchegaray (production director), assisted by Franck Bouvat and Bathsabée Dreyfus, La Sept Cinéma, with Canal + and Sofilmka
Cast: Melvil Poupard (Gaspard), Amanda Langlet (Margot), Gwenaëlle Simon (Solène), Aurélia Nolin (Léna), Aimé Lefèvre (the Newfoundlander), Alain Guellauf (Uncle Alan), Evelyne Lahana (Aunt Maïwenn), Yves Guérin (the accordion player), Franck Cabot (Léna's cousin)
Length: 112 minutes
Format: 35mm, color, 1.66

TALES OF THE FOUR SEASONS: CONTE D'AUTOMNE/ AN AUTUMN TALE (1998)
Direction and Script: **Eric Rohmer**
Image: Diane Baratier, assisted by Thierry Faure, Franck Bouvat, Bethsabée Dreyfus, and Jérôme Duc-Maugé
Sound: Pascal Ribier, assisted by Frédéric de Ravignan and Nathalie Vidal
Editing: Mary Stephen
Music: Claude Marti, Gérard Pansanel, Pierre Peyras, Antonello Salis
Production: Margaret Ménégoz (Les Films du Losange), Françoise Etchegaray (production director), assisted by Florence Rauscher, La Sept Cinéma, with Canal +, Sofilmka, and Rhônes-Alpes Cinéma

Cast: Marie Rivière (Isabelle), Béatrice Romand (Magali), Alain Libolt (Gérard), Didier Sandre (Etienne), Alexia Portal (Rosine), Stéphane Darmon (Léo), Aurélia Alcaïs (Emilia), Matthieu Davette (Grégoire), Yves Alcaïs (Jean-Jacques), Claire Mathurin (Augustine)
Length: 110 minutes
Format: 35mm, color, 1.33, stereo sound

L'ANGLAISE ET LE DUC/ THE LADY AND THE DUKE (2001)
Direction and Script: **Eric Rohmer**, adapted from the memoirs by Grace Elliott
Historical Research: Hervé Grandsart
Image: Diane Baratier, assisted by Florent Bazin, Romain Bailly, and Mathias Peysson
Electricity and Cameras: Christian Héreau, Marc Mulero, Patrick Vachon, Stéphane Rochera, Robert Bosch, Lionel Bailly, Olivier Martin, Jean Trinci, Thierry Jouanjan, and Cédric Riou
Staging: Les Ateliers de Bercy, Eric Faivre, and Dominique Corbin; Video: Frédéric Vitadier
Sets: Antoine Fontaine; Construction: Jérôme Pouvaret , Hubert de Forcade, and Aligna Sadakhom; Painting: Xavier Morange, Régis Lebourg, Benoît Magny, Audrey Vuong, Amanda Ponsa, Magali Mussotte, Xavier Pascual, Escriba and Clémentine Marchand; Carpentry: Xavier Planson; Furniture: Jean-Jacques Lecerf and La Brocante du Moutet; Portraits: Brigitte Coucoureux, Edith Dufaux, and Sylvie Mitault
Outside Sets (Paintings): Jean-Baptiste Marot, assisted by Damien Laurens, Dorothée Marot, and Mette Ivers
Accessories: Lucien Eymard, Nicolas Betran, Alexandre Nicoll, and Katell Postic
Costumes: Jean-Pierre Larroque, Nathalie Chesnais, Gilles Bodu-Lemoine, Pierre Betoulle, Maridza Reitzman, Les Ateliers du Costume, Danielle Boutard, Mantille and Sombrero, Géraldine Ingreneau, Rémy Tremble, Valérie Dansaert, Sevrine Garnier, Marguerite Parvelesco, Yves Lima, and Dalia Abed
Wigs: Les Marandino; Shoes: Pompéi Hire; Wardrobe Supervision: Véronique Portebois, Julien Reignoux, Gil Noir, and Germaine Ribel
Hair: Annie Mandarin and Véronique Hébet
Makeup: Jacques "Paillette" Maistre and Marie Luiset
Administration: Julien Sabourdin, Jean-Pierre de Olivera, and Jean-Baptiste Villechaize

Assistance: Marion Touitou, Renaud Gonzalez, Florence Rauscher, Bethsabée Dreyfus, and Philippe Papadopoulos
Set Stills Photography: Patrick Messina
Sound: Pascal Ribier, assisted by Frédéric de Ravignan and Nathalie Vidal
Editing: Mary Stephen
Special Effects: BUF Compagnie, Olivier Dumont, Jean-Philippe Leclercq, Patricia Boulogne, Stéphanie Fribourg, Francesco Grisi, Anne-Gros Lafaige, Wilfried Jeanblanc, Jonathan Lagache, Halim Negadi, and Hervé Thouement
Sound Mixing: Pascal Ribier
Dubbing: Jonathan Liebling, assisted by Fabien Adelin
Music: Bécourt, Claude Balbastre, and Jean-Louis Valéro
Production: François Ivernel, Romain Le Grand, Léonard Glowinski (executive producers, Pathé Image), Françoise Etchegarary (CER), Antoine Beau (director of production), France 3 Cinéma, KC Medien AG, Rolland Pelligrino, Dieter Meyer, Canal +, Pierre Rissent, Pierre Cottrell (associate producers)
Cast: Lucy Russell (Grace Elliott), Jean-Claude Dreyfus (the Duke of Orléans), François Marthouret (Dumouriez), Léonard Cobiant (Champcenetz), Caroline Morin (Nanon), Alain Libolt (the Duke of Biron), Héléna Dubiel (Mme Meyler), Laurent le Doyen, Georges Benoît and Serge Wolfsperger (the Miromesnil section), Daniel Tarrare (Justin the porter), Charlotte Véry (Pulchérie, the cook), Rosette (Fanchette), Marie Rivière (Mme Laurent), Michel Demierre (Chabot), Serge Renko (Verginaud), Christian Ameri (Guadet), Eric Veillard (Osselin), François-Marie Banier (Robespierre), Henry Ambert (officer in Meudon), Charles Borg, Claude Koener, and Jean-Paul Rouvray (the three officers at Vaugirard), Axel Colombel and Gérard Martin (the walkers at Carmes convent), Gérard Baume (a man on boulevard St Martin), Joël Templeur (an officer of the Versailles patrol), Bruno Flender and Thierry Bois (soldiers), William Darlin (a drunk soldier), Anne-Marie Jabraud (Mme de Gramont), Isabelle Auroy (Mme de Châtelet), Jean-Louis Valéro (the singer), Michel Duprey (the porter on rue de Lancry), Pascal Ribier (a soldier), Emma Le Doyen, Anthony Dunand, Elisabeth Morat, Marc Ligaudien, Maria Da Silveira, Luc-Antoine Salmont, Alain Uguen, François Rauscher, Edwige Shaki, Antoine Beau, Jérôme Beaudet, Jacques Meunier, Pierre Sambert, Lucette Labreuil, Guy d'Agences, Martine Hatrisse
Length: 126 minutes
Format: Betacam digital transferred to 35mm, color, 1.77, stereo sound

TRIPLE AGENT (2004)
Direction and Script: **Eric Rohmer**
Historical Research: Irène Skobline
Translation: Pierre Léon
Image: Diane Baratier, assisted by David Grinberg (trainee: Sébastien Bustamante)
Electricity and Cameras: Christian Héreau, assisted by Marc Mulero and Tom Mitaux; Michel Strasser, assisted by Marc Casi, Jacques Le Meilleur, Clarence Beaumont, Guillaume Diehl, and Quentin Lestienne
Set: Antoine Fontaine, assisted by Audrey Vuong and Cécile Deleu; Construction: Jérôme Pouvaret and Hubert de Forcade; Painting: Benoît Magny, Régis Lebourg, Xavier Morange, Matthieu Lemarie, Amanda Ponsa, Sylviane Lievremont, Laurence Raphel, Philippe Binard, Raphaelle Comte, and Julien Roger; Carpentry: Franck Thévenon, Eric Thévenon, Nicolas Héretier, Aligna Sadakhom, François Aissa, and Patrice Massida; Locks: Auguste Fontaine and Samuel Guille; Flags and Blazons: Valentina La Roca
Accessories: Bernard Ducrocq
Paintings and Drawings: Pascale Boillot and Charlotte Véry
Tapestry: Frédéric Devillers
Costumes: Jean-Pierre Larroque, assisted by Gilles Bodu-Lemoine and Maritza Reitzman
Hair: Annie Marandin
Makeup: Jacques Maistre
Weapons: Maratier
Vehicles: Rétromobile
Continuity: Bethsabée Dreyfus
On-Set Production: Sybil Nicolas , assisted by Nicolas Leclère (trainee: Thomas Douineau)
On-Set Still Photography: Nicolas Leclère and Jean-Claude Moireau
Sound: Pascal Ribier, assisted by Laurent Charbonnier
Editing: Mary Stephen; Digital Correction: Christian Revère
Sound Mixing: Pascal Ribier
Dubbing: Jonathan Liebling
Music: Dimitri Shostakovitch
Production: Philippe Liégois, Jean-Michel Rey (Rezo Productions), Françoise Etchegarary (CER), Pierre Wallon (production director), with France 2 Cinéma, Valerio De Paolis (BIM Distributions), Enrique Gonzalez Macho (Alta Productions), Gerardo Herrerro, Mariela Besuievsky (Tornasol Films), Takis Vetemis (Strada Productions), Yvan Solovov

(Mentor Cinema Company), Laurent Daniélou (associate producer), Eurimages, Cofimage 15, Canal +, CinéCinéma
Cast: Katerina Didasakalou (Arsinoé), Serge Renko (Fiodor), Amanda Langlet (Janine), Emmanuel Salinger (André), Jeanne Rambur (Dany), Cyrielle Clair (Maguy), Grigori Manouknov (Boris), Dimitri Rafalsky (General Dobrinsky), Nathalia Krougly (the general), Vitaliy Cheremet (Alexis Tcherepnine), Bernard Peysson (a doctor), Laurent Le Doyen (the journalist), Emilie Fourrier (sewing assistant), Alexandre Koltchak (Planton), Vladimir Léon (Chernov), Alexandre Tcherkassof (Admiral Galinine), Alexandre Koumpan (General Malinski), Jorg Schass (the German policeman), Georges Benoît (the French policeman), and for the ball: Jean-Claude Tchevrekdjian (first violin), Gilberto Cortes Alcayaga (second violin), Arnaud Limonaire (violist), Chahan Dinanian (cellist), Marc Goldfeder (pianist), Pierre Chydivar, Danièle Rezzi-Gouhier, Antoine Fontaine, Nicolas Leclère, Alexandre Louschik, Pierre-Jean Larroque, Elena Rivas, Léon Kolasa, Danielle Boutard, Maurice Lemperd, Petr Kaplichenko, Daniel Dumartin, Giovanni Portincasa, Lothar Olschewski, Thomas Sekula, Istvan Van Heuverzwyn, Marie Anne Guerin
Length: 112 minutes
Format: 35mm, color, 1.33, stereo sound

LES AMOURS D'ASTRÉE ET DE CÉLADON/ THE ROMANCE OF ASTREA AND CELADON (2007)
Director: **Eric Rohmer**, assisted by Hadrien Bichet
Script: **Eric Rohmer**, adapted from the novel by Honoré d'Urfé
Image: Diane Baratier
Sound: Pascal Ribier, assisted by Armel Durassier
Dubbing: Jonathan Liebling
Camera and Electrical: Françoise Etchegaray, David Grinberg
Editing: Mary Stephen, assisted by Nicolas Criqui, Tristan Meunier, Philippe Reinaudo, Anita Ribeyrol
On-Set Production: Hadrien Bichet assisted by Christian Palmier and Yann Jouannic
Music: Jean-Louis Valéro
Production Design: Marie Dos Santas and Jérôme Pouvaret
Costume: Pierre-Jean Larroque, assisted by Pu-Laï
Hair and Makeup: Milou Sanner
Continuity: Bethsabée Dreyfus

Production: Valerio De Paolis, Françoise Etchegaray, Enrique Gonzalez Macho, Philippe Liégois, Jean-Michel Rey
Cast: André Gillet (Céladon), Stéphanie Crayencour (Astrée), Cécile Cassal (Léonide), Véronique Reymond (Galathée), Rosette (Sylvie), Jocelyn Quivrin (Lycidas), Mathilde Mosnier (Phylis), Rodolphe Pauly (Hylas), Serge Renko (Adamas), Arthur Dupont (Semyre), Priscilla Galland (Amynthe), Olivier Blond (a shepherd), Alexandre Everest (a shepherd), Fanny Vambacas (a shepherdess), Caroline Blotière (a shepherdess), Marie Rivière (Céladon's mother), Alain Libolt (the narrator)
Length: 109 minutes
Format: 16mm blown up to 35mm, color, 1.37

Shorts

JOURNAL D'UN SCÉLÉRAT (1949)
Direction, Script, Editing: **Eric Rohmer**
Cast: Paul Gégauff
Estimated Length: 30 minutes
Format: 16mm, black and white, silent

PRÉSENTATION or CHARLOTTE ET SON STEAK (in the series *Charlotte et Véronique*) (1951)
Direction and Script: **Eric Rohmer**
Editing: Agnès Guillemot (1960)
Music: Maurice le Roux (1960)
Production: Guy de Ray
Cast: Jean-Luc Godard (Walter), Anne Coudret, dubbed by Stéphane Audran (Charlotte [Alice in 1951]), Andrée Bertrand, dubbed by Anna Karina (Clara)
Length: 10 minutes
Format: 16mm blown up to 35mm (1960), black and white

BÉRÉNICE (1954)
Direction and Script: **Eric Rohmer**, from the story by Edgar Allen Poe
Image: Jacques Rivette
Editing: **Eric Rohmer**, Jacques Rivette
Cast: Teresa Gratia (Bérénice), **Eric Rohmer** (Egaeus)
Estimated Length: 15 minutes
Format: 16mm, black and white

LA SONATE À KREUTZER (1956)
Direction and Script: **Eric Rohmer**, from the novel by Tolstoy
Editing: **Eric Rohmer**, Jacques Rivette
Production: Jean-Luc Godard
Cast: **Eric Rohmer** (the husband), Françoise Martinelli (the wife), Jean-Claude Brialy (the violinist)
Estimated Length: 45 minutes
Format: 16mm, black and white

VÉRONIQUE ET SON CANCRE (1959)
Direction and Script: **Eric Rohmer**
Image: Charles Bitsch, assisted by Alan Levant
Editing: Jacques Gaillard, assisted by Gisèle Chézeau
Production: Jean Lavie, Claude Chabrol (Ajym Films)
Cast: Nicole Berger (Véronique), Alain Delrieu (Jean-Christophe), Stella Dassas (mother)
Length: 18 minutes
Format: 35mm, black and white

SIX MORAL TALES, 1: LA BOULANGÈRE DE MONCEAU/ THE GIRL AT THE MONCEAU BAKERY (1962)
Director: **Eric Rohmer**, assisted by Jean-Louis Comolli
Script: **Eric Rohmer**
Image: Jean-Michel Meurice and Bruno Bathey
Editing: Eric Rohmer
Production: Georges Derocles (Studios Africa), Barbet Schroeder (Les Films du Losange)
Cast: Barbet Schroeder (dubbed by Bertrand Tavernier), Claudine Soubrier (Jacqueline), Michèle Girardon (Sylvie), Fred Junk (Schmidt), Michel Madore (a customer at the bakery)
Length: 22 minutes
Format: 16mm, black and white, 1.33

SIX MORAL TALES, 2: LA CARRIÈRE DE SUZANNE (1963)
Director: **Eric Rohmer**, assisted by Jean-Louis Comolli and Barbet Schroeder
Script: **Eric Rohmer**
Image: Daniel Lacambre
Music: Mozart
Production: Barbet Schroeder (Les Films du Losange)

Cast: Catherine Sée (Suzanne Hocquelot), Philippe Beuzen (Bertrand), Christian Charrière (Guillaume Peuch-Drumont), Diane Wilkinson (Sophie), Jean-Claude Biette (Jean-Louis), Patrick Bachau (Frank), Pierre Cottrell (the collector), Jean-Louis Comolli
Length: 53 minutes
Format: 16mm, black and white, 1.33

NADJA À PARIS (1964)
Director: **Eric Rohmer**, assisted by Pierre-Richard Bré
Text: Nadja Tesich
Image: Nestor Almendros
Continuity: Patricia Fourrescarles
Sound: Bernard Ortion
Editing: Jacqueline Raynal
Production: Barbet Schroeder (Les Films du Losange)
Cast: Nadja Tesich (herself)
Length: 13 minutes
Format: 16mm, black and white, 1.33

PLACE DE L'ETOILE (in the sketch film *Paris vu par...*) (1964)
Direction and Script: **Eric Rohmer**
Image: Alain Levent and Nestor Almendros
Editing: Jacqueline Raynal
Production: Barbet Schroeder (Les Films du Losange), assisted by Pierre Cottrell
Cast: Jean-Michel Rouzière (Jean-Marc), Marcel Gallant (a passer-by), Jean Douchet and Philippe Sollers (two clients), Maya Josse (a woman in the metro), Sarah Georges-Picot, Georges Bez
Length: 15 minutes
Format: 16mm blown up to 35mm, black and white, 1.33

UNE ÉTUDIANTE D'AUJOURD'HUI (1966)
Direction and Script: **Eric Rohmer**, from an original idea by Denise Basdevant
Image: Nestor Almendros
Editing: Jacqueline Raynal
Production: Pierre Cottrell (Les Films du Losange)
Cast: Denise Basdevant (herself), with the voice of Antoine Vitez
Length: 12 minutes
Format: 16mm, black and white, 1.33

FERMIÈRE À MONTFAUCON (1968)
Direction: **Eric Rohmer**
Text: Denise Basdevant
Production: Barbet Schroeder (Les Films du Losange), with assistance from the Ministry of Agriculture and Fishing
Cast: Monique Sendron (herself), and the town of Montfaucon
Length: 13 minutes
Format: 16mm, black and white, 1.33

DES GOÛTS ET DES COULEURS (in the series *Anniversaires*) (1996)
Direction and Script: Anne-Sophie Rouvillois and **Eric Rohmer**
Image: Diane Baratier, assisted by Sebastien Leclerq
Dresses: Marguerite Parvulesco
Sound: Pascal Ribier
Editing: Mary Stephen
Music: Konrad Max Kunz
Production: Françoise Etchegaray
Cast: Laure Marsac, Eric Viellard
Length: 20 minutes
Format: 16mm, color

HEURTS DIVERS (in the series *Anniversaires*) (1997)
Direction and Script: François and Florence Rauscher and **Eric Rohmer**
Image: Diane Baratier, assisted by Thierry Faure
Sound: Pascal Ribier, assisted by Laurent Lafran and Jean-Paul Mugel
Editing: Mary Stephen
Music: Marc Bredel and Mathieu Davette
Production: Françoise Etchegaray (CER)
Cast: François Rauscher (brother), Florence Rauscher (sister), Julie Debazac (Sophie), Laurent Le Doyen (the journalist), Jean-Claude Balard (the father), Pascaline Dargant (the young girl), Laurent Rouquet (the driver), Mathieu Davette (the cyclist), Bethsabée Dreyfus (the cyclist), and at the bar in Le Rallye: Simon and Norbert
Length: 24 minutes
Format: 16mm, color

LES AMIS DE NINON (in the series *Anniversaires*) (1998)
Direction and Script: Rosette and **Eric Rohmer**
Image: Diane Baratier, assisted by Sebastien Leclerq
Hair: Jean-Jacques Ambrosi

Sound: Pascal Ribier
Editing: Mary Stephen
Music: Ronan Girre and Jean-Louis Valéro
Production: Françoise Etchegaray (CER)
Cast: Rosette (Ninon), Julie Jézéquel (Marie), Philippe Caroit (Baptiste), Mickaël Kraft (Frédéric), Dominique Lyon (Xavier), Pascal Greggory (Nicolas), Arielle Dombasle (the customer), Isild le Besco (Fifie), Bethsabée Dreyfus (Natacha), Maud Buquet (Zazie), Julie Leibowitch (Julie), Thomas Raynal (Thomas), Olivier Oumanar (Olivier), Jean-Michel Savy (Frank), Eric Castets (a young man)
Length: 25 minutes
Format: 16mm, color

UN DENTISTE EXEMPLAIRE (in the series *Le modèle*) (1998)
Direction and Script: Aurélia Alcaïs, Haydée Caillot, Stéphane Pioffet, and **Eric Rohmer**
Image: Diane Baratier, assisted by Thierry Faure
Sound: Pascal Ribier
Editing: Mary Stephen
Music: Sébastien Erms [**Eric Rohmer** and Mary Stephen]
Production: Françoise Etchegaray (CER)
Cast: Aurélia Alcaïs (Mélanie), Laura Faveli (Alexandre), Stéphane Pioffet (the dentist), Jeanloup Sieff (the photographer), Joël Barbouth (the customer)
Length: 12 minutes
Format: 16mm, color

UNE HISTOIRE QUI SE DESSINE (in the series *Le modèle*) (1999)
Direction and Script: Rosette and **Eric Rohmer**
Image: Diane Baratier
Sound: Pascal Ribier
Editing: Mary Stephen
Production: Françoise Etchegaray (CER), assisted by Florence Rauscher
Cast: Rosette (Ninon), Emmanuel Salinger (Vincent), Vincent Dieutre (Pierre Vidal), Michiko Sato (the Japanese woman), Mashiro Miyata (the Japanese man)
Length: 10 minutes
Format: DV, color, stereo sound

LA CAMBRURE (in the series *Le modèle*) (1999)
Direction and Script: Edwige Shaki and **Eric Rohmer**
Image: Diane Baratier
Sound: Pascal Ribier
Editing: Mary Stephen
Music: Debussy
Production: Françoise Etchegaray (CER)
Cast: Edwige Shaki (Eva), François Rauscher (Romain), André Del Debbio (the sculpter)
Length: 16 minutes
Format: DV, color, stereo

LE CANAPÉ ROUGE (in the series *Le modèle*) (2004)
Direction and Script: Marie Rivière and **Eric Rohmer**
Image: Diane Baratier
Paintings: Charlotte Véry
Sound: Pascal Ribier
Music: Schumann
Production: Françoise Etchegaray (CER), assisted by Bethsabée Dreyfus
Cast: Marie Rivière (Lucie), Charlotte Véry (Eva), Phillippe Magnan (Alain)
Length: 32 minutes
Format: Beta digital, color, stereo

Eric Rohmer: Interviews

Eric Rohmer: An Interview

Graham Petrie / 1971

From *Film Quarterly* 24, no. 4 (Summer 1971): 34–41. Reprinted by permission of University Press of California.

Graham Petrie: Where and when were you born?
Eric Rohmer: What I say most often—and I don't want to stake my life that it's true—is that I was born at Nancy on April 4, 1923. Sometimes I give other dates, but if you use that one you'll be in agreement with other biographers. It was certainly 1923. [Rohmer was in fact born in 1920—editor's note].

GP: Have you always been interested in the cinema?
ER: No, I couldn't say that. I became interested in cinema very late, when I was a student. Up till then I despised the cinema, I didn't like it, I just liked reading, painting, then music a little later. I didn't take any part in theater, I didn't go to it very much. I liked classical French theater, Racine, Corneille, Molière, but to read it rather than see it. I discovered the cinema at the Cinémathèque. I came to like cinema because I liked silent films, but I didn't discover film through just going to the movies.

GP: And then you began to write for *Cahiers du Cinéma*?
ER: When I discovered the silent film, then I wanted to make films. I tried to make amateur films, but I didn't have any money, I didn't have any equipment, I didn't have anything at all, and so I had difficulties. I joined film societies and got involved in organizing these and I made friends there and with these friends we had the idea—we were all very young then—of publishing a Film Societies bulletin, and then we wanted to start a critical review. It was at the time when *L'Ecran Français* had just folded up and there was no weekly film journal. So we tried to found a very small film journal for we hadn't much money, and this published

five issues, one a month. It was called the *Gazette du Cinéma* and was in the same format as *Combat* was at that time. And those who wrote for that review besides myself were Jacques Rivette, who published his first article there, and also Jean-Luc Godard published his first article there. I don't think Truffaut wrote for it, but he was one of our friends. As for Chabrol he didn't write for it either, though I knew him by then. And after the *Gazette du Cinéma*—there was a review called *Revue du Cinéma* after the war which had gone through various stages, there was a first series of the *Revue du Cinéma* in the thirties. It was founded by a critic called Jean Georges Auriol, then it disappeared, and it reappeared after the war, published by Gallimard and André Bazin wrote for this *Revue du Cinéma*. And the editor was Jacques Doniol-Valcroze. Then Gallimard stopped publishing it and moreover Jean Georges Auriol died in an accident. So Jacques Doniol-Valcroze and André Bazin decided to start another film review with the help of a distributor in Paris called Léonide de Quéjème who acted as a sleeping partner. So they began to publish *Cahiers du Cinéma*—they wanted to keep the title *Revue du Cinéma* but as that still belonged to Gallimard they couldn't. And at first a good many very different kinds of people started off writing for that review. There was a little core of young men, who were known as the young Turks because they had rather violent ideas, and these were François Truffaut, Jacques Rivette, Jean-Luc Godard, Claude Chabrol, and myself, and André Bazin called us "Hitchcocko-Hawksiens" because we admired both Hitchcock and Hawks. I made my debut as a critic as one of this little group. On the whole we were very unified because we had very similar tastes. Then Truffaut wrote a very violent article for *Cahiers du Cinéma* attacking the French "quality" cinema, people like Autant-Lara, René Clement, and so on. A weekly magazine called *Arts* noticed this article and asked François Truffaut to become its film critic, or at least to do some film criticism for it. Truffaut was still very young, only twenty-one or twenty-two, and he became the film critic for *Arts* and as there were plenty of films to write about and he couldn't handle them all himself, he called on his friends and most of the *Cahiers* people lent a hand, especially myself, and for a time Truffaut and I did the film review for *Arts*. At this time the *Cahiers* people were spreading out into all the magazines: André Bazin was writing for the *Nouvel Observateur*.

GP: During this time did you still want to make films yourself?
ER: I hadn't given up the idea, we all tried now and then, but it was very difficult. We all made some amateur films, using whatever means we had,

but in general these films weren't very successful because we didn't have anything—not even a camera. When we asked people to lend us their cameras they wanted to do the camerawork themselves and sometimes the photography was pretty bad as a result. We had problems. Then my own story gets involved with that of the Nouvelle Vague, at least with the most important part of it because most of the Nouvelle Vague people were also *Cahiers* people. We didn't call ourselves that, it was the press who decided that one year there was a Nouvelle Vague. It was Chabrol who got us started, he had succeeded in making a film [*Le Beau Serge*] all on his own without having done anything before, by setting up his own production company with money of his own. He was very worried because the film almost didn't get released, and if it hadn't, then the adventure of the Nouvelle Vague might have stopped there, but he succeeded in making the film and even in making another one [*Les Cousins*] because the first film impressed the Committee that gave out subsidies and so he got a subsidy to make another one, and then the first one was released and was a big success. Then a little after Chabrol came Truffaut's *Les 400 Coups*, though this wasn't his first film as he had already made a short in 35mm, *Les Mistons*. Then, or even a little before that, in an almost desperate attempt, for he had practically no money, nothing but the film stock itself, Rivette made *Paris Nous Appartient*, but he too had previously made a short film, *Le Coup du Berger*. I too had made some 16mm films, and my first real film was produced by Chabrol's production company in 1959, a year after *Les Cousins*, and that was *Le Signe du Lion*. And at the same time Godard made *A Bout de Souffle*, but he turned to a producer outside the *Cahiers* group, Georges de Beauregard, and that's how he met Raoul Coutard. So that's how I got started, at the same time as what came to be called the Nouvelle Vague.

GP: I've heard that you recently re-edited *Le Signe du Lion*, that the producer had made some cuts in it when it was first released.
ER: No, what happened was that I made the film as I wanted to. It was produced by Chabrol, but for personal reasons, family reasons, he had to give up the company to someone else. The person who was managing the company didn't like my film, he thought it was too long and he cut it. So there is in existence a shortened version of *Le Signe du Lion*, to which I objected, but I couldn't take the matter to court and I settled for a compromise by which this version could be distributed in the provinces, but in art cinemas and abroad only my version was to be shown. And as the film in fact was shown only in art cinemas, I was really the

winner. Les Films du Losange have now bought the rights to the film and if we find a copy of the shortened version of the film we have the right to destroy it. So the only version of *Le Signe du Lion* which is valid is the one that lasts one hour and forty minutes with music by Louis Saguer. But the version that was shown in London, I'm told, and this was contrary to the agreement we made, is the shortened version which is one hour twenty-five minutes long and has symphonic music by Brahms. And that isn't my version of the film, it's the producer's one.

GP: And then you began your series of *Contes Moraux* with two films in 16mm?

ER: Yes, the first two are in 16mm. This was because the Nouvelle Vague had established itself; those whose films had done well were setting out on a successful career, but those whose films hadn't done so well, like myself with *Le Signe du Lion*, were having problems with continuing. So I decided to go on filming, no matter what, and instead of looking for a subject that might be attractive to the public or a producer, I decided that I would find a subject that I liked and that a producer would refuse. So here you have someone doing exactly what he wants to. And as you can't do this on 35mm, I made the films on 16mm. That way it didn't cost very much, just the price of the film stock. I found people willing to work for me out of friendship, either as technicians or actors. The first was a very short film, only twenty-five minutes long, the second a bit longer than that and then I decided to make the third, which was *La Collectionneuse* and I realized that as long as you were economical with the amount of film you used, it wouldn't really cost much more to do it on 35mm, especially if you used color. Fortunately I met a friend who could advance me enough to pay for film stock and we used 5,000 meters for a film that ended up 2,500 meters long—that means almost a 2:1 ratio. And that is how I made *La Collectionneuse*, with no money.

GP: Can you tell me something about the subject matter of these first two films?

ER: In the first two *Contes Moraux* I'm telling the story of a young man who meets up with a young girl or woman at a time when he's looking for another woman. You find this idea very clearly in the first film, which is about a boy who sees a girl in the street and falls in love with her but doesn't know how to become acquainted with her. He tries to follow her to find out where she lives, but loses track of her. So he makes up his mind to make a systematic search for her, and as he usually eats in a restaurant frequented by students he decides to go without dinner and use the time to look for her in the district round about. And as he gets hungry he starts going into a baker's shop every day and buys some cakes to eat while he's exploring the area. He notices that the assistant in the shop is becoming interested in him, perhaps falling in love, and as he is getting a bit bored, he starts flirting with her. He gets caught up in the game he's playing with her and finally makes a date with her, just to see what will happen. But just as he's going to meet her, he comes across the first girl, the one he'd seen right at the beginning of the story, who lives just opposite the baker's but had sprained her ankle and couldn't go out, which is why he hadn't seen her. She had seen him go in there every day, but, thinking that he knew where she lived, she assumed that he just went in there so that she would notice him. She doesn't know anything about the girl in the bakery. It's a very slight story, an anecdote really.

The second film is a little more complex because it lasts longer. It's the story of a young boy who has a great admiration for one of his friends, a student; he's younger than him and rather dominated by him. At the same time he holds it against the other that he sees him a lot with girls he doesn't like very much. For example, the other one has a girl that he doesn't like, she's not even a student, she has a job in an office and he finds this a bit vulgar. The friend neglects her, he wants to get rid of her, and this girl, who is in love with his friend, attaches herself to him and begins to flirt with him just because of his friendship with the one she really likes, and he wants to get rid of her too and can't. So it's the story of this boy who spends all his time with this girl who's trying to make advances to him, and at the same time his friend amuses himself by jeering at the girl and making fun of her, he even takes all her money from her because she's ready to do anything to keep him. The boy is ashamed of all this and at the same time he daren't do anything to antagonize the friend he admires so much. So that's the situation: he's ashamed of going along with the game his friend is playing, but he doesn't dare to reproach him frankly and say "no." There's a second woman here too, an attractive young girl, and the young boy the film is about is a little bit in love with her, but she looks on him as just a youngster and isn't interested in him. There's really nothing but failure in the film: the boy spends all his time with a girl he doesn't like and the one he would like to go out with is inaccessible and each time he sees her he doesn't know what to say and is aware anyway that she would refuse him. The characters are all very young: the boy is eighteen and his friend is twenty-one.

GP: Do you plan to release these films ever?
ER: No, because they were made on 16mm. If I were ever to show them it would have to be in a very small cinema and I think the public would just find them too amateurish anyway.

GP: Do you think this idea of the man who hesitates between two women is the connecting link between all the *Contes Moraux*?
ER: He doesn't really hesitate, it just happens that at the very moment that he's made his choice, made up his mind, another woman turns up. But there isn't really any hesitation, all that happens is that this confirms his choice. In *La Collectionneuse* for example, he just spends a week with her and then leaves her. In *Maud* too it's an adventure for him, but he doesn't hesitate between one girl and the other; if he'd had an affair with Maud it would have lasted a week and then it would have been over. in my latest film the hero's choice is already made, he's going to get married, and if he has an adventure it's nothing more than that.

GP: Did you start this series with very precise ideas about the subject matter?
ER: Yes, I had had the stories in my mind for a long time, and when I started the series I knew what the theme of each *Conte* would be. But I hadn't developed them, they were still very vague.

GP: You've made some in color and some in black-and-white...
ER: Three in black-and-white, two of them in 16mm and *Maud* in 35. *La Collectionneuse* and *Le Genou de Claire* are in color and the final one, for which I haven't decided on a title yet, will be too. I haven't written the script for it yet, I'm still thinking about it.

GP: What did you choose black-and-white for?
ER: *Maud*, because it suited the nature of the subject matter. Color wouldn't have added anything positive to it; on the contrary, it would only have destroyed the atmosphere of the film and introduced distracting elements that had no useful purpose. It's a film that I saw in black-and-white; I couldn't see any color in it. There is nothing in it which brings colors to mind, and in fact there weren't any colors in what I filmed—for example I filmed a town in which the houses were grey, certainly there were a few colored boardings and road-signs, but I avoided these, you don't see them because they weren't interesting. There is a stone church and there are no colors in that church. Then there is snow—no color

there either. The people are really dressed in black or in grey; they're not wearing anything colored. The apartment too didn't have any color in it; it was decorated in grey already. I was concerned above all with exploiting the contrast between black and white, between light and shadow. It's a film in color in a way, except that the colors are black and white. There's a sheet which is white, it's not colorless, it's white in the same way the snow is white, white in a positive way, whereas if I had shot it in color, it wouldn't have been white any more, it would have been smudged, and I wanted it really white.

GP: So you don't agree with directors like Antonioni who say it's no longer possible to make films in black-and-white and that all films should be in color?
ER: I would agree that nowadays the normal thing would be to make films in color, and it might seem a bit archaic to film in black-and-white. And yet I don't agree really. I think that man has a very strong feeling for black-and-white; it doesn't just exist in photography, it's there in drawings and engravings too—painters created pictures in color, but they also worked in black-and-white for drawings and engravings, in order to create a certain effect. As a result I think that black-and-white is now accepted by the public, and so I think that people are wrong when they say that black-and-white is impossible nowadays. It's a very curious phenomenon. I think that black-and-white will always exist, even if it's true that it will be an exception and the use of color will be standard. However, it's quite certain that at the moment filmmakers aren't particularly inspired by color; most films in color have the same banal look about them and might as well be in black-and-white. Color adds nothing to them. For me color has to contribute something to a film, if it doesn't do this, I prefer black-and-white for, despite everything, it gives a kind of basis, a unity, which is more useful to a film than color badly used.

GP: What would you say color contributes to *La Collectionneuse* and *Le Genou de Claire*?
ER: I didn't use color as a dramatic element, as some filmmakers have done. For me it's something inherent in the film as a whole. I think that in *La Collectionneuse* color above all heightens the sense of reality and increases the immediacy of the settings. In this film color acts in an indirect way; it's not direct and there aren't any color effects, as there are for example in Bergman's most recent film, his second one in color, where the color is very deliberately worked out and he gets his effects mainly

by the way he uses red. I've never tried for dramatic effects of this kind, but, for example, the sense of time—evening, morning, and so on—can be rendered in a much more precise way through color. Color can also give a stronger sense of warmth, of heat, for when the film is in black-and-white you get less of a feeling of the different moments of the day, and there is less of what you might call a tactile impression about it. In *Le Genou de Claire* I think it works in the same way: the presence of the lake and the mountains is stronger in color than in black-and-white, it's a film I couldn't imagine in black-and-white. The color green seems to me essential in that film; I couldn't imagine it without the green in it. And the blue too—the cold color as a whole. This film would have no value for me in black-and-white. It's a very difficult thing to explain. It's more a feeling I have that can't be reasoned out logically.

GP: What exactly do you mean by the word "moral" in the title of this series of films?

ER: In French there is a word *moraliste* that I don't think has any equivalent in English. It doesn't really have much connection with the word "moral," a *moraliste* is someone who is interested in the description of what goes on inside man. He's concerned with states of mind and feelings. For example in the eighteenth century Pascal was a *moraliste*, and a *moraliste* is a particularly French kind of writer like La Bruyère or La Rochefoucauld, and you could also call Stendhal a *moraliste* because he describes what people feel and think. So *Contes Moraux* doesn't really mean that there's a moral contained in them, even though there might be one and all the characters in these films act according to certain moral ideas that are fairly clearly worked out. In *Ma Nuit chez Maud* these ideas are very precise; for all the characters in the other films they are rather more vague, and morality is a very personal matter. But they try to justify everything in their behavior and that fits the word "moral" in its narrowest sense. But "moral" can also mean that they are people who like to bring their motives, the reasons for their actions, into the open, they try to analyze, and they are not people who act without thinking about what they are doing. What matters is what they think about their behavior, rather than their behavior itself. They aren't films of action, they aren't films in which physical action takes place, they aren't films in which there is anything very dramatic, they are films in which a particular feeling is analyzed and where even the characters themselves analyze their feelings and are very introspective. That's what *Conte Morale* means.

GP: In *Maud* and *Le Genou de Claire* in particular you show us some people around thirty-five to forty years old and also some who are very much younger. Do you think there is now a real disparity between these age groups, in the way that people often talk of the new generation having a completely different set of customs and moral values?
ER: My films are pure works of fiction, I don't claim to be a sociologist, and I'm not making investigations or collecting statistics. I simply take particular cases that I have invented myself, they aren't meant to be scientific, and they are works of imagination. Personally, I've never believed very much in the idea of a difference between age groups, I don't think it's very strong and it's certainly not an opposition between one group and another, and I don't thinks it's so very much stronger nowadays than it was before. And even if it is true, it doesn't interest me very much. It's not something I'm concerned with. The fact that the young generation today in 1971 might as a whole have a certain kind of mentality doesn't interest me. What interests me is to show young people as they really are just now, but also as they might be if they were fifty years old or a hundred years old, and the events of the film could have taken place in Ancient Greece, for things haven't changed all that much. For me what is interesting in mankind is what is permanent and eternal and doesn't change, rather than what changes, and that's what I m interested in showing.

GP: I read in an interview in *Les Nouvelles Littéraires* that once you had finished this series you planned to do something completely different, perhaps a film with a historical setting?
ER: No, I didn't really mean that. Certainly once I've finished the *Contes Moraux* I want to do something else, I want to have a change and I don't want to go on with them. I'll do six, that's all, and I've still one to go. But I don't know what I'll do next.

GP: You've done some work for television, haven't you?
ER: No—I've worked for educational television, which is rather different. Television itself is intended for a huge audience, but educational television is intended for a very restricted public because, until now, there was a lot of difficulty in even finding an audience. There were very few television sets in schools and they weren't available in every classroom. Now, with the coming of cassettes, things will change. I did some educational films on different subjects, just as other people did documentaries, and what I found very interesting was that I learned a great deal and I was free

to do what I wanted. I was on my own; I wrote the scripts as well as filming them. It was a very interesting experience. But I don't know if these films would interest a wider audience.

GP: What do you think about what is happening in films just now? Do you think a new kind of cinema is coming into being?
ER: I've no idea. There may be people who are creating a "new" kind of cinema, but you have to ask how new it really is, if it doesn't just form part of the "eternal *avant-garde*," which sometimes just rediscovers ideas that were avant-garde years ago. For me what is really new is those ideas that never date. But what is certain is that lots of new ideas find their way into films that the public never gets to see. It seems to me that it would be desirable to be able to see everything that was being made by young people in the cinema, even if it wasn't completely successful, and in France, which is a country where you can see plenty of films, I think it's the country with the largest number of specialist cinemas in Europe, we haven't been given the chance to see what is really new, and there's no place to show truly experimental films except the Cinémathèque. And so I can't pass judgment on this new cinema, though the films I make myself haven't any of the characteristics of what is called the avant-garde, and I feel that this "traditional *avant-garde*" isn't the route the cinema ought to follow. But I don't know very much about this new cinema, especially the young American cinema. I don't want to judge it; I make films that are right for me, and other people have their own ways to follow. What I want is for everyone to be able to take his own way and find his own public. But I go very seldom to the cinema, I don't write criticism any more, and I don't have enough knowledge to reply properly to your question.

GP: Have you ever wanted to make a film in the United States?
ER: No. First of all I don't speak English and I couldn't work in a country where I don't know the language. And I want to show the reality of life in France, I don't want to deal with a way of life I don't understand. At a pinch I could make a documentary about life in a foreign country, but that's a different matter. Also I have a very personal way of working and in France I have a great deal of freedom in this respect. I work with an extremely small crew; I have no assistant director, no script-girl, and I take care of the continuity myself. Perhaps I make mistakes and put an ashtray here when it should be there, but that's just too bad. And as usually there are no special clothes for the actors and few objects of

special importance; in the long run there are no problems with this way of working. I use very few technicians because there are very few camera movements, but those technicians that I have are excellent, even though there aren't many of them. In other countries you have crews that are quite terrifying. I use five or six people and there you have sixty. That frightens me and I would be quite incapable of working in that way. I don't like to be the big boss who dominates everyone else; I like to be close to everyone, and I don't see how I could work under these conditions in the United States. Certainly that applies to traditional filmmaking; "underground" films would be a different matter. But I can show on the screen only those things I know about, and I think that there's still a lot to deal with in France. There's the question of language too: I place a lot of importance on speech, on style, on voice quality and intonation, and it's very important. The French language counts for a great deal in my films. I'm a writer too, I write my own scripts, and as a writer the French language is important to me. I couldn't write something and give it to someone else to translate, for my own author in my films. So I could only make films in France.

GP: What films or directors have most influenced your own, in style or themes?
ER: Silent films above all, though I don't know how direct the influence is. People say that there is a lot of talk in my films; that I express myself through speech rather than images, and yet in actual fact I learned about cinema by seeing the films of Griffith, Stroheim, and Murnau, and even the silent comedies. That's how I learned about cinema. There are two directors after the silent period whom I like very much and these are Jean Renoir and Roberto Rossellini; they are the people who most influenced me. As for the others, I admire Americans like Hitchcock, but I don't think I've been really influenced by them; if I have, it's quite unconsciously. I can tell you whom I admire, but influence is a different matter, for sometimes you don't even know yourself who has influenced you and I'm perhaps not the right person to talk about it.

GP: Do you prefer to work for a small audience that will appreciate what you are doing, rather than for a large public?
ER: Yes, certainly. If it depended only on me, instead of attracting people to my films, I would try to drive them away. I would tell them the films are more difficult than they really are, because I don't like to deceive people, I like to show my films to people who can appreciate them.

I'm not interested in the number of spectators. Having said that, it's true that a film is a commercial undertaking and ought to recover its costs. But as my films don't cost much, I don't think I need a very large audience, and I've always thought that they should be shown in theaters that aren't too big. The intimate character of my films doesn't suit a theater or an audience too large for them. And I don't think they are suited to a mass reaction or a collective reaction. It's better if the spectator feels he is experiencing a completely personal reaction to it. Each reaction should be unique, individual, and different. I think the film is enjoyed better if the spectators aren't sitting too near one another, if the theater isn't too full, and they don't know each other. Then each has a different reaction. That's better than a theater where there's a uniform reaction. I don't like watching one of my films in public and it distresses me if everyone laughs in the same place, as my film wasn't made with that in mind. I didn't write something just to make everyone laugh at the same time. It's all right if someone smiles, but it shouldn't happen at exactly the same place in the film. Perhaps this is because my films are more like reading than like watching a spectacle; they are made more to be read like a book than seen like something on the stage. So it distresses me to see a collective reaction.

GP: Would you agree that the endings of your films tend to be rather sad?

ER: They are not what one is expecting to happen; they are to some extent against the person concerned. What happens is against the wishes of the character, it's a kind of disillusionment, a conflict—not exactly a failure on his part but a disillusionment. The character has made a mistake; he realizes he has created an illusion for himself. He had created a kind of world for himself, with himself at the center, and it all seemed perfectly logical that he should be the ruler or the god of this world. Everything seemed very simple and all my characters are a bit obsessed with logic. They have a system and principles, and they build up a world that can be explained by this system. And then the conclusion of the film demolishes their system and their illusions collapse. It's not exactly happy, but that's what the films are all about.

[Translated by Graham Petrie]

Eric Rohmer: Choice and Chance

Rui Nogueira / 1971

From *Sight and Sound* 40, no. 3 (1971): 118–22. Reprinted by permission of the British Film Institute.

Eric Rohmer: Unlike my colleagues on *Cahiers du Cinema*, I came rather late to films. Until I was sixteen I hadn't seen a thing. It was only after the war that I really became interested, when I started going to the Cinémathèque, which in those days was called "Le Cercle du Cinéma," and then it was the silent films that attracted me most. Murnau was the great revelation. In those days he wasn't so highly thought of. Even Bazin considered his work dated—though of course he didn't feel that about Stroheim. I suppose *Nosferatu* was the only Murnau film that was really appreciated (and of course *Tabu*, although that was because everyone credited it to Flaherty). So *Sunrise, Faust, Tartuffe, The Last Laugh* really were revelations. I wrote somewhere that Murnau was the greatest of all filmmakers, the one with the richest imagination. And I still think so.

Rui Nogueira: Your first feature film, *Le Signe du Lion*, was something of a commercial failure. Do you feel that you now know the reasons?
ER: The critics spoke highly of the film, but not in a way that made people want to see it, whereas they did make people want to see *La Collectionneuse, Ma Nuit Chez Maud*, and *Le Genou de Claire*. And *Le Signe du Lion* never found its proper audience. Nowadays films like mine have a following, a select public that knows what kind of film it is being offered. There must be a process of selection, of segregation (and I don't care if that's a pejorative word!). There are different publics for different types of painting, music, books. So why do people still think that in cinema there is only the one big general public? The mass audience enjoys television, variety, adventure. Rightly so; it's foolish to try to force on it what it doesn't want. But films like mine appeal to people with a certain filmic

or literary background; an audience, I now realize, which is actually much larger than I once supposed. Of course there are films much more difficult than mine which still haven't managed to find their audience, outside the Cinémathèque.

RN: You have done some TV work. What do you feel about television?
ER: I have directed a couple of programs for French television in the series *Cinéastes de Notre Temps*. That was an extension of my work as a critic; it certainly wasn't filmmaking. With Educational Television it was different: I've made some documentary shorts for them which were real films and which I like a lot. Or, rather, I like them as much as the work I have done elsewhere. I also work occasionally simply as a "director," in collaboration with an educationist, but those are just bread-and-butter jobs. Television does teach you to produce "readable" images. Though, oddly enough, I have noticed that films made for public cinemas are often actually more "readable" than material filmed directly for television, in spite of the inevitable losses. When you show a film on TV, the framing goes to pieces, straight lines are warped, the decor no longer looks solid and three-dimensional. As for the feeling of "immediate time," which is central to a film like *La Collectionneuse*, that goes completely. Take a film like *La Carrière de Suzanne*, which depends on the problem of deciding whether a girl is pretty or plain. On the average television set, the picture quality is so poor that you couldn't tell anyway. A person's charm comes across on television almost exclusively in close-up; and even then it is often helped by the voice, which does come across well. But the way people stand and walk and move, the whole physical dimension . . . all that is lost. Personally, I don't take the view that television is an intimate medium. It's a mini-spectacle, perhaps, but it's still a spectacle. It's really closer to theatre than cinema, because when you watch television you are not sitting in total darkness, isolated from the world outside; you're in front of the screen, but you're not inside it. Whereas cinema, as I see it, is a continual and continuous involvement.

RN: Before talking about your films, would you mind answering a question you must have been asked dozens of times: how did the idea of the *Contes Moraux* occur to you?
ER: I can try. Partly because I wanted to follow the same idea through several films; partly because I thought audiences and producers would be more likely to accept my idea in this form than in another. Instead of asking myself what subjects were most likely to appeal to audiences, I

persuaded myself that the best thing would be to treat the same subject six times over. In the hope that by the sixth time the audience would come to me. I am still carrying out the program I mapped out for myself ten years ago. I was determined to be inflexible and intractable, because if you persist in an idea it seems to me that in the end you do secure a following. Even with a distributor . . . it's much more difficult for him to put up arguments and criticisms about a scenario which is part of a group of six than about an isolated script. No one, for instance, is going to ask me to work a bit of a crime story into *Le Genou de Claire*, because it's the fifth of the *Contes Moraux* and the *Contes Moraux* aren't detective stories. So really my aim was to persuade people to accept this style of cinema—which is not new, for in films as in novels nothing is ever really new. What I call a *conte moral* is not a tale with a moral, but a story which deals less with what people do than with what is going on in their minds, while they are doing it. A cinema of thoughts rather than actions. The people in my films are not expressing abstract ideas—there is no "ideology" in them, or very little—but revealing what they think about relationships between men and women, about friendship, love, desire, their conception of life, happiness (perhaps in my next film I'll talk more about happiness . . .), boredom, work, leisure . . . Things which have of course been spoken about previously in the cinema, but usually indirectly, in the context of a dramatic plot. Whereas in the *Contes Moraux* this just doesn't exist, and in particular there's no clear-cut line of tragedy or comedy. You can say that my work is closer to the novel—to a certain classic style of novel which the cinema is now taking over—than to other forms of entertainment, like the theatre. And that, for me, is significant. I think I have contributed towards leading the cinema even further away from the theatre than it had already gone. My characters may do a lot of talking, but it takes more than dialogue to make a play. They don't talk at all like people in a play—at least, I hope they don't.

RN: Why did you number the *Contes Moraux*?
ER: Because once you have decided on a collection of stories, it's best that it should end somewhere. I don't want to become "the moral stories man" in the sense that Edgar Allan Poe, for instance, is "the extraordinary stories man." I can make—and one day if I want to I shall make—fantasies, thrillers, historical novels. The *Contes Moraux* are a phase, while at the same time I see them as variations on a given theme. In *Le Genou de Claire*, as in the earlier films, the story is about a man meeting a woman at the very moment when he is about to commit himself to

someone else. In *Claire*, this woman is double—or even triple, if you regard Aurora as more than just a confidante. The man is fully aware that this meeting isn't going to disrupt his life: there is nothing dramatic about it, no moment of decision. What is in question is his way of thinking, his way of looking at life, rather than his course of action. In my previous film, the encounter with Maud enriches the engineer morally; in *Le Genou de Claire*, the man's meeting with the two young girls will perhaps add something to his ideas before he marries Lucinda, whether it serves to confirm his opinions or undermines them.

RN: One might almost say that this encounter enables the man to draw up a sort of introspective balance-sheet . . . ?
ER: Yes, for him it amounts to a kind of halt, a respite, a breathing-space, a parenthesis in his life, a moment for taking stock. What interest me are the thoughts that fill his mind at that particular moment. And I wanted to use the cinema to show them, even though as the art of objective and exterior images, it might seem the least appropriate.

RN: Although he is resolute about his decision, Trintignant in *Ma Nuit Chez Maud* can't stop himself proposing to Maud.
ER: But he does it whimsically: it isn't serious. Which doesn't alter the fact that everything always remains in question, even after the decision has been made.

RN: Could we go back to *La Collectionneuse*? It was a daring venture, because I believe you had no distribution guarantee. Where did you get the money from?
ER: Nowhere. We hadn't any money, or only a very little. There was the cash from the sale to television of my two previous *Contes Moraux*; and that was just enough to pay for the film stock, rent a house in St. Tropez (in June, when it's reasonably cheap), and hire a cook . . . The actors and technicians agreed to work without salaries, on a profit-sharing basis. I made it a rule that I would only have one take for each shot, and I used less than seventeen thousand feet of film. That kind of hard discipline has its advantages: once the actors are used to it, they can actually be more relaxed and more consistent in their performances. It's much easier to achieve perfection in a single bound than step by step. It's like the high jump: there's no point in trying more than once. With some directors, actors must not be allowed any independence; and that kind of director has to do a number of takes to get the effect which corresponds to

his own intentions. But if you think, as I do, that the actor's spontaneity should be expressed in each take, then it's in your best interests to shoot as little as possible.

RN: But didn't you rehearse before every take in *La Collectionneuse*?
ER: Of course I did. I couldn't have done without rehearsals, particularly as the film was very carefully planned and in no way improvised. I wrote the dialogue myself with the actors, sometimes only the evening or the morning before we shot the scene. But the fact remains that the dialogue was written.

RN: You used a rather different method of working with the actors and dialogue in *Maud*, and then in *Le Genou de Claire* reverted to the technique of *La Collectionneuse*.
ER: Yes, on *Ma Nuit Chez Maud* I had written the whole script myself two years before the film was made—except for Antoine Vitez's "Marxist' speech which we worked out together. And in *Claire*, Brialy's part was scripted from start to finish, with only two exceptions. For the two girls, about half of their dialogue was scripted and the rest was worked out much later, through discussions and conversations. This is particularly evident in the dialogue of Beatrice Romand (Laura), where you can sense the improvisation. *Claire* is really a mixture of everything: scenes I wrote earlier, and scenes which I worked out with the actors, sometimes weeks and sometimes only a day or two before shooting. We would get together and talk around a cassette recorder, and I could see what was natural and what was less so and make a choice. There are even some wholly improvised scenes in which Brialy made up his own lines—for the first time in his career, I believe. Of course I told him what to talk about, but the actual words are not mine. For instance, the scene of the quarrel with the lifeguard at the camp site: I was very anxious that this should retain an authentic, slightly incoherent quality which a written script would have eliminated. As it was, there was some tension while the scene was being shot. Afterwards everyone dived into the water; with some pleasure, I might add. We shot one take and it was the right one.

RN: What struck me most, in terms of the performances in *Le Genou de Claire*, was the subtlety of the actors' inflections. It appears to be very conscious, and yet the result sounds wholly natural.
ER: I did encourage this type of voice modulation, the use of different inflections . . . you couldn't say I ordered or imposed it, but helped it

along. And that is one of the advantages of using actors who have not been spoiled by professionalism. Aurora's voice, for instance, has a tendency towards harshness which she herself thought was excessive. Instead of checking her, I would compliment her every time she said that she was scared of her own voice . . . I really like it a lot. It's the musical side of my films; because, as you know, I never use music itself. The only music in my films is the music of people's voices. You know, I find this idea of "directing" actors somewhat contentious—it's a dangerous idea to practice or at least a delicate one, especially in contemporary cinema. In Chaplin's *The Countess from Hong Kong* the actors are "directed" to an extraordinary degree; but I don't think that a young filmmaker could or should do as much. Chaplin is capable of repeating the same take literally dozens of times. I very seldom do more than one take, and when I do repeat a take it is rarely because of the actors. This implies a conception of "acting" that is entirely different from Chaplin's, though he was right in his time and is still right for himself . . . And, you know, *The Countess from Hong Kong* is an extremely modern film: it's a source of ideas, it really does offer something new, whereas all that these so-called "new" films offer me is a hotchpotch of half-assimilated influences.

RN: Do you supervise the framing and editing on your films?
ER: I do indeed: I keep a close watch on everything. The editing is always a key element, and on *La Collectionneuse* I did my own cutting, only bringing in the editor for the sound. When I shoot with direct sound I don't actually handle the film myself, but I'm never out of the cutting-room.
Framing, too, is vitally important. I always have a look through the viewfinder, and if I leave Nestor Almendros considerable initiative it is because after several years of working together we see things in the same way. Besides, he has a visual culture, a highly developed pictorial sense, and that is extremely rare in France.

RN: Do you think that *La Collectionneuse* was one of the first observations of the times we live in . . . of young people, that is, in that kind of setting?
ER: Inevitably it was. Every film is a witness to its own time, the moment it shows things as they are. In the cinema nothing is easier than to show what is: you only have to look around you. I really admire people who manage to show what is *not*, or what no longer is . . . There's achievement for you! Yet you still occasionally see, and in France especially, films of a truly staggering unreality . . . When I say that the cinema is adept at

showing what is, I mean what is in life: not what's in the magazine articles or on television screens. It's the medium for raw reality, not predigested by the press or the opinion polls or the popular myths. The cinema's role, precisely, is to create the myths, as it did in Chaplin's time, not to find all its sources of inspiration outside itself. Film, for instance, used to provide the themes for strip cartoons; now it's the other way round.

RN: What struck me particularly in *La Collectionneuse* was your care for a particular kind of detail: the books the characters are reading for instance, the complete works of Rousseau and the book on German Romanticism...
ER: I wanted my character to be reading some monument of world literature, the sort of big book one takes away with one on holiday. Patrick Bauchau (Adrien) felt like re-reading Rousseau, though he says the book could just as well have been *Don Quixote*. As for *Romantisme Allemand*: that was a book belonging to Daniel Pommereulle which Haydée flipped through and then put aside, just as she does on the screen. I was very concerned about the authenticity of the Pommereulle character: I didn't want the painter to be played by anyone except a painter. And I chose that paint-tin with the razor blades from among his works because he was fond of it and talked about it. It's possible to see the tin as having symbolic meaning in the film; but although I wouldn't disagree, it's a meaning which derives from the character himself and not from me.

RN: You also had the Marxist in *Ma Nuit Chez Maud* played by an actual Marxist (Antoine Vitez), and the novelist in *Le Genou de Claire* played by a novelist (Aurora Cornu).
ER: Yes, a thinker or writer or an artist cannot be interpreted by anyone else. The same is true of a workman, as far as his work is concerned.

RN: Can one identify the characters in *La Collectionneuse* with the actors?
ER: No. They have nothing in common except their style; the way they talk or the way they look. I didn't want to make a psychodrama but a work of pure fiction, with the conscious collaboration of the cast. I never tried to film them unawares, but asked them to give the best part of themselves.

RN: Still on *La Collectionneuse*, one notices that in the "voice-off" passages Adrien is using a very formal, eighteenth-century manner, whereas the dialogue is always very modern in style. Did you intend to suggest the dichotomy between thought and speech, or was there another reason?

ER: I don't find Adrien's commentary at all "eighteenth-century" though of course the style is "literary." Let's say that these are extracts from a journal, written in the style such a man would probably use, however slangy he may be in conversation. Anyhow, it's a dandified slang... But the dichotomy is certainly intentional: rightly or wrongly, I wanted that difference in tone.

RN: But there's no such difference with Trintignant, the narrator of *Ma Nuit Chez Maud*; his dairy notes correspond exactly with the way he speaks.

ER: But here it's no longer a question of a private diary; merely a couple of observations which he's making to himself, and which I wanted expressed as briefly and neutrally as possible.

RN: How did you choose the actors for *Le Genou de Claire*?

ER: I have known Jean-Claude Brialy for a long time, and I chose him for this part because I've always felt that he was a very good actor who had got trapped in a series of parts well below his potential: he has a sharp and subtle mind, and he is always playing hare-brained, rather childish young men. His beard was also a help, because it aged him just that little bit more and gave him the maturity I wanted. As for the others... Aurora, the novelist, has been a friend of mine for several years; I met her in Paris and as soon as I saw her I had the idea of giving her a part... this part. Béatrice was unearthed, with some difficulty I might say, by some photographer friends who spread the word that I was preparing a film. She was doing modelling work for teenage fashion magazines. And Laurence (Claire) was a schoolgirl.

RN: Béatrice Romand, the girl who plays Laura, is really amazing. A star is born...

ER: That's what everyone tells me, and that's what I thought when I chose her. There is something about her... you don't meet girls like her every day, maybe once every five or ten years. I don't know how the character would have worked out if I hadn't found her: I know Laura would have been less interesting. I developed the character for her. And I'm sure she can play very different types of role from the one I gave her here: she is more conventionally beautiful in real life than she looks in the film, because I had to make her seem a little younger. I see her perhaps as a Dostoievsky or a Chekhov heroine—very touching. But she can play anything, and whatever she does she will bring an extraordinary power to it.

RN: And for *Ma Nuit Chez Maud*?
ER: There the actors were all professionals, and they identified miraculously with their characters. It was the more remarkable because, as I've said, the script was written long before the film was cast.

RN: People tend to discuss the women in your films rather than the men. Perhaps it's because the women always seem to be pulling the strings; the men in your films are often dupes . . .
ER: The central character in my films tends, first and foremost, to be complacent about himself. You could say that he's constantly being taken in by his own philosophy, his self-justification. My own view of him is rather critical. His complacency is always attacked by the other characters. My female characters are not necessarily more sympathetic, but they are more clear- minded. You should never think of me as the apologist for my male character, even (or especially) when he is being his own apologist. On the contrary; the men in my films are not meant to be particularly sympathetic characters.

RN: Does Claire represent for Jerome a possibility that he has lost?
ER: If you like, she stands for an attraction that is purely erotic, in the most refined sense of the word. Jerome has a Proustian side to him: not a libertine, but an "amateur." He's fascinated by a single part of her body. He dreams of a woman who has a special kind of lightness and slightness and fragility. But this is exactly the kind of woman who is not for him. You have the impression—as far as you can tell from Lucinda's photograph—that he'd get on much better with a woman of more force and personality. Yet his desire drives him towards a girl who, physically as well as morally, is somehow at once more fragile and more unassuming. It's a common enough thing in men: the contradiction—even within desire itself—between what is purely desired and only desired, and what is possessed. The object of desire is not necessarily the object of possession. That's what I was interested in showing. Proust, of course, described it admirably: it's a twentieth-century rather than an eighteenth-century preoccupation. And even with our present rampant eroticism, one wonders whether the ordinary man really would be satisfied if he could possess the women he sees in the magazines. I think there is a type

of woman who is made to be looked at and another type who is made to . . . be touched. All the senses cannot be satisfied by the same object; and the contradiction is clearer today than ever before, since visual eroticism has become so general. At any rate, that's the case with Jerome: from the woman who, to his sense of sight, appears the most desirable, he wants nothing, or only something extremely symbolic. Ultimately, touching her knee is simply a way of being able to say "I touched it," like children when they're playing tag . . . Possession for him adds nothing to desire. On the contrary, his desire feeds on the absence of possession. That's what satisfies him. It's not an unusual state, and there's nothing morbid about it.

On top of that, I think Jerome simply wants to dazzle the novelist, to do something that will make people talk about him. And he does say to her: "It's no longer you who are shaping the novel, it's me." But I don't know . I can't really answer questions like this, because, in so far as the central character asks himself the same sort of questions, the audience can do likewise. In my films, there are things you hear and things you see, and the rest is supposition.

RN: When Jerome justifies his gesture by talking about the good deed he has done, is that just a case of the libertine's moral camouflage?
ER: Absolutely not. Jerome is in no sense a libertine, even if what he did was rather unpleasant: it was extremely hateful of him to make the girl cry for no good reason. But his motive was that he deeply and sincerely despised the other boy. The characters in my *Contes Moraux* are never cynics. They always find justifications for their actions, as people in real life always do . . . Of course, they can be wrong . . . they may often give false reasons, but at least they always have reasons. And they have them sincerely. At the end of the film, when the novelist sees the reconciliation between the boy and girl after Jerome has left, she laughs quietly to herself because she realizes that he was mistaken. He's more naive than blasé. At least that is my interpretation, but it isn't necessarily the right one . . .

RN: The fact that the boy comes to see Claire the day after and tells her the complete truth not only destroys the whole story Jerome had imagined, but makes his gesture useless . . .
ER: Yes, but the boy too could be lying. There is nothing to prove that what he tells her is the exact truth. His explanations seem very embarrassed and you get the impression that he's not entirely innocent.

Definitely not. So that Claire is right to hold it against him. So the story really has no ending ... In all these *Contes Moraux* it is a mistake to define feelings too precisely—they are always a little cloudy and ambiguous. When you find an explanation—and you always can—there is always another explanation behind the first one. I never really manage to finish my stories, since the endings I find all have multiple repercussions. Like an echo. You might say that the end is a way of going back over the story. As in *Ma Nuit Chez Maud*: a ball bounces on the ground and turns the story around so that we see it in a different light. *La Collectionneuse* was a little like that as well. At the end, Haydée leaves Adrien on the road, and that forces us to reconsider everything, right from the beginning. It's a device which I've used in all my *Contes Moraux*, but it is also an essential part of the theme, or the chemical ingredients which go to make up the theme: this way of ending on an echo.

RN: *Claire* is presented in the form of a diary. Why?
ER: One can suppose that it corresponds to the notes taken by the novelist. The dates, written on the pink paper, are in her handwriting.

RN: The kiss on the hilltop: why did you set this particular scene in the midst of the mountains?
ER: On this film, I didn't look for locations to fit a story I had written; I found the places first and it was only afterwards that I wrote the film. The settings gave me an idea of which I only became fully conscious at the editing stage. I noticed that my whole mise-en-scène was structured along one dominant line: a diagonal running from the surface of the lake to the mountain-tops. It's along this diagonal that Laura is looking when she gazes up at Jerome; and along which his arm travels as it approaches Claire's knee. In the scene you mention, it's very sharply defined: all the movements converge on the circle of the mountains. I've also noticed that I tend to set my love scenes in what could be described as natural amphitheatres: the cove in *La Collectionneuse*, the snowy hills lowering over the town in *Ma Nuit Chez Maud*. Perhaps there is a symbol there. I avoid symbols on principle, but this one imposed itself on me anyway. The symbolism was really willed by Laura, who had said the day before (and the phrase came from the actress herself, because I was letting her improvise in that scene), "The mountain is protecting us." The relationship between the Laura-Jerome couple and the mountain is a sort of symbolic echo of the one between the adolescent girl and the mature man. She leans on him, leans back on him, rather as they

both lean against the mountain. So that the circle of mountains does in fact turn out to be the ideal frame, the ideal receptacle for this scene; and even if there isn't a specific symbol, there's still a surprising similarity of forms. What matters to me is that my characters should develop within the settings on which they can leave the clearest mark. But, as I said, the particular relationship here was one that only struck me when I was watching the film on a viewer. I chose that particular countryside, quite simply, because I had discovered it during my wanderings and was fascinated by its beauty.

RN: Like the role of water in your films: ambiguous and free-flowing . . .
ER: Yes, water too, I'll agree with that . . . water is the first element . . . the idea of tears and of rain . . . And there's also perhaps a childhood memory involved, one of my earliest memories, of a little girl crying in a barn or under a shed while it was raining outside, and her sister comforting her. I suppose that I had always envisaged the scene where he caresses her knee as happening in the rain. That was my first idea. The lake came later, it was slightly superfluous, but since I'm very fond of water there is a lot of it in my films; I like water to look at, and to touch. There's water in *Le Genou de Claire*, in La *Collectionneuse*, in *Le Signe du Lion*. In Ma *Nuit Chez Maud* there is snow instead. And—yes, you're quite right—there is the sea at the end of the film.

I am not very fond of the arid Mediterranean landscape, the setting of *La Collectionneuse*. The country I like best is the temperate zone, in central France. I wanted to have trees in the film. And then the cherry trees, the fruit and flowers—they're all things I find enormously pleasing. There are very few manufactured objects in my films; there's furniture, of course, but you won't find any fetishism about clothes or objects. At least, I don't think you will. Yesterday I saw Stroheim's *Merry Widow* again—a marvellous film, by the way. I hadn't seen it for a long time, and I was struck by the sheer frenzy of the costumes and sets. Personally, I don't belong to the baroque family, the Stroheims and Sternbergs, who attach such extreme importance to artificial things. I don't like artifice; I prefer nature.

RN: But the framework is very significant, since I can't imagine your characters in settings other than those you've chosen for them. You never separate your characters from the setting.
ER: That's exactly right. And Nestor Almendros's camerawork does a great deal to relate characters to a landscape. They are bathed in light.

It is a type of camerawork that has more to do with the modelling of figures than with outline. And I like painters who really use light, who drown their subjects in light rather than isolating one object from another. I dislike, for instance, that surrealist trick of detaching the object, enclosing it, making a sort of entity out of it. The painters I prefer are Rembrandt or Turner or Cézanne.

Moral Tales: Eric Rohmer Reviewed and Interviewed

Beverly Walker / 1973

From *Women and Film* 1, no. 3–4 (1973): 15–22.

When *My Night at Maud's* hit the film scene four years ago, I breathed a sigh of relief that someone had, at last, created a character with whom I could readily identify. The fascinating Maud was perfect: she was educated and self-supporting (a doctor by profession). She enjoyed being a mother to her daughter but made no apologies for her divorcee status. Her beauty and sex appeal were not surface artifice, manufactured by Hollywood: they were totally integral to her character and personality. No passive "sex object," she was perfectly capable of letting a man know she desired him. Brilliantly played by Françoise Fabian, Maud captivated everybody—men as well as women. The filmmaker, an unknown Frenchman named Eric Rohmer, had done something most unusual: he had presented an unorthodox woman without any dark insinuations about her character. She stood alone in counterpoint to a conventional married couple. And Rohmer showed his bias: marriage was portrayed as a refuge for silly, frightened people.

The plot was simple: An engineer (Jean-Louis Trintignant) meets, by chance, Maud. Forced by a snow storm to spend the night in her apartment, they pass the night discussing their conflicting philosophies of life. She attempts to seduce him but he explains that he has already seen in church a girl he intends to marry. In mind he has committed himself to her and must, therefore, remain faithful. They go their separate ways and he eventually contrives to meet the girl—a blonde-haired student (Marie-Christine Barrault) who, like himself, is Catholic. They marry and have children. A few years pass. A brief epilogue shows an accidental encounter between Maud and her happy family. A sharp glance between the two women indicates that the wife is the student with whom Maud's first husband was having an affair when their marriage ended. Their mouths are closed, however, and the husband will never know. He bids Maud adieu and scampers down the beach to build sandcastles with his kids.

The real substance of the film lay in its subtle ambience of characterization and mood. Maud was free and open and ready to accept life as it happened. The engineer lived according to a preconceived outline, a blend of tradition and Catholicism. The wife, laden with guilt over her affair, saw marriage as an escape from temptation. (And, perhaps, atonement for her sins?)

My enthusiasm for *My Night at Maud's* lasted quite awhile. Being a maverick was hard enough without constant reminders from movies and TV that a woman is condemned if she doesn't go down the route of marriage and children. Eric Rohmer became my hero. Then a friend, a film critic and essayist, planted a seed of doubt. The scenario went something like this:

HE: You're crazy to think that director is against marriage. You've misread the film.
ME: I don't see how. Maud is clearly superior to that uptight married couple. Imagine a man picking out his wife at Mass, the way a horse breeder might choose a fine mare from a line-up. Absurd. The man cuts himself off from life's possibilities by playing it so safe whereas Maud participates in all of life's possibilities.
HE: You're forgetting the epilogue. Maud stands there all alone, confessing that things haven't been so great. The engineer is happy as a lark with his wife and kids.
ME: No, you've got it wrong! Maud has courage. She's so secure she can admit mistakes without feeling annihilated. And at least she *knows* she's unhappy. The engineer is so cut off from his feelings that he wouldn't recognize dissatisfaction in himself or in his wife. How could he experience joy? He's fixed things so that only a catastrophe could shake his boat. And his smugness is shown to be foolish by the fact that even the people around him protect him from reality. Neither Maud nor his own wife will ever reveal his wife's contribution to the breakup of Maud's marriage.
HE: (Patience exhausted.) I know the man. He's a devout Catholic who is

absolutely devoted to his wife and children. He lives a monastic life and has never, ever been known to get involved with another woman.

Well, you may have a point, I said unconvinced. Hope dies hard.

My curiosity about Rohmer increased. I pried into every corner of his life by reading everything I could about him and questioning anyone I met who knew him. I learned that he was already close to fifty, and had been one of the founders of *Cahiers du Cinema*. *My Night at Maud's* was number three in a series he called "Moral Tales." He had written the scripts twenty years earlier and each story was to be a permutation on the same theme, that of temptation mastered. Each was to have a common, symmetrical construction: A man in love with one woman meets another. For a brief interlude, he flirts with the idea of a liaison. In the end, he decides against it and returns to the first. It was a variation of the perennial triangle. Parisian film gossip revealed that Rohmer kept his personal and professional lives totally separate. Almost no one had ever met his wife and children, or been invited to his home. There was conjecture that his wife didn't even know he was a filmmaker—and that his mother didn't, for sure. He had *been* a professor for years, teaching under a pseudonym. So devoted was he to his students that he stopped shooting his first film when he discovered it was taking too much time away from his students. It was never completed. That information only served to make him more interesting. A man of real moral conviction. Every filmmaker I knew would have sold his grandmother into slavery to finish a film.

As subsequent Rohmer films came forth, it became less clear what he was up to. *La Collectionneuse* (Moral Tale #IV but made before *Maud*) is the thinnest of the series: A promiscuous girl named Haydée (Haydée Politoff), the "collector" of the title, bewitches a couple of intellectual dandies one summer in St. Tropez. One of them (Daniel Pommereulle) finally gets her out of his system by sleeping with her but the other, Adrien (Patrick Bauchau) remains thoroughly befuddled. He alternates between indignation at her behavior and enchantment-mixed-with-envy at her freedom. He finally manages to get away without ever having really confronted his desire for her, driving off to his fiancée with a clear conscience.

Claire's Knee (#V) tells of Jerome (Jean-Claude Brialy), a writer, who encounters by chance an old friend (Aurora Cornu) while vacationing near Annecy. While visiting Aurora, he becomes intrigued by her hostess's daughter, a beautiful young girl named Claire (Laurence de

Monaghan). Already engaged to be married, he feels guilty about his attraction to the girl. Aurora is amused by his discomfort and urges him to pursue Claire . . . see what happens. A poet, she enjoys manipulating people as well as characters. Claire's stepsister Laura (Béatrice Romand) is there, too. Less beautiful than Claire, she is more interesting—in the tradition of Maud—and develops a crush on Jerome. Thus he has a double temptation. He finds Laura good company but not desirable. His interest in Claire mounts. Frustrated by her aloofness, he tries to break up her relationship with her boyfriend. His machinations fail, but Claire's distress provides him an opportunity to satisfy his obsession—to caress her knee! Just before he leaves, Aurora discloses her engagement. Peeved that she hasn't told him before now, he nonetheless congratulates her for making such a sound decision and departs in a boat for his fiancée in Switzerland.

Claire's Knee has the most complex structure of all the Moral Tales. Two parts of the triangle are doubled. The role of the narrator is split between the man and his friend, Aurora. Each of them has already made a decision to marry and live a normal life before the film begins. Her vicarious enjoyment of Jerome's crisis implies that she has already passed a similar temptation. An added complexity is the question of their relationship. Were they lovers? Was she a temptation he passed up—perhaps because of her former independence? Therefore, Aurora might also be seen as a temptress out of his past, thus tripling that side of the triangle. At the time of the film, however, she seems to have "sowed her wild oats" and be reconciled to the safety and tranquility of marriage. She has taken a rather dull fellow as her fiancé.

The "temptress" or "liberated woman" side of the triangle is likewise shared by the two young girls. Claire is similar to the wife in *Maud* and therefore an inadvertent "temptress." We know she'll settle down one of these days and become a good wife. Laura, the more unconventional of the two, is rejected by Jerome.

By the time I had seen the two additional films, I began to wonder if my friend hadn't been right. Perhaps I had misread Rohmer. He had continued to create off-beat, free-spirited females. But it appeared to me that some kind of subtle judgment was being made against them.
a) They were always portrayed as a "temptation."
b) They were always pitted against a more conventional woman.
c) They always lost the man.
There seemed to be an implication that the independent woman was never going to find "true happiness"—not on *this* earth, anyway. It was

perplexing because these women were always far more interesting than the wife or fiancée—when the latter was even present in the film. In *La Collectionneuse* and *Claire's Knee* we see her only in a photograph! Even though each of the films was named after the independent woman, the central character was always a man. It was his story, his crisis: will he or won't he be unfaithful? Could *that* be the "moral" Eric Rohmer was talking about in his "Six Moral Tales"?

In his final film of the series, *Chloe in the Afternoon*, the battle lines were clearly drawn; all points of the triangle were visible in the story. The wife, for the first time, was given almost equal time on screen. The situation was the same as in the previous films: a man already promised to one woman (in *Chloe*, he is married) meets, by chance, another. He flirts with the idea of an affair but ultimately conquers the temptation and returns to his wife. And Rohmer switched things around a bit this time, loading the dice: The man's wife, Hélène (Françoise Verley), is educated, impeccably dressed and comports herself with dignity and grace. She's a most sympathetic figure. The independent woman, Chloe (Zouzou), is an "unkempt hippie," promiscuous and unable to hold a job. Worse, she is conniving and treacherous, bent on seducing the man despite his stated protestations. Fredric (Bernard Verley) is the weakest of all Rohmer's protagonists. He goes further toward completion of the unmentionable act than any of the others. While Chloe awaits him, naked in her bed, he begins to undress in the bathroom. Suddenly getting hold of himself, he dashes out a side door, hastily turning on the faucet to disguise the sounds of his exit! The last shot of Chloe shows her stretched out on the bed à la Ingres. Fredric races home to his wife in the middle of the afternoon, making the excuse that he just had to see her. She, who has known that something was up all along, breaks into tears as her husband undresses her and leads her to the A-Okay marriage bed. Virtue intact. Marriage triumphant. The independent woman humiliated.

I interviewed Eric Rohmer in Paris last August, before *Chloe in the Afternoon* had opened either there or in America. He looks and acts like an older version of any one of his protagonists, particularly the engineer from *Maud*. One senses that the problems he has put on the screen are personal and deeply meaningful to him. As movies everywhere have become increasingly schematic and depersonalized, one can't help but admire him for his courage. I came away from the interview with a deepened respect for the man. While I do not agree with his conclusions, I certainly did share his concern about finding a way to live in harmony with oneself. At a time when conflicts between men and women seem almost insurmountable, we are fortunate indeed to have an artist who confronts the problem with such honesty. A modern consciousness has given his work a dimension he could never have anticipated when he conceived the stories some twenty years ago. The values he espouses in his films are held in contempt by a probable majority of the film-going public. And yet his love for all of his characters, and especially, I think, for the woman who dares to be different, has given his work a depth unique in modern cinema. This is possible only because of his ruthless— and undoubtedly painful—self-examination coupled with an extraordinary integrity.

What follows is an edited version of an almost three-hour interview. Rohmer is a quintessential European intellectual, speaking in long, convoluted sentences and constantly refining every statement. Since his replies to my questions were simultaneously translated by his indefatigable producer and friend, Pierre Cottrell, it was sometimes impossible to catch every word. It was also difficult to challenge some of his statements.

BW: M. Rohmer, Nestor Almendros (cinematographer for all of Rohmer's films) told me that you are the most conscious filmmaker he has ever seen. That there is not one element of your films over which you do not have total control. Do you feel this is true?
ER: Yes!

BW: Does that mean that your films always correspond exactly to what you wrote and envisioned?
ER: The first day's shooting corresponds to the idea. But as each day's filming progresses, the rhythm is controlled by other factors. And you feel betrayed by the technique. But gradually you get used to this version and begin to see the film not the way you imagined it in your mind's eye, but for what it is on the screen. When it's finished, it somehow corresponds to the idea that you had . . . or the idea that has been transformed through the process of shooting. As to *Chloe in the Afternoon*, it is extremely faithful to the letter of the script.

BW: Are you never surprised?
ER: The greatest difference comes in the way the actors play, which makes my intentions more clear and, yet, somehow modifies them, too. For example, when you read a novel there is always a certain freedom to imagine the character from its literary description. In film, impossible.

He is what he is on the screen. If the same words were said by a different actress than Zouzou, the character would be different. She brought a personal touch—and this is what interests me in cinema: to put together things that exist with things you are not totally master of. I like the actors to bring me something; I want them to interpret. This way, the film always surprises me—and this is what I want. It's necessary that something happen during the shooting, even in films as elaborated in their scenarios as mine are. And I will add this is what makes the cinema interesting for me; this is why I make films instead of writing books.

BW: Which is more interesting for you, the writing of your scripts or the shooting?
ER: They're equally interesting: I'm not interested in making adaptations. In the Moral Tales, I never considered myself only a *metteur en scene*. I couldn't conceive one without the other. (Pause) I notice nowadays there are more and more *auteurs* in the cinema.

BW: What is the genesis of the Moral Tales?
ER: Two or three came from little stories I wrote when I was very young, that I thought of publishing. But I modified them completely and never published them. When I became interested in the cinema, I didn't think these stories were filmable. Then one day I had an idea for a film (*La Boulangère de Monceau*)—one that was not written out. And I realized this little scenario had something in common with the tales I had written before. Splitting hairs, I realized the stories had a common theme and I decided to point out this theme and make six. I thought that instead of looking for a producer before making the films, it would be better to make one film and *then* get a producer. I felt the producer or the public would come later. And finally they came!

BW: How did you decide their order? (Note: Rohmer lists *My Night at Maud's* as III though it was shot after *La Collectionneuse* which is number IV.)
ER: The order was that of the easiest to shoot. At the same time, the first one was a simple story and the last enriched by all the others. In both *La Boulangère de Monceau* (I) and *Chloe* (VI), the theme is apparent. It's like a musical composition when the theme returns in the last movement. I also felt the last three had to be done in color so they must come when it was possible to shoot in color. (Note: Meaning when there was a sufficient budget.) Except for *Maud* which was always conceived in black

and white. And, of course, it was easier to make the first films with young people because there are more of them not doing anything and they will make movies without being paid. The first ones were also better realized with non-professionals whereas mature actors were needed for the last three.

BW: I find it extraordinary that you could have conceived the stories for these films twenty years ago and filmed them with almost no change. In other words, that you, as a person, as an artist, didn't change and therefore find it necessary to alter your scripts. Did you never feel at odds with yourself?
ER: You can judge from reading the scripts that I always remained faithful to myself. There were some changes: for example, I wrote Maud right after the war and the hero was retained in the girl's apartment not by snow but the curfew. He had already decided to marry the girl whom he had seen, however. And there was no religion, originally.

BW: Why did you add that element?
ER: The concept of the Moral Tales was that there would be an explicit philosophy expounded . . . not my own but that of the character . . . although this is difficult in cinema and there is the danger of doing a thesis movie. It was a reaction to a certain conception of modern literature. When I wrote the stories that led to the Moral Tales, I was discovering American literature between the wars—what was called "behavior literature." It was the painting of situations: what people said was less important than the literature that preceded it. This eventually led to the French *nouvelle roman*. I felt the cinema had to do something different from literature, so I acted against this tendency.

I think that in life—in our Occidental society since I know very little of others— conversation often involves things other than the frivolous. Rather, ideas and feelings. Those were the subjects I wanted to show in my films. "Moral" means that each person expresses his philosophy of life. I don't want to sound too pretentious . . .

Of course, the young man in *La Collectionneuse* (Patrick Bauchau), the girls in *Claire* and in *Chloe* have very different conceptions of life. And express it differently. In life that's how people are. And cinema is to show life. It's because I'm a realist I do that, not to express my own philosophy. In the world I see, that's how it goes. The difficulty is that these philosophies must be integrated in the story, not merely *hors d'oeuvres*. But for me this was not too difficult since the story and the philosophy of the story are one. This is particularly evident in *Claire* but also in *Chloe*. The characters in *Chloe* say more banal things but, still, they act in accordance with their concept of life. Even if they don't elaborate, it becomes clear by their actions. Morals change less than people, at least in this area which is mine. Superficial things change, but not deep things. Still, I modified. I adapted my films to the period in which they were happening. Even though my original idea was ancient, the final writing took place only just before shooting began.

BW: I should think audience reaction to the character of Chloe—as well as Maud would have been very different twenty years ago. Far less approving.
ER: The bohemian tradition always exists and this character could have been conceived even in the last century. You could put the story in 1890, at the time of Maupassant, with only a few changes.

BW: That is true, but the literature of the last century wasn't read by the same masses of people that see movies today. I can't imagine how, even ten years ago, audiences would have responded so sympathetically to Chloe. Women like Chloe, Maud, Haydée (in *La Collectionneuse*) could never have been cheered then, as they are now.
ER: It is true there's been a change in mores, which I would date from around 1965, when I made *La Collectionneuse*. And maybe the public will find them demodé, but I wrote them before this change. When I conceived the character of Chloe, there were existentialists.

But this thing about mores is very exterior. The fact that morals are a bit freer changes very little the basic relationship between men and women. What makes my subject free from fashion is that my characters do not claim a certain freedom against the rules of society. They do not try to free themselves from social pressure. There is not a conflict between the individual and society. The conflict is more between the freedom of the character and the rule he imposes on himself. Frederick (the husband in *Chloe*) has a rule which is to be a good husband; Chloe, not to get married. And inasmuch as in any society there are rules—whatever they may be—these subjects are valid. If it's not bourgeois morality, it's anti-bourgeois morality. (Pause.) Some say that the very idea of morals is passé, but I do not feel that.

BW: Why is it that audiences always dislike your leading man?
ER: The male character examines his own conduct and doesn't see

himself in the most favorable light. I don't want to make my male character sympathetic but the contrary. He's someone with certain beliefs who becomes intrigued by a woman with different beliefs. He thinks they're wrong but, somehow, better than his. And so the audience, too. They're attorneys for the other party.

BW: But you evidently agree with him because he never makes a decision to go with the woman who intrigues him.
ER: In the long run, even if he thinks woman #1 (wife or fiancee) is not worth as much in the abstract as woman #2 (the tempting woman), she's really worth more. They're compatible. The man and woman #2 don't make a good couple.

BW: You, as their creator, don't want them to make a "good couple."
ER: Since they're right for each other in real life, the fact they're together onscreen cannot be criticized. In *La Collectionneuse* there was the Bauchau couple (Patrick Bauchau's real-life girlfriend was the one in the photograph) and in *Chloe*, the Verley couple (Bernard Verley and his real-life wife, Françoise). And I've always found certain antagonisms between actress #2 and the male actor. In all of my films I've never had the bad surprise of the male character and the temptress falling in love. On the contrary, there's always been a little teasing game. There's no compatibility between the independent woman and the narrator.

BW: Are you a crusader for marriage?
ER: No, the tales only analyze situations that exist in life. The traditional moral values seem to win over, even if they're criticized in the process of the movie. That made Zouzou call me a reactionary. But I don't feel it is my role to fight roles or to defend them. (Note: I think he means he is not a propagandist for either party.)

Still, I think morals are an important thing. Moral judgment still has meaning. Literature and cinema that show the animal rather than the moral side of people is less interesting . . .

BW: For you?
ER: No, for the audience. Modern literature and cinema are very often critical and derisive and make fun of the people presented. I find in that direction there is little to say. It's a small subject. For me, what makes the human being different from an animal is that he imposes obligations upon himself. Man is looking for a certain rule of life. "And who can go

with humor to heroism," says the dandy in *La Collectionneuse*. My characters refuse heroism. They want to live in the everyday life and heroism is not part of everyday life. I think it's an interesting problem because it concerns everybody—how to live each day according to certain ideas. What is tragic in modern life is when the idea of life is lost.

BW: Your point of view toward the women in your films is controversial. Some feel you disapprove of the independent woman.
ER: The tales are moral inasmuch as the characters follow a certain idea of life, even in common everyday situations. But you must realize that woman #1 has just as equally a strong notion of life as woman #2. If the public has more sympathy for woman #2's idea of life, it may be because it seems less conformist than the man's. But maybe it's just as conformist. (Long pause.)

The public is free to be critical of my characters, but I am not. On the contrary, I am an admirer. I show only things I like. What I like about the temptresses is not an abstract idea of their prettiness, but because they have a variety, a richness of life. What I like about them—as in all of life—is the fact they are unique. And the cinema, of all the arts, is the best to show the unique aspect of a human being.

The great ambition of the Moral Tales was to take everyday situations and make from them stories that do not look like any other. I like to find a situation in which I could find myself . . . If my Moral Tales appeal a little to the public, it is because they show that life is not as dull as reading magazines or statistics. And that passions and feelings cannot be reduced to figures and percentages.

BW: Forgive me for staying on this subject of your women a little longer. Why is it that in all of your films the independent woman always loses the man?
ER: The Moral Tales happen in the past: before the story begins, the man has already chosen his woman. He might wonder about the independent woman. "If, instead of my wife, I'd have married another . . ." And why not. There might be millions of women he could marry. But I don't write to justify his choice of one or the other. I'm writing to show what is happening in the heads of the people.

BW: It's difficult not to take sides. Your independent woman or temptress is always far more interesting than the wife. Françoise Fabian ran away with *Maud*.

ER: It's necessary that the merits of the two women be approximately equivalent. I realized, after the films were made, that audiences had more sympathy for one or the other of the two ladies. There were many people who, contrary to you, loved the Marie-Christine character in *Maud*. And the actor. By the same token, for some the character of Chloe is the height of horror.

I like the fact that the character must hesitate between the two women. And I like the fact that audiences hold for one or the other. But you must start from the fact that he's married to one woman and not wonder why he doesn't marry the other one.

BW: Are you implying that the independent woman, whom you call the temptress, can never find marital happiness?
ER: You can say the following: I choose two women who interest me. I'm not a director who shows only one type of woman in his films. I'm more interested in Chloe. This it proven by the fact that she's longer on the screen. *But interest is one thing, sympathy another.* (Italics mine.) The characters of the wives have not been developed as much as those of the temptress because the subject of the film is the interest and time spent by a man with a woman who doesn't correspond to his notions. If some despise my narrator because he's not in love with the independent woman, that's okay. It might be proof of his humility.

Eric Rohmer is a shy and secretive man about whom, for years, little was known. His professional life is conducted under a pseudonym and he once published a novel under yet a third name. He lives quietly in Paris with his wife and two children. He claims to have been born in Nancy in 1920. Rohmer's professional life is well charted, however. He taught literature for a number of years, at the same time writing criticism for several publications and ultimately becoming editor of *Cahiers du cinéma*. His compatriots on the influential French magazine were Godard, Chabrol, Truffaut, Rivette; together they forged the *politique des auteurs* and have helped each other throughout their respective careers as filmmakers. Rohmer coauthored (with Chabrol) a book on Hitchcock who, along with Hawks and Murnau, he accounts his favorite directors. While preparing *Chloe in the Afternoon* Rohmer completed his doctoral thesis on "The Organization of Space in Murnau's *Faust*."

In addition to his journalistic work, Rohmer made several short films and worked extensively in television. He made a number of documentaries, of an educational nature, on a wide variety of subjects, from Poe and

Pascal to a study on the use of concrete in architecture. This work influenced the style of his moral tales. "For me, television was a way of studying the relationship between text and image. It taught me how people react, and I learned from television not to use too many effects, to leave the camera immobile in front of the speakers."

Rohmer made two feature-length films prior to the Moral Tales, the non-completed *Les Petites Filles Modeles* (1952) and *Le Signe du Lion* (1959). In 1962, he made *La Boulangere de Monceau*, the first of his Moral Tales. Made in 16mm, black and white, it was twenty-six minutes long and starred Barbet Schroeder, the executive producer of all his subsequent films. The following year he made the second of the series, *La Carrière de Suzanne*. These films were eventually sold to French television, providing the funding for *La Collectionneuse*. Each of his films has, in turn, financed a successor.

Rohmer spends a long time preparing his films and then shoots them in six weeks, rarely repeating a take. The preparation time is divided between research and actors. Locations are scouted with great care, with special concern for the best light of day for each. Rohmer is influenced by certain painters and studies their work carefully; a touch of Ingres may be noted in *Chloe in the Afternoon*. He is always accompanied by his director of photography, Nester Almendros. "Rohmer avoids easy beauty but, at the same time, he wants every shot to be beautiful," says Almendros. Rohmer chooses his players with utmost care and has demonstrated an eye for unusual personalities, particularly in his choice of women. He spends a lot of time with each of his leading players. "He gets you thinking about the character," says Bernard Verley, "and by the time shooting begins you are very electric." Rohmer often tailors his dialogue for the specific actor, giving it to him or her a few days prior to the shooting of a scene.

A sports enthusiast, Rohmer runs three miles every day and, as part of his thirty-year crusade against pollution, refuses to own a car. An occasional cigar or glass of wine are his only known vices; tea is served promptly at 5:00 P.M. every day on his set

Rohmer's future plans include publication of the moral tales and, in 1975, a new movie.

Rohmer's Perceval

Gilbert Adair / 1978

From *Sight and Sound* 67, no. 4 (1978): 230–34. Reprinted by permission of the British Film Institute.

Eric Rohmer has always cut a somewhat solitary figure. At a time when most of his New Wave contemporaries were freely subverting minor American thrillers, he was serenely plotting the course of his *Contes Moraux*, six cool, epigrammatic variations on a theme whose place in cinema might be compared to that, in literature, of eighteenth-century epistolary novels. At a time when sexual explicitness on the screen had already become dully commonplace, the most shocking moment in a Rohmer film was, perhaps, when we were finally permitted to feast our eyes on Claire's charming knee, full-frontal, being fondled by Jean-Claude Brialy. Now, when French cinema is passing through a *crise d'inspiration*, Rohmer, as sure of purpose as ever, has embarked on another series, this time of ambitious literary adaptations. The first was, of course, *Die Marquise von O . . .* , filmed in German. The latest, *Perceval*, based on the twelfth-century epic of Chrétien de Troyes, was still being mixed when I recorded this interview with Rohmer in his office at Films du Losange, the production company he founded with Barbet Schroeder.

Gilbert Adair: Before dealing with *Perceval* itself, I'd like to ask you about your habit of making films in series.
Eric Rohmer: Is *Perceval* part of a series? Perhaps. It is, in any case, less deliberately so than the *Contes Moraux*. But it's only in the cinema, after all, that series are unusual. Literature offers any number of examples: poems centered round a common theme and published as a collection, short stories published together in a single volume. And a film, by its length, is closer to the short story than to a novel. There are always enormous problems to be faced when one tries to adapt a novel to the screen.

Die Marquise von O . . . , on the other hand, was easy. Kleist's novella barely fills forty pages and yet it contained quite enough matter for a ninety-minute film. The idea that some magical correspondence exists between the cinema's hour and a half and the 250 pages or so of a novel is a received one and totally false. But the filmmaker, no less than the author of short stories, may require more space to express himself than that afforded by a single film. So you see the usefulness of the series.

I gave another reason, though, in my preface to the *Contes Moraux* when they were published recently—and published, precisely, in short story form. I claimed that for the filmmaker personal inspiration was next to impossible, that the *film d'auteur* was perhaps a myth. Writing a scenario and shooting a film are not only different stages of the filmmaking process, they are two quite separate acts of creation. In general, when one speaks of an original screenplay, it was written first and, if it's good, might just as well have been printed. It is not the same in the theatre: no matter how badly a play is performed, its own qualities remain on the printed page and, if the play is well known, the spectator takes that into account. But in the cinema, if one has written a text and brought it to a certain degree of perfection, it may well lose by being filmed. The cinema will not necessarily be a plus, it will be something else, an adaptation—even where one's own work is concerned.

So the filmmaker will be torn between two roles: that of author, in the literary sense, and that of director. I am not at all sure that this coheres into what is called an *auteur*. Not unless a kind of unity is established, however arbitrarily. After all, a director in the theatre can turn his hand to Shakespeare, then Chekhov, then Beckett, say. Many do just that, and in theory nothing stops the film director from doing likewise. It might be very interesting, though . . . No, I feel he must be more than that, more of a composer than the conductor of an orchestra. And for me the series, which is a constraint but, as is the way with artistic constraints, capable of stimulating the imagination, provides the necessary unity.

GA: Do you consciously separate these roles when preparing and shooting a film?
ER: With the *Contes Moraux* I considered that I was, above all, a writer and questions of *mise en scène* seemed less important; with *Die Marquise* and *Perceval* I am more truly a *metteur en scène*. Then again, what I have just said strikes me as completely false . . .

GA: Why six *Contes Moraux*?

ER: I had one idea, one small but very precise idea. I developed it. I fed it into an imaginary computer, adding a few accessory elements, and the computer came up with six tales. But I was pleased to limit myself to six because what I complain of in many otherwise intelligent directors is that they don't know how or when to stop. The crisis currently besetting our profession stems partly from that. Nowadays—in France, at least—making a film seems to consist primarily in telling some personal story. Everyone has at least one personal story to tell, which is fine, except that becoming an artist almost always depends on the ability to advance beyond the autobiographical stage. This was, of course, a concept of cinema advocated by my New Wave friends and myself in the 1960s; but what was then an important and healthy reaction has ended by boring the public. Of *cinéastes* working today I can only think of Bergman who continues to film the same story, more or less, without losing his capacity to surprise us. With the others there is a constant danger of diminishing returns and the lack of a really solid scenario.

GA: But for most filmmakers a screenplay is not intended to be comparable to a literary text. Could you envisage shooting a film with the original material in a more embryonic state?
ER: I repeat, I believe more and more strongly in the importance of the scenario. And, speaking for myself, I couldn't begin to shoot with a text devoid of intrinsic literary qualities. It's something I feel as a spectator, too. I'm very quickly bored by films whose dialogue, construction, characterization do not excite me in themselves. I can't conceive of a film which would be the pure *mise en scène* of nothing. It was an idea that was kicked around in the sixties, but I don't believe in it. I believe in the subject. The notion of an abstract or even non-narrative cinema seems to me passé. Take Antonioni, for example, not that his scripts were ever weak. But I particularly like *The Passenger* because it has a real story, a plot, even if the plot is not that original.

GA: Why *Perceval*?
ER: Well, I read the text and liked it. It had the added advantage of being relatively little known. In France it is hardly read at all any longer; or else it's read in a flat prose translation. My idea was to make a double translation, as it were: to translate it into verse that would be much closer to the original, then into film, where I felt that Chrétien's masterpiece could make a much stronger impression today. You understand, I made *Perceval* as much out of love for the text itself as for the cinema, which

I treated, as was the case with *Die Marquise von O . . .* , more as a means than an end. A means of serving literature. Why not, after all?

Filmmaking is of course my vocation, but filmmaking can be anything one pleases. If Kleist's novella is now better known and more widely read than it was, if I have managed to clean *Perceval* of the patina with which it was encrusted so that it may reach a public to whom the literary text is a closed book, I'll feel that—in one respect, at least—my films are successes. But making *Perceval* was also a means of getting off certain well-trodden paths, of avoiding the trap of naturalism, which I feel has completely exhausted its possibilities. In the relation between literary and filmic narratives, in the way my actors learned to speak, in the play between the stylized and the real, I hope I may have enriched cinema a little . . . well, let's just say I don't believe I'm in the rear guard.

GA: The visuals of *Die Marquise von O . . .* were inspired by the Empire style in painting and furniture; you even staged one or two rather Greuzian *tableaux vivants*. Will *Perceval* have the look of art works of the period?
ER: I had no desire to reconstruct the Middle Ages such as they were, or as we imagine they were. *Perceval* is less historical, in that sense, even than *Die Marquise*. My aim was to give as authentic an expression as possible to Chrétien's intentions—not to interpret the text from a modern viewpoint, as Frank Cassenti did in his film *Chanson de Roland*, but to visualize the events Chrétien narrated as medieval paintings or miniatures might have done. Of course, I don't give a hang if the *result* is authentic. It would be wishful thinking to suppose that one could portray a period in history and its ideology as they presented themselves to the people who were living at the time. Only the starting point has a claim to authenticity. I used twelfth-century literature and painting and music—there is a lot of music in my film—to arrive at something else, a totally personal creation which, I hope, will also offer a less than conventional view of the Middle Ages.

Because working in the past has enabled me to discover certain *new* possibilities of expression which would otherwise have escaped my attention. For instance, the coats of mail worn by the actors are absolutely faithful to those of the period, i.e., made mail by mail. Well, we discovered a kind of truth in those coats of mail. They were extremely heavy, the actors and stuntmen were forced to invent ways of moving in them, which finally inspired a whole new approach to the kind of gesture to be used in riding horses, battle scenes, and so on. Something not seen before in historical films.

GA: Gesture would seem to be very important for you. But in *Die Marquise von O...*, where the actors ape the gestural rhetoric of eighteenth-century anecdotal paintings, the spectator who in a museum would accept the conventions, or at most smile at them, is tempted to laugh outright when they are animated on an enormous screen and in a quite different cultural context.

ER: I don't mind. I'll be surprised if it happens with *Perceval*, though, partly because it doesn't pretend to the spatial realism of the earlier film. And there is in medieval art no pathos, none of that rather weepy, sentimental side of the eighteenth century, which may well strike us as comical today. *Perceval* is very far from that, it's more poetic, more *fantastique*, even. The stylization is much stronger, although not constant; I didn't want it to become stilted or artificial. As to gesture, in medieval art it is always very stylized. A hand, for instance, is always shown stretched wide open, you'll rarely see one closed. So I sought an overall system of gesticulation which would justify every such movement. And finding the key was less tricky than I thought. I observed that it was enough to pivot the forearm around the elbow, keeping the elbow close to the body and never moving the upper arm.

In *Die Marquise von O...* the actors made dramatic, declamatory gestures—an arm stretched out, a forefinger pointed accusingly, and so on. These are eighteenth-century gestures *par excellence*, Roman or revolutionary gestures, if you like. Whereas in the Middle Ages, no matter what the situation, the expressive movement is always governed by the elbow remaining tight against the body. By constantly thinking of this code, the actors soon managed to arrive at a natural style; and during the year in which we rehearsed they would practice it every day, like scales. As I say, I avoided systematization. Perceval himself is depicted as a man of nature, a *naif* whose reactions are quite spontaneous, and he was permitted a great deal of freedom in his gestures. The courtiers and musicians, on the other hand, who represent the manners of a society—and this was an excessively mannered, precious society—adhered much more rigidly to the code. So gesture sets up an opposition between Perceval, who is unversed in courtly manners, and the ladies and gentlemen of breeding. But it was never a question of slavishly imitating earlier works of art, it was a means of access to a new kind of expression which enabled us to rediscover—in particular, with the women—a certain behavioral grace, close to that of the dance and now quite obsolete. Women today behave as they please, unlike those of earlier periods on whom a strict etiquette of gesture was imposed.

GA: It seems that the actors were not only called upon to speak their lines, but also to comment on their actions.

ER: Yes. In the text of *Perceval* there is a narrative which I found so beautiful that I decided to keep it, instead of merely filming the actions it depicts. The Grail, for instance. It might have been considered enough in a film version to show it. Not for me: I wanted it to be described in Chrétien's own words. In fact, the Grail is a poor example, since it's quite straightforwardly done: there is a voice commenting off. But in other passages characters shift from the first to the third person and vice versa; even, on occasion, adding "says he." Well, it poses no problem. Perceval will say, "Make of me a knight, says he." During rehearsals the actor, Fabrice Luchini, was afraid to say "says he." He would alter his voice, lower it. He would try to swallow the words. So I had him say, "Make of me a knight, says he" all in the same tone and exactly as if the character were speaking every word. It's fine, I assure you. No problem at all. I'm certain that, after perhaps a few uneasy moments, the spectator will cease to notice it. There were passages concerning Perceval that I had originally given to a chorus—for instance, "And he who has no sense of day, nor of hour, nor of time, replies: What day is it?" Well, now it is Perceval himself who comments on his otherworldliness. Or Gauvain, when courting a young girl, will say, "He is alone with the maiden."

GA: Is this said to the girl or is it spoken to the camera?

ER: To her. It's part of their conversation. Instead of a long dialogue scene between them in which they might express their love for each other, I simply have her say, "Of love they speak without end." It's all quite natural, especially after the beginning of the film which is sung, more or less, which is more like an opera. The first few minutes are extremely stylized. When Perceval appears, saying, "And he throws his lances in the air, one behind him, one in front, one up, one down," it could hardly be more artificial. He doesn't even throw the lances, in fact. He merely speaks of throwing them. But, as a style, that seemed a little too balletic: afterwards, the film becomes progressively "naturalistic."

GA: When I saw the decor it appeared equally false, more like some enormous maquette than a proper set.

ER: But the decor, too, will end up by appearing natural to the spectator. There is in this film, you see, a stylization of forms but a realism of space. I pondered for a long time on the problem of representing in three dimensions the flat, one-dimensional space of medieval paintings. In my opinion, whenever cinéastes have attempted to flatten perspective, it has been a failure. Photography is photography. So I decided that if I was going to stylize the image, it wouldn't be by photography but by the conception of decor. I had the idea, which might appear paradoxical, of rendering the absence of the third dimension by an exaggeration of that same dimension, which is to say, rendering the flat by the curved. After all, the frames of medieval paintings aren't always square. They're frequently in the form of letters, as in the famous illuminated manuscripts from Ireland. When this is so, the edges of the frame, which are generally ornamental, weigh very heavily on what is depicted within. The painting seems to curve under them. If a painted character finds himself, as it were, at the edge of the frame, he is obliged to bend slightly, as if a pressure were being exerted on him. Now the shape of the cinema is rectangular. No getting away from that. But what I did was to curve the whole set—for it was one unique set—into a semi-circle so that, when a character walks straight ahead, his walk must in fact describe a curve. The trees, the castles also follow the contours of the set. I don't suppose the spectator will be particularly conscious that everything is revolving, but he'll doubtless feel it as a general impression.

GA: Are there any false perspectives?
ER: None. I didn't want to do what Laurence Olivier did in *Henry V*. The film was shot in an entirely realistic manner. The towers may be much smaller than life-size but they are recognized as such. They stand firmly on the ground, or rather the studio floor, one can walk around them, there is absolutely no attempt at *trompe l'oeil*. My first decision was that everything should be practical. One should be able to climb the stairs or live in the castles, however small. The horses just manage to pass through the castle gates, but they *do* pass. We believe it.

GA: Truffaut once remarked, *a propos* of historical films, that he was willing to accept the existence of cameras in the Middle Ages, or whenever, but not the existence of zooms. Did you decide from the outset on a definite style of photography and lighting?
ER: All the work went into the decor. Once the set had been constructed, we shot it as we might have shot a modern one. There are no *visual* effects. Except, of course, that *Perceval* was photographed in a manner completely opposed to Nestor Almendros' previous film, *La Chambre Verte*, which Truffaut wanted all in chiaroscuro. We were looking for a much more evenly spread light. Not that we deliberately set out to avoid

shadows, on the grounds that there were none in medieval paintings. It's simply that the set, as constructed, cast very few shadows; even if we had wanted them, it would have been awkward. By using lots of gold—on the walls, for instance—we couldn't help but obtain an effect of flatness without shadows. But, thanks again to the curve, I don't think one ever has the impression of a backdrop.

GA: How did the actors manage to establish a relationship with such an artificial, toy-like decor?

ER: It's a very different one from the relationship with the real world, or even when one is filming in exteriors. In *Perceval*, the actors hardly *touch* the decor. There is no tactile relationship as we have in life with our surroundings. When the characters are seated on the dainty little benches we had made for them, they hardly seem to sit at all, they sit on the very edge and place almost no weight on them. What we were trying to generate, by means of this airiness, was a kind of magnetism between actors and decor, a perpetual play of attraction and repulsion, especially when they move, a certain distance is maintained. A rider on horseback is forced each time to take the same curving route. Even in the interiors, space is emphasized by numerous curved corridors, arches, colonnades, and so on. This creates tension.

GA: Do the battle scenes resemble those in films by Eisenstein or Welles?

ER: Not at all. First, because they aren't like that in the text. Chrétien generally says little more than, "Useless for me to recount yet another battle." It's always the same, after all, and it obviously bored him. He wasn't writing a *chanson de geste*. In the film, however, there are no ellipses: you see the battles, you see the lances clashing, the knights falling dead. But it's very rapid. It's all over in a flash. There are no frightful open wounds visible, almost no blood. Except once at the very beginning, when Perceval, still very young and cruel, unlearned in chivalry, pierces a knight's eye with his lance. In the context of the film this is an extremely strong moment, but again it's very, very rapid. And it all ties in with the set, which is simplified in accordance with Chrétien and medieval art. A tree stands for a forest, stands for several forests, in fact; the same castle is used for many different castles. Only the interiors change. And in the battle scenes, finally, very few knights participate.

GA: For such a complicated film the shooting schedule was astonishingly short—eight weeks.

ER: We rehearsed for a whole year, don't forget. Luchini knew not only his own lines by heart but all the other roles. Everyone applied himself to the film with an extraordinary kind of devotion: Luchini, for instance, took a job working nights for a TV repair company during the year of rehearsals. As it happens, we were able to bring the film in three or four days under schedule.

GA: The characters of the *Contes Moraux* were gifted with intelligence and a capacity for articulating their problems which was—and still is—rare in the cinema. But Perceval is a *naif*: is he a Rohmerian hero?

ER: I like Perceval, who is, I should say, closer to the feminine characters of the *Contes*. One could compare him perhaps to the *Collectionneuse*, in the rather insouciant way he collects his adventures.

GA: One final question—for our English readers, as they say. If *Perceval* may be considered part of a series, is there any chance of your choosing an English classic?

ER: Who knows? Stevenson, I might enjoy filming. But there is the problem of the language. My German, you know, is very weak, but that didn't bother me during the shooting of *Die Marquise von O* . . . I had learned all the classics at school so that, even if I spoke it badly, it was good German that I was speaking. Unfortunately, I have no knowledge of English at all. And the English literature I know best is American detective stories . . .

Comedies and Proverbs: An Interview with Eric Rohmer

Fabrice Ziolkowski / 1981

From *Wide Angle* 5, no. 1 (1982): 62–67.

Eric Rohmer's career has been an extremely varied one: teacher, critic, editor, producer, director. François Truffaut and Jacques Doniol-Valcroze called on him in the late fifties to take over the editorship of *Cahiers du Cinéma* which had just felt the blow of André Bazin's death. Rohmer, who signed his first articles in *Cahiers* as Maurice Schérer, led the review for some six years and finally devoted himself solely to filmmaking. He grouped his first films in a series of what he called *Moral Tales*. They include *My Night at Maud's*, *La Collectioneuse*, *Chloe in the Afternoon*, and *Claire's Knee*. His two most recent films, *The Marquise of O* and *Perceval* explore more historical subjects. The sixty-one-year-old director is lanky and speaks in a staccato rhythm which often betrays the fact that he is thinking aloud. We met on March 31, 1981, in the offices of his production company (which he owns with Barbet Schroeder) to speak about his latest film, *La Femme de l'Aviateur*. With this film, Rohmer returns to a limited group of characters given to lengthy discussions about their relationships. On Rohmer's desk is a copy of the new issue of *Cahiers du Cinéma* which includes an article on *La Femme de l'Aviateur* by Pascal Bonitzer. "Is it positive?" I ask. "It's a typical *Cahiers* piece," Rohmer explains. "It's positive, but the things they say about the film could just as well be said to be negative!"

I would like to thank Mr. Rohmer for his time and cooperation in editing the final version of this interview.

FZ: Why *La Femme de l'Aviateur* now, after two "historical" films, *The Marquise of O* and *Perceval*? Is this some kind of return to earlier concerns?

ER: You might well ask why those two films after the Moral Tales. They represented a kind of interlude, an intermission. I write very slowly and shoot the films well after having conceived the subject. After the *Moral Tales*, I needed a break; there was even some laziness involved. *Comedies and Proverbs* came to me while I was shooting *Perceval*. A new way of composing a story presented itself to me; a new structure became evident. The structure of the *Moral Tales* could have been prolonged but I limited myself to the six Tales, while I don't think I'll stop with *Comedies and Proverbs*. I can continue indefinitely inasmuch as this structure is a larger one without a specific theme.

The subtitle of the film—*On ne saurait penser a rien* [One Cannot Think of Nothing]—is a deformed proverb. It refers to a bit of dialogue in the film: "What are you thinking about?" "Nothing." One always thinks about something. But my proverbs will always be either false ones or those taken against the grain. I don't believe in proverbs any more than did Alfred de Musset who also wrote *Comedies and Proverbs*. It's to show that I have no moralizing intention—the opposite of the Moral Tales. The opposite of any truth is correct. There is no formula for truth; it isn't found in assertions. But I mean to stay superficial with these films. I don't want to make profound films. Bazin used to say that there was a profundity of the superficial in American film, but I also think that there is a superficiality to profundity.

FZ: Your mention of Bazin reminds me of something Chabrol said about films with "small subjects." In this respect *La Femme de l'Aviateur* seems to effect a tie with the New Wave in its early period, not only in its economy of production, but in its choice of a fictional subject—in this case a very brief action is the pretext for the entire story.

ER: It's difficult to pin down. For example, is *Claire's Knee* a "small" subject? But if we're talking about area covered, all my films, including *The Marquise of O*, have been taken from short stories (*Perceval* is the exception). I wrote them in that form. They're not taken from novels. In other words, I have rather limited material which could be presented in two or three pages and which I have expanded. What really disappoints me when I see novels which have been adapted to film is that everything has had to be tightened up and contracted. I think that cinematic mise-en-scène is an art of expansion rather than contraction. I believe that we must expand the life of something which, when told, would be very short. *La Femme de l'Aviateur* was written in the form of a fifteen-page short story (as I've written the next one). At first, I don't think there's enough material, that all I've got is a short film. I then realize that it isn't a short and that I've even almost been led to write too much.

By the way, I'd like to say that television has brought something that didn't exist before, which is to allow for the adaptation of novels. They are better suited to television series, for example. But I think that a one-and-a-half hour film corresponds more to the short story in literature than the novel. If I were inspired in a novelistic vein, I would be tempted by television. But the conditions under which series are filmed for television are not those which allow for completely free expression. There are too many constraints.

FZ: Did your recent experience in the theater influence your work methods on this film, especially in terms of the acting? How does your conception of acting (which some have called flat in this film) differ from Bresson's?

ER: My interest in the theater came from a certain lack of enthusiasm for the raw documentary. A certain type of filmmaking like that of the New Wave went to the limits and has found its logical continuation in television. We are no longer impressed by someone who speaks as they would in real life because, at one point, actors thought they had to *act*. It's not as rare as before. I was drawn by something a little more stylized, a kind of expression not as close to the platitude of everyday life. At the same time, I never left the natural element in my theatrical experience. I've always refused theatrical oratory. After this experience in the theater I wanted once again to show people as they speak every day. But, what was once a goal at the time of the New Wave is now a normal method. The goal of my story is not only to show people who speak in a more-or-less natural way, but to show them speaking that way in order to go somewhere else. In the same way, shooting in the street, a little on the sly as the New Wave used to do, is no longer a goal but normal. It is a natural thing, but also almost obligatory. It's impossible to show extras like they once did in Marcel Carné films.

At the same time, we must learn from the experience of the sixties in order to master the street. In the sixties we went down into the street; in the eighties we are masters of it. We can organize a mise-en-scène in the street as complex as in the theater. I wanted to do theater in a place which wasn't built for that purpose. I wanted to master completely all the elements from a visual and aural standpoint, and to do this I used advanced techniques which didn't exist at the beginning of the New Wave. We shot with 16mm equipment and blew it up to 35mm. But we'll soon shoot the same way in 35mm. In terms of sound, we mustn't forget that the first films of the New Wave were shot in post-synchronous sound. There have been considerable advances, especially the invention of transmitter microphones and multiple-track systems. We had two microphones for this film and double tracks which were only mixed later. There was a great deal of work during the mix. I used the Buttes Chaumont area, for example, and found myself as comfortable there as in the studio during the shooting of *Perceval*. The constraints of the studio—the heat, the noise from the fans, the schedule, the horses, etc.—were no worse than those I found in the park—the sightseers, the constantly changing settings, the weather. Therefore, I was as comfortable in the park as in the studio. There was the added pleasure of breathing air which, even if it isn't the best for you, was very pleasant at that time of year.

As far as the acting is concerned, I don't agree that it is "flat." I'm looking for what is natural, but everyone has their conception of what is natural. I'm very particular about this point. There are actors who seem to me to speak correctly and those who sound false. Of course, these notions are rather subjective. I'm not really drawn to non-professionals; I think actors speak more correctly than non-actors. There is a certain false theatrical quality into which the actors can be drawn and which I avoided. But I'm also not pleased by the singing quality of the voice of someone who doesn't know how to master his or her voice. I think I'm very far from Bresson in that respect, since he doesn't have these categories of correct or false and is looking for a blank voice, a voice without intonations. On the contrary, I play on intonations even though they may not be the same as those found in a classic film. I think that if Bresson sees the film, he'll be horrified.

FZ: I was struck by a conception, not only of the city, but of Paris specifically. It reminded me of the surrealist conception of the city as a character. Can you say something about the song at the end which has to do with the city?
ER: It may look more like a Parisian film to you than to a Parisian writer, but I'm happy to see that people notice this. The love of Paris had a lot to do with the return to a contemporary subject matter. The disaffection I felt for Paris at one point was the reason for my historical films. Paris has always interested me, inasmuch as I am not from the city and see it with an outsider's eye. I wouldn't be interested in shooting in foreign locations, for example, and if I shot in Germany [*The Marquise of*

O], it was because I was thinking of German Romanticism. But I would be incapable of dealing with contemporary German reality. My generation in France greatly admired American cinema. There was a whole myth around the U.S.: the least little thing that took place there became sublime. It took on an epic quality while everything that took place in France did not exist. For example, many French intellectuals have difficulty accepting French detective films because they find them incomplete somehow. Even though Americans have a certain mastery of this genre, there are great French examples like Simenon and Melville. But the French have a complex about it—as long as it comes from the U.S., it's more interesting. *Cahiers* had some role to play in this and, as editor, I had some hand in it. We greatly admired Dashiell Hammett, for example. I recently saw *Quai des Orfèvres* by Clouzot and even though I'm no great admirer of Clouzot, I truly think that the police story there is as good as in some American films. But as long as it was French, we liked it less than if it had been made by an American.

It's a little bit the same for Paris. I became conscious that without being old-fashioned one needn't be systematically modern. I don't think that modern Paris is to be found in its modern architecture, which is only superficial. I chose a Paris that has existed for a very long time, a very banal Paris, where there has been a lot of filming [the Buttes-Chaumont area] because Feuillade shot there since the Gaumont studios were nearby and because television is there today. I stayed there longer than usual instead of simply presenting postcards of the place. I wanted to give the train station at the beginning of the film more space. I had to choose, for the opening title sequence, between the train station and the postal workers. Before them, there were to be a number of shots of the train station which would have been very much like Carné. I wanted to show how in this nineteenth-century city a modern way of life had installed itself: the appropriation of an old setting by young people who feel as comfortable in it as if it were something of their generation. I think this is something specific to Europe, especially to France and Italy—an appropriation of an architectural setting each time by a new generation.

The song was to express this nostalgia for a certain tradition. There is a musical tradition in Paris which is making a comeback in the streets. It seems to be superseding jazz. There's an old-fashioned quality to it. I think it's a living tradition and on this point I'm very nationalistic. In the nineteenth century there was a German imperialism in music with the waltz which was the popular music, and in the twentieth century there has been an American imperialism: jazz, etc. But I don't think that

European traditions have died off. I think they're enjoying a revival. This is true of Occitan traditions which connect with the Middle Ages, and *Perceval* also had music which tried to be European. I was amused by an American review of *Perceval* which showed me to what point Americans were often insensitive to this music. It said, "It's only good for making school children of Parisian suburbs dance on Saturday nights." For them it was totally naive and childish music. There is also the Parisian tradition of music. You see, the character was supposed to whistle and I first thought of having him whistle a blues melody and then thought, "Why? After all, we're in Paris!"

FZ: What about the production itself? It seems to have been made on a very limited budget.
ER: The subject matter didn't require a lot of money, but there is also a statement that a film without a large budget is possible. That's important given the situation of the industry at this time. It is good to know how to make films with little money. You know that there's no necessary relationship between the amount of money spent on a film and its quality. You can spend a lot of money on films that look poor and vice versa. Waste must be avoided. All these notions are not so widespread in the U.S. where there is a larger public. There is no art house [*art at essai*] circuit like there is here. I didn't get state money for this film [*Avances sur Recette*]. I really didn't get any support and this is why the film is somewhat exemplary. I didn't need state or television money. It will later be sold to television. The film cost about $400,000 and was shot with a small crew.

FZ: I heard that you insisted on releasing the film in only two theaters in Paris!
ER: I also realized that there is a distribution system in France which consists of releasing a film in numerous theaters in Paris and the provinces, the final result of which is that a film stays around only for a very short time, no more than three weeks in some cases. That's the way Belmondo's films are released. A Belmondo film will sell 280,000 tickets in one week, but the second week will be about half of that. Of course, people go see the film because of the recognized value of the star.

But for more personal films [*films d'auteur*], films which must be recognized on the merit of the story they tell, we need a certain amount of time. Word of mouth must go out. It's the only way. Otherwise we'll encounter the auteur star system which is just as bad. A Bergman film is released and people go see it because it's "a Bergman," while they should be given the time to make up their minds. The distributor releases it in a great number of theaters and if people are disappointed it won't hurt him because they will already have seen it. Sometimes, the more difficult a film is, the more theaters it is released in.

I'm taking a risk, but the film isn't much of a financial liability since it cost so little. It will certainly break even. It's more advantageous to have fifty thousand people in ten weeks than fifty thousand in two weeks with the slim hope of getting two or three thousand more in the next two weeks. Of course, we needed less money for publicity and for prints. And for a filmmaker, it's totally different; fifty thousand people in two weeks is a failure while the same number in ten weeks is a success. I think that exhibitors will finally see it this way. If they don't, the more personal films will only be able to make it if they contain an element capable of attracting crowds right away. That's a little threatening right now!

FZ: You didn't work with Nestor Almendros this time. Were you looking for something different in the cinematography?
ER: Nestor was taken up with other commitments in the U.S. with Robert Benton. I like Nestor and I like working with him, but I can also work with someone else with different methods.

Of course, this is 16mm blown up to 35mm and it therefore has a less looked-after quality than Nestor's work. Technically, at the time of shooting, we had to be more careful than usual. Nestor is very refined and subtle, and he uses very simple means. The other reason is that since it is blown-up 16mm, we had to take great care in the use of small lens openings like f5.6 or f8. I had the feeling of having done a more professional job.

Why did I use 16mm? It was because we were more at ease in the street, but it wasn't the only reason. I also think that the present 35mm cinematography in color is too beautiful, too smooth, too shiny. It has an almost hyperrealist side to it. That kind of 35mm cinematography looks American and gives the Parisian environment a shine which doesn't belong there. For me, that isn't Paris. Paris has more muted colors. Jean Renoir used to say that he liked a particular gray which is only found in Paris. It isn't a bluish gray, because in photography gray takes on a bluish cast. For me, Parisian colors are to be dampened. And even if the photography here looks a little rough, there is a unity of color from one end to the other of the film which I hadn't been able to achieve until now. There's a unity not only between the different interiors, but also between the interiors and the exteriors. There are green-blue dominants. I encountered this problem in *Chloe in the Afternoon* which took place in a Parisian setting, and I know that Nestor and I had some trouble dominating the colors. I recently saw it on television and liked it a lot, but I think that the television image mutes colors a bit. When it is shown in a theater, there are sometimes colors—especially in exteriors—that shock me.

FZ: What will the next Proverb and Comedy be?
ER: The next one will not take place in Paris but in a town outside the city which will not be Clermont-Ferrand. It will largely be made up of interiors. The proverb will come at the last minute.

Eric Rohmer on Film Scripts and Film Plans

Robert Hammond and Jean-Pierre Pagliano / 1982

From *Literature/Film Quarterly* 10, no. 4 (1982): 219–25. Reprinted by permission of *Literature/Film Quarterly* © Salisbury University, Salisbury, MD 21801.

Since Eric Rohmer has already spoken of his ideas on film in the introduction to his *Moral Tales*, this interview concerns the relative importance of the script as opposed to the rest of the film.

Question: What are your current film projects?
Eric Rohmer: Let me give you a bit of information: now that I've written a cycle of films based on original scenarios—what they call in France "author films"—*Moral Tales*—and now that I've stopped for a few years to film *The Marquise of O* and *Perceval*, I'm going back to a new cycle, called *Comedies and Proverbs*. So you see, my answer can differ depending on the periods. If you had seen me two years ago, perhaps I would have answered differently.

Q: *Comedies and Proverbs* . . . is there a connection with Musset?
ER: Yes, there is. That is, just as you have *Moral Tales* as a title that already existed (especially since Marmontel—whom I haven't read—wrote some *Moral Tales*) you have Proverbs that are a traditional genre. You have them in Shakespeare's *Much Ado About Nothing*; Carmontelle, whom I haven't read, was famous for his proverbs; and not only Musset, but also the Countess of Ségur, who wrote the little book that I always loved when I was small, called it *Comedies and Proverbs*.

But in the last analysis, just as the *Moral Tales* have nothing to do with Marmontel, neither will my *Comedies and Proverbs* have anything to do with the people who managed to write *Proverbs* and *Comedies*. Moral

Tales is simply a means of stressing the *tale* side, the narrative side, the story, which I didn't initiate in cinema—since other people had already done that—but that I used in a slightly more systematic fashion. As far as my *Comedies and Proverbs* is concerned, that has another spirit, the spirit of social games, something too of the actors' work. That's what interests me—this new project.

Q: Will there be, as with the *Moral Tales*, variations on a theme?
ER: No, in this case there will not be variations on a theme. Maybe someone will discover a common theme, maybe I myself will discover a common theme, but a priori there is none. I couldn't identify the least theme except that the stories have a rather unhappy ending, but anyway it's an apparent black that is really white, an evil which is a good. The *Moral Tales* ended happily, but that was only a transitory white which was perhaps a black insofar as this happy ending closed, stopped the story, and dropped the character back into his banality, whereas in the *Comedies and Proverbs* the ending is more open. The outcome of the story being played out is more of a failure—as a matter of fact, in general, proverbs are rather negative: like "you shouldn't do that," "there is no reason to. . . ." etc.—but, in the last analysis, it leaves the door open for something more positive. The character has set out on a road which, it appears, is not really his. In the *Moral Tales*, the character felt rather sure of himself—in an often rather pretentious way and which he has been criticized for—but which is attributable to the character and not to the author. (It is pretentious of the character to think of having found his own way and of securing his own happiness. This pretense is part of his character, however, and is not to be claimed by the author.) In my new project, inversely, the character has something more to be pitied for, doesn't know very well where he is going and he goes wrong. But in a comic way, whence the title *Comedies and Proverbs*. Comic, within the limits which I have always drawn, that is, a comedy. . . . You say "a la Musset," if you wish, but anyway it isn't exactly the same tone: a serious comedy, a comedy which doesn't have the effect which triggers a laugh in any violent way.

Q: Knowing your current interest in the stage. . . .
ER: The fact that I call these films "comedies" and not "tales" shows that the connection with the theater is more specific. In the *Moral Tales*, there was a connection with the novel, the art of storytelling, and here there would be a sort of connection with comedy. Having said this the

first, the one I'm about to shoot, everybody is going to tell me: "After all, it's like a moral tale, there's no great difference." The only difference is that there won't be any commentary at all in the first person. There is no character who can say, "I." You can't do that. If you put in a commentary with "I," it would change the tone completely. And there we leave the main character sometimes, whereas in the *Moral Tales* you might say we never leave the main character (except in *Claire's Knee*, for just a few seconds). I think we'll follow the main character from one end to the other, but we won't necessarily identify with him—or at least we won't imagine at all that the story could be in the first person.

As a matter of fact, there's a point that has always interested me: what is cinema in the first person and cinema that isn't in the first person? It doesn't depend necessarily on whether or not there is commentary. You could very easily make a film in the first person without having any text. There are films in which you'd have liked to introduce a commentary to make things easier, but it's frequently disastrous: it produces a complicity with the character and completely destroys the kind of objectivity necessary for the film. So I think it would be better to make it impersonal, and that is often difficult because at that very moment you have to imagine an observer, and that's not always so easy. There is a Howard Hawks film, *The Big Sky* [1952], where the commentary says, "We." It's a bunch of men. I like that "we." It's not the main character speaking; it's one of the members of the crew so that you get back to a sort of objectivity. It's a simple storytelling device and there you can use short-cuts.

Anyway, in the present project, there isn't going to be any voice-over. So it will be more like a comedy, divided into acts, but that's all the theater there will be. The acting will be cinematographic, but maybe a little more extreme than in the others. In the *Moral Tales*, I had arranged for the acting to be more "in-turned." There weren't any very sentimental scenes. People had the attitude that there was running conversation. There were lots of conversations. In the new series, there are conversations as well, but I think there will be scenes that will be more actors' numbers. That interests me: *The Marquise of O, Perceval,* and my recent experience with the theater have given me a taste for acting. I think that the kind of barrier that has been put up between theater and cinema (and that some people, like Bresson, persist in maintaining) hasn't any meaning anymore.

Q: In that case, the actor has to have a good text.
ER: Yes, of course. I'm writing my texts as I go along. I don't even have

all the subjects ready yet. I have a few. I'd like to do more than for *Moral Tales*. I have done the first subject. The text here is very important for me, too. It's a text written from beginning to end, not at all improvised. For the most part, it will be written. But it is quite possible that I may reserve, as in the *Moral Tales*, a few little nooks and crannies for improvisation. Anyway, for the moment, I'm not going down that road; for the moment, I'm writing it all down.

Q: But the *Moral Tales*, wasn't the greatest part written out?
ER: Yes, it was written out. Sometimes it was written after conversation with the actors. I try to put familiar words in the mouths of the actors, words familiar to them personally. The text is very often made as a function of the actor. So there I'll be doing the same thing. It will be a subject for which I have done some research. I talk with a lot of people . . . you might say I have guinea pigs. In *Moral Tales* contrary to what you might think there had been a lot of research. I've always said that they were not personal stories. In the current stories, the research side will be perhaps still more emphasized; that is, I'm having conversations with the actors themselves and other people who are not the actors, and from these conversations . . . I'm not constructing my story, perhaps because the story is already constructed, but I'm trying to find the tone for the dialogue in order to vary my own tone; for the danger when you are your own scriptwriter and your own dialoguist, is a certain uniformity of tone that is perhaps acceptable in literature or in the theater, but that in film I find tiresome. I like to vary the tone of the dialogues. In *Moral Tales*, I succeeded in varying it enough: for instance, there is no common measure between *The Collector*, which is a language which belongs to the characters themselves and *My Night with Maud*, which I wrote myself as a function of the people I know in a university society, let's say. In *Claire's Knee*, as well, there are ways of speaking that came to me via the characters, either characters who were not French—like the novelist—or young people who have their own language, one that is peculiar to the generation. And so here, too, I'll be using elements like those; in that sense I won't be changing.

Q: So your manner of developing a scenario is a dialectical process: you begin with a story-line, then you shift to conversation-research?
ER: That's rather hard to say. For instance, for the first subject, I started from something very old. It was a sketch. I can tell you that quite frankly that I have very great difficulty inventing stories, I had a very fertile

period when I was very young, let's say between twenty and twenty-five, prolonged to around thirty. After thirty, I found myself rather dried up. At the time I suffered a lot from this, telling myself I'd never succeed in finding subjects independently. And at the same time I really wanted to make films on *my own* subjects. Probably that's one of the reasons I've made films (I've explained this in the preface to *Moral Tales*). Why be a filmmaker if you can be a novelist? If you really want to write stories, you write them and then you're happy, and you don't have any desire to make films afterward. The novelists who make films do it perhaps because writing causes them some problems. They want to branch out into something else. The case of Marguerite Duras is quite clear. I think that there is someone who, in the last analysis, has an inspiration which is at once very rich and very limited. She had very few subjects, and, at the same time, she redoes those subjects, re-combines them, etc.

As for me, my case is a little different. I had written stories, and besides, at the beginning I didn't even want to make films. I would rather have written a novel. Anyway, I didn't complete it. It's remained in rough draft. I haven't published it. In the sixties I suddenly thought I might take up some of the stories I'd written a little after twenty-five and that I could make *Moral Tales* out of them. *My Night with Maud* for example was a little, extremely short, short story (I thought I had more of a gift for very short, short stories than for novels). It wasn't situated anywhere near Clermont-Ferrond. There wasn't the business about Pascal, Christianity, Marxism, absolutely nothing. It was simply a situation: someone was forced to spend the night at someone else's house. *Claire's Knee*—people think it's the reflection of a forty-year-old on youth, but in reality when I wrote it I was twenty-four years old. I was more the age of the guys in the film than the narrator. As a result, it isn't a biographical story in any way. At that moment, I confess I had wanted to imagine a character I might have known, a person about forty years old. After *Moral Tales*, I kept hoping to find subjects, and then I noticed that I had a big problem. All the same, I had this idea of *Comedies and Proverbs*, and I felt that they needed a common theme. I looked and even found some vague themes, but it really didn't get organized. And then I began to re-read what I'd written, not at twenty-five, but before, and that I'd completely dropped. I noticed that there were things there that I could use. From the time that you find two or three stories you can make out the others by relationships (opposition, similarity, symmetry, etc.). So I took a very short story, thinking I might make a short film out of it, and then I noticed after all was said and done this story was not short at all and that I could easily make a one-and-half-hour film out of it.

Q: Don't you think that novels are too unwieldy to be made into a film? There's too much....
ER: I feel that film is nearer to the short story than to the novel. What makes many adaptations of novels bad is that they have to be cut terrifically. *The Marquise of O*, which is an extremely short, short story and is followed exactly from beginning to end . . . well that made a film that is an hour and thirty-five minutes long. As a result, the scale of length for a film is that of the short, short story.

Q: But you have to expand . . . you must elaborate on the original somewhat?
ER: Well, I am not ashamed of developing ideas. I say to myself that there is a time for the invention of situations and there is a time for.... What amuses me, besides, is that all the people who have read this story that I'm going to shoot have said to me, "Now that's a story that depicts the youth of today very well!"

Q: In the last analysis, you have always done adaptations, whether it be Kleist, Chretien de Troyes, or yourself....
ER: . . . or myself, yes. I don't believe in "direct writing" in cinema. There are not so many examples of that, and in general the films that have been made like that are not among the most successful. There is no such thing as what Alexandre Astruc has called the "camera-pen," that is, anyone who makes a film the way he writes a book. The work in films is always a job of staging, and staging begins by an adaptation of a work which exists by itself in a literary way. There is no film which cannot exist literarily in one way or another. And the criterion which would state, "This film would be worth nothing literarily; it exists only by the film" is a criterion which is only rarely valid. When all is said and done, I don't see any film for which it would be valid. Even things which are very cinematographic, which renew cinematographic language, *Citizen Kane*, for example, or *Stromboli*....

Q: Or *Breathless*?
ER: Or *Breathless*. They have literary equivalents. Now, these literary equivalents may be less interesting. What is original in the film would

not be so in literature, not in the same way. There is, all the same, a literary existence of those works, their subject can exist literarily and it does exist literarily. *Breathless* is after all a story which wasn't born with. . . . Even if Godard improvised a little, it's a thing which he thought and wrote, after all. There was a script. In other words, I believe in the script.

Q: It does my heart good to hear someone say those words at last.
ER: I believe in the script, but I'm wary of script-writers. I find the position of the script-writer, especially in France, a very uncomfortable position. Because the script-writer, when you come right down to it, is a mender; he's someone who is in the service of someone else, etc. It is better, in France at least, for the director to be his own script-writer. We don't have the example, in France, especially today, of a script-writer who is really. . . . Script-writers are people who come to patch up things, to help the director when he doesn't have any ideas. I think that in England and in the United States it's different. I think that in Italy, too, it's different, that there is an effort to collaborate with the script-writer that is more productive than in France.

Q: There are cases, all the same, in France. Gruault, for instance, is certainly more than a mender.
ER: Gruault is after all. . . . Yes, I know Gruault very well, but anyway. . . . It's certain that the Resnais film, *My Uncle from America*, has a slight Truffaut aspect, that educational side that up to now hasn't been in Resnais. There is a slightly instructional side, that manner of explaining to people, to put within their reach that fastidious side, slightly teacherish like the Truffaut of *Day for Night* or *The Wild Child*. I wondered if that came from Gruault. You can't be sure. It could come from Resnais. Certainly his authority is very, very comprehensive. Resnais's relationship with his scenarists is very individual. I don't believe that there is an example, in French cinema, of anyone who has such a definite personality and who at the same time really needs a script-writer.

Q: Yes, they are Resnais films, and at one and the same time Duras films, Robbe-Grillet films, etc.
ER: Right. He is a rather rare case in France.

Q: But you are a rather rare case yourself. A director who is his own script-writer doing without any interlocutor.
ER: France is characterized by the very fact that there are nothing but

individual cases. Everyone works in his own way. That's what makes French cinema interesting. There is no common line; there are very distinct individualities.

Q: American script-writers are very much the servants of the directors. Perhaps more than in France. Professionally it's very difficult to get into the system because the producers have their stable of script-writers.
ER: In France, a young author can succeed more easily in doing a film based on his own subject than on someone else's. If you come saying, "I want to adapt such and such a thing," or, "I'm working with a script-writer," you won't be taken so seriously. Whereas, in the United States, according to what I'm told anyway, if a new director wants to make a film based on his own subject, he can't. Nestor Almendros, my cameraman, told me about the case of Benton, who did *Kramer versus Kramer*. He told me that Benton had succeeded in making the film only because his own subjects had been filmed before by others. Or, inversely, you won't get to make a film if you don't have a known script-writer; whereas, in France you can very well get along without a script-writer. In France, at present, I believe that there is not a script-writer who carries really great weight, in whom producers can have confidence. And then, in France, the production system is a little different. What counts more and more are the Commissions (of advance on receipts, television, etc.) and the Distributors. Those are the great powers. Beneath, there are the directors and the producers on more or less the same footing.

Q: In your work, on the level of the script, you don't feel the need of an interlocutor, even just to test your ideas?
ER: There are people, like Resnais, who like to talk with someone. For me, my interlocutors are my guinea pigs. It has even happened that my actors have served as my guinea pigs, not for the film in which they played, but for the next film. . . . No, I don't need collaboration. Not at all. I work all alone. I speak to no one. Only when I have finished do I have someone read it.

Q: This manner of working with the actors is also Tacchella's, isn't it?
ER: Tacchella was a script-writer before. The position of the script-writer is always uncomfortable. The script-writer is either a novelist who isn't very much at ease, or someone who wants to become a director. There were once people who were more at home writing with the script. Charles Spaak was really *the* script-writer. Prevert, while not being a real cinema

person, had an extraordinary reputation anyway. A Prevert script was a thing which had a value in itself, independently of the director with whom he worked. Nowadays, there are certainly no people of this kind.

Q: I have been astonished to hear script-writers in France say, "I am not a writer," or to make a distinction between "ecrivain" and "ecrivant." . . .
ER: That whole story is really rather complicated. One thing is certain; that is, that a play is a literary work. It can be produced by anyone; it can be simply read, never played. It is nonetheless a work which exists in and of itself. But there is no script which has the same literary value as a play. Why not? That is a question I keep asking myself without being really able to answer it. The play relies entirely on the dialogue, which has a certain continuity; it makes a whole. If you take a script that has a certain quality, a Prevert script, there must be blanks, moments where the story is handled simply by the acting, by the image, whereas in the theater—at least traditional theater—the moments where the expression doesn't come from the text are really rather rare. But then, in contemporary theater, there are indeed things which seem more like cinema, that's certain. So there I won't theorize; I'll just observe: I don't see many examples of scripts that are the literary equivalent of a play. A play exists independently from a production. It is written. You feel like having the text; people can learn it; others can feel like producing it. But the film script, in general, is made for one production. There are forty thousand directors who want to redo *The Misanthrope* or *Hamlet*; no one wants to remake *Citizen Kane*, obviously.

Interview: *Pauline at the Beach*

Serge Daney and Louella Interim / 1983

From *Libération* newspaper, March 23, 1983. Reprinted by permission; translated from the French by FH.

Question: What is the status of the actors in your films? Are they professional artists?
Eric Rohmer: Yes. I won't have any debate on this point now. I've asked for professional actors. In the *Moral Tales*, with *La Collectionneuse* for example, there were people with whom I indulged in a cinema-verité kind of documentary style filmmaking. It's really not the case here. The text was written in advance, and there was absolutely no improvisation.

Q: But didn't how they present themselves in real life, privately, socially, influence how you used them in the film?
ER: I'm going to tell you something. The story's theme is rather old now, I sketched it out a long time ago. At the time, the character played by Arielle Dombasle I imagined being played by Brigitte Bardot. No. I wrote all the dialogue before knowing who the actors would be.

Q: Have you ever written a character for a specific actor?
ER: Not really, no. I'm very lucky—I won't say it's a miracle, that's too strong a word—but I am extremely lucky with my actors. The text that I've written suits them well. In this film, it's particularly clear: the actors have been almost impregnated by the text. They have made it theirs. In fact, I don't really work with them and I have very little to do with that process. When people talk about my "relationships with my actors," I feel slightly embarrassed because it happens naturally. And I think it's very important in the cinema to trust the natural movement of things, without trying to interfere too much. The default position in most films is that you interfere, that you want to put too much in front of the

camera, to direct too much, and say too much. So, yes, on that point, I'm very "New Wave," like others, Godard for example, but in a less systematic way than him. And then there's something else: most of my actors have also been directors, either in the theatre or in the cinema—Atkine, Dombasle, Rosette in *Pauline*. I like appealing to their intelligence.

Q: How do you write your scripts?
ER: The writing process takes several years. Everything is always old. All my subjects are old and I will always use these subjects. Their roots go back to the period of my own youth and that's no doubt why I work with relatively young people.

Q: Do you read your own scripts out loud, to test how it sounds when it's spoken?
ER: It's difficult to say because I don't consider myself a dramaturge, but nor am I a writer. Let's say I like to write dialogues. I'm a dialogueist. I'm really surprised when people ask for help with dialogues! For me, the difficult thing is the initial situation, the idea, that's difficult and laborious, but once I have my characters they speak for themselves and off we go. I'm not afraid that I won't have enough for them to say, I even have the impression that they have a lot to say and my job is to rein them in. Like many people who aren't specialist writers, I'm terrified of writer's block, so I try not to stop writing. I take notes and my work consists of copying them again and again. But when it comes to dialogues, it goes so quickly that I don't even think about what I'm writing and sometimes I can find my words difficult to read because I have such bad handwriting when I write so quickly, and I can't type.

Q: It's true that your characters sometimes seem rather intoxicated by words . . .
ER: Yes, that's true, people have said that to me and I can recognize that. In the *Comedies and Proverbs*, more than in the *Moral Tales*, there is a kind of intoxication with words: people talk a lot, and are aware of it. These are people who find themselves in situations that invite confidences and that are pulled along by these confidences. This film, from Pauline's point of view, puts speech on trial—can we trust what people say? She doesn't say very much. It's the critical gaze of a teenager on adults who say too much, there you are. At that age, people don't really like speaking, and are rather suspicious of people who talk too much; you like to be a bit reticent.

Q: There's an interesting categorization in *Pauline*: the young, the old (who aren't really that old) . . .
ER: Well personally I'm quite against those kinds of categories. And I think they're less clear cut in France than elsewhere. But often it's young people themselves who use these kinds of categories. And of course, it's useful in a comedy. But even if I seem to use these categories I would differ myself markedly from them. I don't like groups at all, of whatever kind. My young people aren't the same as young people in other films. What interests me in this story is not so much showing young people at odds with their relatives, but rather in a more unusual situation: on equal footing with the adults.

Q: Let's get back to the actors. They are not debutants, but they're not stars either. Could you work with a star, with everything that implies about the profession, the star image and their brand?
ER: I'm going to be very critical towards French cinema on this issue. I think that 1982 has been lamentable: there hasn't been any mass-appeal decent French film, for sure. And I think what's bad is precisely this: we always use the same actors, we have a kind of star system. If I claim a certain originality for myself, I would say it comes from my refusal to use these stars; they bring in money but my films would lose out. I'm going to be even more severe: I think that at the moment, television, and by this I mean made-for-TV movies, are better than the cinema. Watching made-for-television films as a whole, you'll find that for a portrayal of French society, for new audio-visual techniques, or even simply for more interest, television is better than cinema. Often, when I see films made for cinema on television, I find them badly made with bad acting. Whereas on television there are a variety of actors who aren't stars and are excellent. On the other hand, made-for-TV movies have a charm that cinema films no longer have because they have lower production values and are made more quickly. I can't give any names because I think the quality of this kind of film doesn't depend on the script or the director, but more on its actors, its themes, its subjects, things like that (like 1930s French or American cinema).

Q: The French cinema, the so called "cinema of quality," tries very hard to distinguish itself from television. Something like the Césars is used to reward films that aren't always terrible, but that are usually superficial and serious, that don't have the charm of the "B" features and which aren't capable of surprising us.

ER: Yes, it's a combination of factors, it's something completely artificial and fabricated, it seems, that prevails at the moment. Having said that, I'm not a critic anymore, I don't want to make myself judge and jury, and I'm only giving a vague and subjective account, because I don't go to the cinema very often.

Q: This year, the Césars ceremony made heavy use of marketing and was very competitive. How did you vote in the Césars?
ER: In the second round, I don't vote because there's never a film that I've liked, or even that I've seen. In the first round, as it's secret, I always vote for my actors and collaborators. For mise-en-scene, I don't put my own name but that of a director of a film that I like. I can talk about the Césars: I find it a ridiculous institution, a stupid copy of the American system which doesn't compare at all to the French one. What works elsewhere can't work here and is simply going to push French cinema into being a pale caricature of this mythical American cinema, that is to say something that is completely inauthentic. There. That's why I think we should protest violently against the Césars.

Q: In your next instalments of the *Comedies and Proverbs*, are you going to investigate other social milieus or other age groups?
ER: I try to vary the places where I film. My films are fiction, but it's hard to depict areas of life one doesn't know at all. Having said that, there's still quite a range. I can paint intellectual circles, middle class and at a push working class milieus, young workers (as in *The Aviator's Wife*, the setting was modest). I would like to do something on young professionals, admittedly it would be more difficult at least from a script that was already written, to film something concerning factory workers or rural farm workers who have a completely different way of speaking.

Q: When will you know that the *Comedies and Proverbs* are finished?
ER: It's an open question. I can stop and start as I please. It's not like the *Moral Tales*, I wanted six because I wanted it to be a pleasing whole. Here it's not the same, it will be without a definitive end.

Q: Were you able to have any control over the commercial release date of this film?
ER: Well, as far as this film is concerned, perhaps I'm being optimistic, but I'm not too worried. I'm very lucky because my films' budgets are almost balanced by international pre-sales. As a consequence, it's not

that important how well they do at the French box office. Everything is determined by marketing: but what you gain in ticket sales, you lose in costs. We give too much importance to figures. For me, *A Good Marriage* was a great success, as it sold ninety-five thousand tickets, but for Godard or Demy that could be a catastrophe. It's meaningless.

Q: Why do you think your films are so successful in America?
ER: It's got a lot to do with subtitles. The films are very rarely dubbed, so there are a lot of nuances in the language which aren't perceived. And they still work despite that. I've even wondered if it's because of that that they work, because such nuance adds an extra difficulty for the audience member, whereas the subtitles are less ambiguous. And another very simple reason is that they don't have stars. They don't need them, because they don't know French stars in America anyway.

Celluloid and Stone

Claude Beylie and Alain Carbonnier / 1984

From *L'Avant-Scène du cinéma* 336 (January 1985): 4–10. Interview conducted in November 1984 in Paris. Reprinted by permission; translated from the French by FH.

Eric Rohmer's corpus has been frequently commented upon, mainly in terms of its elegant simplicity and the subtle psychology of his characters. We preferred to take a different path in our interview, concentrating on the spatio-temporal environment in which his films take place, and the urban perimeter that they circumscribe. Architectural and filmic space are linked. What secret alchemy does Rohmer use?

Q: We have the feeling that you have, since your first films, been interested in questions of architecture, space, and notably urban space, and their relationship to the cinema. Is there an interesting project for a film-maker there, and for you in particular?
ER: Yes, and I'm happy to be asked the question. I've often wondered if my interest in urban planning is demonstrated in my films. It seems some viewers are sensitive to this.

Q: Some great films address these issues: *Metropolis* (Lang, 1927), *The Fountainhead* (Vidor, 1949), *Land of the Pharaohs* (Hawks, 1955) . . .
ER: Fritz Lang is certainly a filmmaker for whom architecture is really important. Now, strangely, I'm more interested in Murnau than Lang. Murnau is more of a visual artist than an architect. I think in general one can distinguish two types of filmmaker: painters and architects. There are those for whom space exists before you film, and those who invent a space during filming, and who conceive a space that no longer has anything to do with the real space. For the former, the architects, the cinema's aim is to make a pre-existing space live before our eyes, a space in which the distances and relations between objects resemble those of the

real world. This is the space that belongs to Fritz Lang, to Renoir, and to Rossellini. I certainly belong to that group.

Q: How does that work for the genesis of your films? Do you have an exact idea beforehand of the space your characters are going to inhabit?
ER: It depends. Sometimes the space is written into the script, sometimes it only appears in the mise-en-scène. Let's take the case of *The Sign of Leo*, my first feature-length film. It's clear that the story was written to take place in Paris, and the film could only be made in Paris, and even only in some specific areas of Paris. It's the same for *The Girl from the Monceau Bakery*, even though it would theoretically have been possible to situate the story in a different arrondissement of Paris. My character goes around the district—that was a problem that was difficult to solve as well, because you can't show a circular journey on the screen: as the screen is flat, straight lines become confused with circles. I made this difficulty work for me in *Perceval*: I only had circular journeys and I turned them into straight lines. In *Monceau Bakery*, I found it difficult to show a person "turning in ever decreasing circles," I don't know if the viewer would have understood the trajectory.

In the films I've just quoted, the space was there before, and I simply had to conform to it. In *Claire's Knee* the script only found its definitive form when I saw the places we were filming. Then there are films such as *La Marquise d'O* where space isn't that important: I'm not talking about the movement of people in the frame here, but the exterior which could easily have been elsewhere. It is tempting to say that there are films where space is open and there are films where space is closed. But things are more complex than that. For example, *Perceval* seems quite open, because of the hero's progress, but in fact he doubles back on himself when he finds the Grail, he meets the same characters again, such as L'Orgueilleux de la Lande, the maiden on her horse. . . . He also turns in circles. I exaggerated this by having a circular set.

In the *Comedies and Proverbs*, space is both part of the script and part of the mise-en-scène, even if one could conceive of *The Aviator's Wife* in a park other than the Buttes-Chaumont. In *A Good Marriage*, space is more contingent, but I did have to find a provincial town within a certain distance of Paris. The mise-en-scène enriches the space, even if it doesn't order it.

Q: You only film rarely in studios.
ER: Very rarely, in fact. I have barely filmed in studios other than for

My Night at Maud's, because I found it difficult to find a flat that had the properties that Maud's flat needed to have. There is a studio scene in *Love in the Afternoon*, because I wanted a particular arrangement of windows looking out onto the street and two juxtaposed offices. In nearly all my other films, I took flats as I found them, and sometimes modified my plots as a consequence.

Q: We're struck by the fact that your characters aren't trapped or imprisoned (the exact opposite to those of Fritz Lang, for example). Even if they turn in circles, they move, they walk, you show them on bicycles, on trains etc. . . .
ER: Yes, you're right, I have a soft spot for people on the move.

Q: Usually in the cinema to signal a change of location, we see a map with a dotted line, or a moving train. In your work, there is a particular focus on movement, on characters walking or running.
ER: Yes, yes, what should I say? All I can say is that in my latest films, and perhaps even in my first, the characters question the place where they live: they are aware that they live somewhere, and that they like it, or that they don't. . . . That's the case in *The Aviator's Wife*, and also with Pauline and Louise. It's the conflict between mobility and fixity.

Q: Well, Pierre Wesselrin in *The Sign of Leo*, as a result of wandering about, becomes a tramp.
ER: Yes, he's the mother figure of my films.

Q: In *Place de l'Etoile*, this becomes frankly obsessive.
ER: Oh, I think I'd say abstract . . . or expressionist if you prefer.

Q: You could have used an aerial view to show your hero walking around the Place. But you stick to his steps . . .
ER: It would have made things easier to have taken a wide view, to have used a helicopter on something like that. I don't actually like those kinds of procedures, which are very common in the cinema. So what if I create difficulties for myself, I like finding original solutions.

Q: When you say you don't like filming in studios, is that mainly for economic reasons?
ER: It's true that filming in studios is expensive. But that's not the only

reason. The real reason is that I am . . . inspired by places. They give me ideas. What pleases me in the cinema is contact with reality.

Q: Are there some places where "the spirit moves you . . ."—the spirit of cinema, of course?
ER: The spirit can be moved anywhere. There are no unfilmable places, even the ugliest, most disagreeable places can be filmed. There is no architecture that isn't interesting somehow, even if it's unpleasant at first sight.

Q: Anyway, you're not on the look out for picturesque locations. In Paris you don't film tourist hot spots such as the Sacré-Coeur or Montmartre. We don't even see the Arc de Triomphe very much in *Place de l'Etoile*.
ER: Hmm, I'm not so sure. When we were young critics who first started writing about the cinema, we thought that French filmmakers didn't show Paris enough, whereas American filmmakers did it really well, even if it was in the form of clichés such as the Eiffel Tower or the Arc de Triomphe. François Truffaut wrote it in the *Cahiers*: the Americans are right to do this, because these places are in Paris. Personally, I don't flee clichés or postcards; in *The Sign of Leo* you've got the quais by the Seine, Notre-Dame, St-Germain-des-Prés . . .

Q: For *The Aviator's Wife* did you think straight away of the park at Buttes-Chaumont?
ER: Not exactly. It was a subject I worked on a long time ago, and that I thought would take place in the Bois de Boulogne. If I finally chose Buttes-Chaumont, it was essentially because of its terraces and landscaping, so that the mise-en-scène could make use of different heights. There aren't many steep, sloping sites in Paris, and I played on the mountainous aspect of the location, that wouldn't have been available in the Bois de Boulogne which is a lot flatter.

Q: It isn't just Paris, you pay attention to the provinces as well.
ER: I am particularly looking for variety. I'm constrained by it to the extent that my themes share an identity, and several of my films embroider the same theme. It was the rule in the *Moral Tales*, so diversity was brought by the places. To the extent that I could have called my films after the places they were set in: Annecy, Clermont-Ferrand, Buttes-Chaumont, Granville, Marne-la-Vallée. I'm from the provinces, like

most Parisians, and it is a fact that people who are not born in Paris prefer Paris to those that are. I like Paris, and I'm content, when my films occur in Paris, to show the city with a certain insistence.

In the provinces, my choices have been dictated by chance. I'm not particularly attached to places I know, I haven't shown places that I'm nostalgic for, it was above all dependent on shooting facilities that were given to me, and collaborations that occurred on site.

Q: Do you prefer the town or the countryside?
ER: Here's another question I find it difficult to answer. I think I prefer the countryside, but I like living in a city! What I don't like is average-size towns, the between the two. I like capital cities. On the other hand, I don't see myself as a painter of provincial life. In my films that take place in the provinces, I prefer the people on the margins, who aren't attached to their milieu. Take for example *La Collectionneuse* or even *My Night at Maud's*. If I show places, it's from the outside, from the point-of-view of someone who isn't fully integrated. I'm not a painter of habits, of either Paris or the countryside.

Q: You're also interested in the Parisian suburbs, notably in one of your films that was made for television, *Métamorphose du paysage industriel/ Metamorphosis of the industrial landscape*.
ER: It's true that the banlieue offers excellent material for a filmmaker. First, because thousands of people live there, next because it's a newer and more varied décor than Paris. There are more and more films where the action happens in the banlieue, crime films in particular, doubtlessly because it is easier to film violent scenes there. I've noticed I haven't given enough attention to the banlieue in my own films, and I want to rectify that.

Q: Are you bothered by the nightmarish tower blocks of certain suburbs?
ER: I've forbidden myself all criticism. I show things. I give things their chance, if I can say that. I have no a priori opinion on places. They take a test, like people: are they photogenic? There's a Godard film I like a lot, *Two or Three Things I Know about Her*. Godard filmed the most bleak and awful things, and succeeded in making them live, in giving them their own beauty. Perhaps he criticized them as well; with Godard one never really knows if he is for or against, and that's what's fascinating. With a panoramic shot over a tower block in Sarcelles, one can make a sublime image, and it is Godard who has achieved this.

Q: In *Full Moon in Paris*, when we see the deserted landscape of the banlieue, we have a feeling of sadness and depression . . .
ER: Of sadness, why? Because the heroine herself is sad, because it's winter, because the building isn't finished yet. . . . When the trees have grown, it will change.

I force myself to describe the feelings of a person at a given moment in time, and to find the most appropriate place to express them. For all that, I don't include any social criticism or pamphleteering.

Q: Would you like to live there?
ER: That's not the question. This architecture is going to age better than the tower blocks we built in the 1950s. The landscape you're describing perhaps seems lonely, but from a pictorial point of view, it's very beautiful. . . . At first, one sees the straight lines of the station, then those large buildings in the background, then we come to the lower level buildings, with their harmony of blue and white. . . . Perhaps it's not very warm, but it pleases me. Aesthetically, it's an interesting place.

Q: But that doesn't prevent the heroine from having only one desire, to leave and return to her Parisian cocoon, in the heart of Paris.
ER: In the provinces, it seems people like to be open to the outside, "to have a shop front" (*avoir pignon sur rue*). In Paris, people shut themselves away more, although you know the world is out there, at hand.

In Marne-la-Vallée, the paradox is that there are many openings to the outside, but outside nothing is happening, well, not yet. It will come later, and then people will have to protect themselves against an invasion. For the time being, let's admit that it's depressing and cold, but it could become extremely warm, or on the contrary, unliveable. A building is like a human being; it ages, for better or worse. An eighteenth-century residence can house modern office buildings and adapt perfectly to its new function, better than a building in steel and glass.

Q: But at least there was something. There, there's nothing.
ER: There's nothing yet, there will be something soon. That's why I made my hero an architect. He's a pioneer, like in the American West. He's in the middle of the desert.

Q: Can we distinguish cold and warm places in your films? On the one hand there's *La Collectionneuse* and *Pauline at the Beach*, on the other *My Night at Maud's* and *Full Moon in Paris*. We could even class the films by season: *Pauline* is the summer, *A Good Marriage* the autumn, *Full Moon in Paris* winter and *The Aviator's Wife* spring . . .

ER: It's a seductive idea, but it's not as simple as that. *The Aviator's Wife* was filmed in September . . . but it's true it could have happened around the end of May, start of June.

Q: We weren't just thinking about simple temporal issues: your characters and stories are affected by season, a bit like *Lola Montès* or *Autumn Sonata*.

ER: I've simply had the privilege of nearly always being able to shoot my films on the dates indicated in my shooting schedule, so I know what season they'll take place in. Truthfully, I'd like to be able to slip from one season to another. I tried it a little in *Love in the Afternoon*, where we see autumn, winter, and spring, the shooting of the film having been spread out over rather a long period. I did a little at the end of September, another section in December, and another in March–April time. I had coldness and greenery, and I played on the contrasts. In *A Good Marriage*, you might notice that at the start we're in summer, and at the end, when the heroine goes to the lawyer's office on Boulevard Raspail, the wind shakes brown leaves, as that sequence was filmed at the start of November. For *Full Moon in Paris*, I marked the months, and I would have liked the film to finish in springtime. Finally however, I stuck to the period of November–February, and I didn't play on the change of the seasons.

In *My Night at Maud's*, I had snow. We did take a big risk, because we could have had a winter without snow, and I didn't want to use false snow at all. For *La Collectionneuse*, we filmed in June, but the Midi area of France makes it feel like high summer. From mid-June onwards in St-Tropez the grass turns red. The summer of *A Good Marriage*, on the other hand, was as cold, windy, and cloudy as one could wish.

Q: We have slipped from questions of space to questions of time, which is perfectly normal. But let's go back to spaces. It seems that it's not so much the difference between rural and urban spaces that's important to you, so much as the desire to *close* these spaces—by finishing the film exactly where it starts.

ER: Yes, I did construct my four *Comedies and Proverbs* along those lines, and perhaps this will surprise you, but it was as an homage to Marcel Carné. I saw and loved Carné's films before those of Renoir, and even if nowadays I feel closer to Renoir I still feel a certain loyalty to Carné, particularly for the way he finishes stories where they started. It's true of *Le Jour se lève/ Daybreak*, *Hotel du Nord*, and *Les Enfants du Paradis*. Maybe it's a bit of a gimmick but it pleased me to make use of it. It tallies with the moral of the tale in my *Comedies and Proverbs*, which is a moral of prudence: you mustn't try and run away, reality will always drag you back to where you started.

Q: The difference in Carné's films is that it's simply a trick of fate, the triumph of the insignificant . . .
ER: Whereas for me, it's a sort of return to enable a better flight next time. In *A Good Marriage*, the young girl finds herself back in the same train, but ready for a new adventure.

Q: In your last proverb, allegedly from the Champagne area, but which you obviously invented, "He who has two wives loses his mind/ he who has two houses loses his soul," we are struck by the idea of place as a kind of cocoon, as if housing is related to the ego and the identity.
ER: Yes, it's obvious. My heroines are either desperately searching for a home, or desperately fleeing a home. *Full Moon in Paris* can be seen in this light as the exact opposite of *A Good Marriage*.

Q: Let's talk a little bit about the names of your characters. Is there not a certain affectation in calling them Aurora or Chloé, or even Pauline or Octave?
ER: It's not very easy to choose names for characters, because you mustn't be too unusual or too common-place. So, usually, I let my actors choose their character's name.

Q: But Octave must be a reference to *La Règle du jeu/ The Rules of the Game*?
ER: No, it's to Alfred de Musset—as are Marianne and Camille.

Q: Oh yes, Renoir himself thought of de Musset!
We'd also like to discuss your use of props, such as the goldfish bowl in *The Aviator's Wife*, or that doorway in *Full Moon in Paris*, which we can see a table and a teapot through. . . . You like objects placed in the background, it seems?
ER: It's not that deliberate, but it's true I like sets with depth—I don't like things to be too flat. It's probably also to do with encouraging depth-of-field: I hate hazy images and like all my film images to be sharp.

Q: A painterly rather than an architectural reflex?
ER: Both.

Q: In the series of articles you wrote for the *Cahiers du cinéma*, "Celluloid and Marble," your views on modern architecture seemed somewhat, let's say, traditional. There was a lot of hope about the tendencies of the period, but also some fear, that architecture would stifle the human scale.
ER: What I wrote then (and that probably needs editing) a lot of architects think today. Bauhaus and le Corbusier were of their time. Then I was called retrograde, now we would say postmodern. Arts evolve in a spiral, through advances and backward steps. That was what I was trying to say by citing Rimbaud as my epigraph for those articles: "We have to be absolutely modern." The use of the word absolutely means we must not fall into a pseudomodernism that will quickly become outdated. Today, it is not the towers at La Défense which are modern, but perhaps the small buildings at Marne-la-Vallée, which are real houses and not "machines for living in." At the start of the century there were architects with overweening pride who wanted to make over the world. They thought architecture would change the world. People don't think that anymore. Their successors have had an important lesson in modesty, they no longer proclaim that people must change to suit the architecture, they have understood that architecture must adapt to people. I never said anything else.

Q: In your work as a filmmaker, which of the Arts do you feel closest to? Architecture, painting, literature, or theatre?
ER: I hope to above all be a filmmaker. But you have to distinguish several stages. During the script stage, I'm above all a writer. Then when the mise-en-scène is developed, in the choice of settings and their organization, I feel more like an architect. I only use a set designer for studio based work. The only exception was my last film, for which the sets were decorated by Pascale Ogier.

Q: Can we conclude with a play on words, another false proverb which could sum up our conversation: "To live happily ever after, you must keep a house?"
ER: Yes, but . . . the reverse proverb could be true too. There's not just a moral in the tale, there's poetry too.

Q: Do you mean that the moral is security, but the poetry is risk?

ER: I'd express it in rather more geometric terms. There's the stable and the unstable, immobility and change. Louise in *Full Moon in Paris* says at one point that she has itchy feet. The heroine of my next film will have itchy feet too, trying to find some stability in her life.

Interview with Eric Rohmer

Gérard Legrand, Hubert Niogret, and François Ramasse / 1986

From *Positif*, November 1986. Interview conducted September 27, 1986. Reprinted by permission; translated from the French by FH.

Question: The last film of the *Moral Tales* is *Love in the Afternoon*. Did you think of Billy Wilder's film of the same name? Having just seen *The Adventures of Reinette and Mirabelle*, we think that, were you a theatre director, you would stage Feydeau or Labiche. How do you see your relationship to comedy?
Eric Rohmer: I did think of the title of Wilder's film. I like Wilder, he has a corrosive edge, joined with a certain vulgarity which means I don't always have a lot in common with him. In the comedy genre, I prefer Lubitsch. But I don't name comic directors when I'm asked to name my favorites. Having said that, amongst the directors I love, some have directed comedies, such as Hawks and Renoir. There are some extraordinary comic passages in Murnau.

Q: In your first and last films, the scenario depends on signs of the zodiac. The fact that the heroine of *The Green Ray* is a Capricorn is very important to her. "L'Heure bleue" section of *The Adventures of Reinette and Mirabelle* doesn't rely so much on astrology as meteorology. And then there's *Full Moon in Paris*. Do you think that you see this as almost a playful element in your films, or is it really part of your ontological vision? Even when Eric Rohmer makes light-hearted films, is there still a precise vision of the world which remains the same, a truth that we might label cosmic?
ER: It's quite complicated, but I can answer your question because you've posed it in a very precise manner. Astrology—which I don't really believe in—plays a similar role in my films to the pagan supernatural in eighteenth-century authors' work, when they had scruples about

discussing Christian miracles. Personally, the Catholic Christian faith which I am attached to has inspired me from time to time. I allude to it in *My Night at Maud's*, but from a sociological rather than a religious point of view. In *Perceval*, I emphasized its Christian character, whereas I could have chosen its Celtic character. Sometimes in my films there are very vague allusions. But I would be incapable of treating a subject such as that of *Therese* [Cavalier, 1986], a film I haven't seen, or [*Onze*] *Fioretti* [*de François d'Assise*] by Rossellini, a film that made a great impression on me. But at the same time, I'm eager to show transcendence in a roundabout way, like a game. That's how I use the theme of the stars, without believing in it, but without being a sceptic either, by which I mean being interested in people who believe in this area. I like people who have faith, even if I don't believe in the thing they have faith in.

There's a second point which is much deeper and more sincere in my work, that's the cosmological or even meteorological side. My films are made using meteorology. If I didn't check the weather forecast everyday, I couldn't make my films because they are filmed according to what the weather's doing. My films are slaves to the weather. To the extent that I don't cheat and that I'm inspired by the weather, I have to be a weatherman. It's the cosmos as a perfect work of art and as a natural marvel which attracts me. These are the miracles of nature. The green ray and the blue hour are the miracles of nature. This feeling about nature that I've always deeply felt I find difficult to integrate into my films which are always more psychological and morose. My last two films have been an opportunity for me to stress this more than in my previous ones.

Q: *The Adventures of Reinette and Mirabelle* is in praise of silence. "The meteorological incident" is the minute of silence at the start and the end of the film.
ER: So much so that this is what gives this rather disparate film unity. At the beginning it was four different stories, I wasn't even sure if they would be a film, because I could have screened them as four short features on television.

Q: Isn't there something frustrating in the fact that with the inevitable degradation of film, waiting a year to capture an image of the green ray is also waiting a year to create something that will degrade on the film stock?
ER: That's a question that concerns all film. You say that film degrades, well, that's true. But you could also say it doesn't degrade that much,

as Langlois pointed out, citing the Lumière brothers' films. These, that are the oldest films, are among the least degraded. Until we have the means to perfectly preserve things (it seems that videodisc is a method of perfect preservation, but, for the time being, it doesn't seem to be being used, and there is poor image definition when the film is projected on a screen), cinema preserves things less well than writing, or painting; the paintings of Van Eyck or from the Renaissance. And we could say the same thing about painting: the oldest works are better preserved than more recent ones. When you dream of cinema, you think of that. When I was at the *Cahiers du cinéma*, I was very interested in the issue of film preservation, and I carried out an interview with Henri Langlois, and if I had stayed at *Cahiers* I would have carried out others . . . it has carried on without me with interviews with directors and film programmers. But when you make films, you don't think about those things anymore. You could reproach certain great painters for having used fragile material, but that isn't their concern.

Q: In *The Green Ray* and *The Advenutres of Reinette and Mirabelle*'s Blue Hour, we are reaching something very simple and very fragile: a certain color appears for a few seconds.
ER: The thing is fragile in terms of the fiction and its representation, but the representative piece of art can be either fragile or not. It's not the same thing. It is certain that cinema attempts to capture fragility and preserve it, to give it duration. But this preserving role is limited, because the film image, and even more so the film stock, is not as solid a material—and here I'm quoting from a series of articles I wrote—as marble. Celluloid is not as solid as marble.

Q: The astrological data begins with *The Sign of Leo*. But even if it isn't as obvious as in *Full Moon in Paris* or *The Green Ray*, it always determines the personalities of some of your characters, such as André Dusollier and Beatrice Romand in *A Good Marriage*, who are so antagonistic that we can see them as such or such a sign placed in opposition. . . . Is there a kind of opposition between this use of the stars and your use of the elements? It's the accidental against the essential, as with your two characters. Events change destiny. The snow fall in *My Night at Maud's*, the rain storm in *Claire's Knee*. There is something that underpins the astrological, and that is the meteorological. It is the essence and the accident in your characters.
ER: You're mentioning things I hadn't thought of, but you're right. My

desire to make films was at first a desire to film natural phenomena. I was wondering how to do this when I was making amateur films—how to film the rain or a storm. Those were things which preoccupied me. I wasn't happy with the artificial studio cheats.

Q: You make use of the elements to express a privileged moment in your characters' lives.
ER: What I can tell you, is what corresponds to will on my part, to my deep desires, and what is chance. What corresponds to my will is the following: a deep love of nature, and a desire to represent nature, but still knowing that that is not enough because it must be attached to a story. Nature has been filmed a thousand and one times. But, a strange thing—no one has ever filmed—and I've checked, but never to my knowledge—the green ray. No one came forward saying, "yes, I've filmed it." And it's something than can be filmed, but no one has the patience. On the other hand, extraordinary things have been filmed, but more things such as volcanoes, earthquakes, avalanches, not such simple things as I have done. As for astrology, there is a side which isn't very serious, and which really owes a lot to chance. Why is Delphine a Capricorn? *The Sign of Leo* makes more sense because the story takes place in August, and therefore the sign had to be Leo. Delphine being Capricorn is pure chance. Her friend hands her over *Elle* magazine, and in the horoscope which is read in its entirety—and which I didn't invent—it was Capricorn that corresponded exactly to her character. The actress wasn't that star sign, but one that's very close [laughter].

Q: Is *The Green Ray* the first of your films to be improvised in dialogue and situation?
ER: *The Green Ray* is totally improvised. Nothing was written. There is not a trace of writing. In certain cases, the actors improvised completely. They said what they wanted to say. For the meal scene, I didn't say anything, I just indicated: "Try to convince her to eat some meat." That was all. The scene with the boy in Biarritz is totally improvised because he didn't know what we wanted from him. I met him three minutes before we started filming, because the boy who should have shown up wasn't there. I found this boy on the beach, and I put him beside the "Swedish girl," and told him, "Sit at this table and try to chat up these two girls." They didn't know what was going to happen. The other boy wasn't totally innocent, because he knew my camera woman. The other, the one with the Midi accent, who mucks about, just said what a boy might say

in that situation. He asked what nationality she was. He thought she was Swedish, whereas in fact, she's Finnish. The other said she could be Spanish, or German. That was totally improvised.

On the other hand, there are moments where the actors knew more or less where they were going. They were the most difficult scenes, and sometimes I was tempted to write them. It's a lot more difficult to make people say what you want them to say—you have to limit yourself, not wonder off topic, and be quite concise, rather than saying, "Say that . . . say that." At the end of the day, there are quite a few scenes like that in the film, which advance the plot, and in which the conversation has to be centred on a precise topic, and specific things must be said to inform the viewer and at the same time there has to be fairly rapid exchange of information between characters. We figured out with the actors what we had to do, but I didn't make them say complete sentences. Those were the most difficult scenes. Those were the ones that needed the most takes. The other scenes were good on the first take. The only thing we had to do after was the reverse shot, so that we could show all the characters (in a conversation with four characters, you can't show everybody), and to be able to cut. We listened to the first take again, and then the actor repeated what he had to say. In *The Adventures of Reinette and Mirabelle*, there was also an improvised scene. It was recorded on cassette, and we listened to the cassette again when they were talking about the theft at the supermarket, so that the discussion could be filmed with both characters. The first shot is more spontaneous than the reverse shot.

Q: Was *The Green Ray* filmed in order?
ER: In this case, we had to film in order. The only change is that we filmed the trip to the mountains before the trip to Cherbourg, for practical reasons, whereas in the film it's the other way round.

Q: Did you use more film stock than usual?
ER: No, less! Which surprised me! When you're using 16mm, you're less worried. In my latest film, *My Girlfriend's Boyfriend*, I filmed a lot more. In *The Green Ray*, I filmed less. Why? Because purely improvised scenes work the first time or they don't work at all. But I could have failed in filming them. We didn't really make any mistakes in filming, because we set everything up carefully. The only things that gave me problems were very simple things, short, transitional scenes, where the actors had to say something precise, to make the other person reply something equally precise. It's very difficult to improvise in pairs.

Q: Isn't there that in the scene with the retired taxi driver?
ER: That's total, pure improvisation. He didn't even know what we were going to talk to him about. I went to him one day to ask his agreement. He said yes. I asked him, "Do you go on holiday?" and he started to reply, and I stopped him. I said, "No, no, we'll talk about that tomorrow." The next day we arrived with the camera and we asked him the question.

Q: Like an interview?
ER: Exactly. The idea for *The Green Ray* came from there. I was struck by how natural people were in TV interviews. On TV, when people are in a natural situation, they're perfect. Whereas someone who is not an actor is awful when they're given a written text or when they're interrogated in the street with a microphone shoved under their nose, in a situation where they're ill at ease. But when they forget all that, when they're sat at a table, people are perfect. During *The Adventures of Reinette and Mirabelle*, the girls asked me, "What style are we going for today?" There were two styles: the Pivot style, and the Polac style.

The Pivot style meant not jumping on the interviewee. You had to let him or her speak, and speak politely afterwards. The Polac style meant speaking at the same time.

Let's say that, here, naturalness is perfect. If you're looking for it, you find it here, because people forget the cameras. These are scenes where people are performing, but not in relation to a possible spectator, but in relation to each other, as in a discussion. So I said to myself, if I put all these people, who are not professional actors, around a table, in an everyday conversation, they will be natural, because they will naturally be performing. At the same time, I couldn't make a film that was just that. There had to be passages that were from a classical fiction film, by which I mean passages of exposition, of plot advancement, and drama. There I was greatly helped by my principal actor Marie Rivière, who was as good in the discussion scenes as in the others. She called the tune, not only through what she said, but the way she could speak, the way she questioned people, the questions that her character provoked. She is someone who inspires, who you want to talk to, and that's very important.

Q: There are two moments where that's obvious: the scene where she cries, alone, a little away from the group, and her friend comes to console her, with a slight movement towards her; and the final scene where she really galvanises the young man when she says to him, "Would you like to come with me?" Here is classical fiction. It's here that you can see you're not simply a realist filmmaker, that there's something else. Realism or sociology are not the same as ontological truth.

ER: To come back to Marie Rivière, she didn't cry at the times I thought she would cry. I had only vaguely planned the moments where she would cry, but the only time she cries when it was planned, which was probably the most forced, which doesn't make it less moving, is the time you've mentioned, when she's away from the group. The other times it just came naturally. For example, when she started crying at La Plagne, which wasn't planned at all. I have a take where she doesn't cry, but when she does, she completely confuses the boy she's talking to, who was surprised. She also cried in the hairdresser's, which was awkward, as it was a very precise scene where we need to explain some of the action. There is nothing more tricky than getting people to say, "I was there, I left, I've come back" and allow the other person to ask questions without it becoming repetitive and boring: "Ah! You went there . . ." I wanted to avoid that kind of dialogue, improvisation as you learn it in class. What saves those moments is that suddenly, she starts to cry. The most extraordinary moment where we didn't know she was going to cry is just before the conversation with the two boys in Biarritz, where she says, "But I'm open, I look at people . . ." and she begins to cry . . . to such an extent that the camerawoman was surprised. The moment where she begins to cry, she had started to zoom out, but when she noticed that Marie Rivière was crying, she advanced the camera towards her again.

Q: In *The Adventures of Reinette and Mirabelle*, Marie Rivière cries and she completely throws the others, in order to get the money (six francs and seventy centimes). Was that a very written moment?

ER: *The Aventures of Reinette and Mirabelle* is both very carefully written and not at all written. It is a completely blended mix, not subtly because it was planned that way, but because I now no longer know what was improvised and what wasn't. The most improvised episode was this one. The last wasn't improvised, it was totally written. Apart from when I let Reinette expand when she's discussing painting. On the other hand, Fabrice Luchini says exactly what's written in his text even though we have the impression he's improvising. In fact, he speaks his text very precisely. At Montparnasse station, there was no text, it was improvised, with all those kinds of misunderstandings and redundancies that this kind of discussion can give rise to.

I could have written it. But it would it have been a question of writing naïve things to be said, because they are naïve? If they are improvised they can be naïve in the positive sense of the word, a sort of truth about things. You can sense the person's sincerity. But if they're written, a critical point of view is adopted and it becomes a kind of record of stupidity—a sort of *Bouvard and Péchuchet* . . .

Q: She reads *Bouvard and Péchuchet* in the Jardin du Luxembourg . . .
ER: I always thought it was *The Idiot*, but maybe she got the wrong book, because she was still reading *The Idiot*. *Bouvard and Péchuchet* is not a saga of stupidity. It's not that, they are not stupid. I wanted there to be a didactic quality. I wanted the girls to say profound things that appeared naïve. In the countryside, that quality was most apparent, then it disappeared. . . . But in that discussion, I wanted there to be something very true that chimed with how young women speak nowadays, with common problems, as people today might talk about them. That's why I let them say what they were thinking, even if I don't agree, and they said things I would never write. It's the only way to do it, to make it acceptable, because it would be unbearable to write it. On the other hand, the other stories, which are more comical, in which common places aren't discussed, can be written. In a very general way, when there is philosophy in my films, whether it is cowardice or prurience on my part, a certain distance, I engage in debate via my characters, very often the actors. In *My Night at Maud's* I engage via Jean-Louis Trintignant but that remains wrapped up in a very complex, ambiguous situation. The Marxist, those were Antoine Vitez's ideas as he expressed them at the time. In *La Collectionneuse*, the theoretical ideas that one can have about art in general were Alain Jouffrey and Daniel Pommereule's ideas.

The small things that can be expressed in my films are often born from reflections from the characters or the actor. Here, I wanted to go a bit further through inspiring myself from the character, through transcribing the thoughts of the character. Perhaps the actors will tell you that these are not their thoughts. We expressed that for the film, but in real life, we think something else. It's possible, it doesn't really matter. What's certain is it hasn't come from me, even if I believe in it in a certain way. But I don't completely agree with either Reinette or Mirabelle: I agree with their conflict. I think what they're discussing is important. Perhaps I wouldn't express myself in the same way, but something in their dialogue affects me.

Q: There are points of contact: the relationship between reality and art. Reinette has a desire to deform reality through art, to transform it, which isn't totally antagonistic to yours. Even if she doesn't completely express your point of view, the film shares it.

ER: I am closer to Reinette than to Mirabelle, who expresses a kind of popular common sense. I am closer to Reinette in her paradoxes and her naivete. My naivete is less assured and more provocative. But I am closer to her, even to her ridiculous side. Even Dostoievsky is close to *The Idiot* in his stupidity. I like ridiculous characters who make us laugh. All my characters have this ridiculous aspect. I want them to be like that, and they all contain a kind of truth.

Q: The heroine of *The Green Ray* is reading *The Idiot*. Was that deliberate?
ER: No, it wasn't a deliberate choice, it was a coincidence, a miracle. In that film, there was nothing but chance. That was pure chance. It just so happened she was reading that book, I don't know why. If she had been reading a book that I didn't like, perhaps I would have said, "Find something else." But as soon as I saw she was reading *The Idiot*, I said, "Oh, that's wonderful, she's reading *The Idiot*."

Q: The choice of books in your films is never innocent. In *La Collectionneuse*, they read Rousseau, that isn't chance.
ER: There are correspondences, but at the same time, there is a certain degree of chance. I brought the Rousseau, so, yes, it was there. . . . At the end of the day, I accept happy coincidences, and unfortunate ones, well, I try to . . . [laughs]

Q: Reinette is someone who tries to be systematic about her thoughts and theorizes accordingly, whereas Mirabelle uses common sense.
ER: *The Adventures of Reinette and Mirabelle* was organized very quickly, because I met Reinette and I found her extraordinary. One of the first things she said to me was, "I organize my life according to principles." "Good, like what, for example?" "When I've decided something, I do it. I decided not to speak, I haven't spoken." And that's where that episode came from. The story in the café happened to her. Then we set it up. Lots of customers will have experienced that kind of thing.

Q: Usually, your films are very carefully planned, but with *The Green Ray* you got to the editing stage that wasn't organized, unlike your previous films. How did this new experience go? Did you try to model the material in some way, or did the story emerge of its own accord?
ER: *The Green Ray* is a film that was too successful. It was easy to film.

There wasn't much waste. It was easy to edit. And then, people liked it, while I didn't think the general public would like it, seeing it as a slightly nostalgic evocation of the New Wave. I can't really learn much from it, because I have the impression it was a one-off, I don't know if we could do it again.

That's why afterwards I began *The Adventures of Reinette and Mirabelle*: I wanted to see if I was going in the right direction. *The Adventures* both confirmed and undermined my decision. I didn't stick exactly to my original idea. I was in the presence of a young woman with a strong personality, who things happen to and who makes things happen. That's the chance of a meeting with someone. Now, in my life as a director I've met people who've inspired me, such as the characters in *La Collectionneuse*, and especially Daniel Pommereule, who, although he doesn't play the main character, is the keystone of the film. Actresses such as Béatrice Romand, Arielle Dombasle, Pascale Ogier, are very inspirational people with strong personalities. I need people with strong personalities. In my last two films, it wasn't only people who were capable of articulating that I needed, but who find themselves in novelistic or comic situations, who bring along with them a whole world of dramatic or comic situations. There again, I'm dependent on meetings.

The editing process was easy too. The only scene that I thought was a failure was the scene that touches most people, that's to say the end. I thought to myself, at the time, I'm not going to be able to do anything with this film, there's no ending. I began by editing this scene to see if I could do something with it. I still didn't have the sunset and it's very hard to edit without that. I made a sunset on a screen that I filmed, then edited that to get some idea of how it would work. Moreover, it was a very difficult scene to film. The characters were ill at ease. They weren't in front of the sea, because it was too noisy. The promontory we were on was between the ocean and the bay. So the characters, instead of being just above the ocean—also because the light was moving—were in front of an embankment, turning their backs to the bay and not looking at the ocean. So that their gaze went the right way, so that they were watching a horizon, I used a towel or a bag, I don't remember which any more. So we weren't filming in good conditions. It was a scene that needed several takes and I chose shots from different times. I had to see what it looked like on the editing table. That was when I said, "This scene won't work if there's not any music." Now, in my films, I never use extra diegetic music, never. But here I think it's needed. Then I had the idea of a musical theme that could be threaded through the film. When I saw that worked, I said to myself, "OK, this end is possible, but it's a film that's a lot stronger at the start and everything that happens in Biarritz doesn't add very much. I don't know if it will work with such a strong start. I'm worried it just peters out." That was my impression, that it was a film that started almost too well. But, once the film was edited, the reverse is true, people feel that there is a progression towards the ending. That was what I thought about when editing.

Q: But during editing, did you change or alter the story or cut elements that seemed important while filming?
ER: No, I hardly cut anything. The intertitles with the dates I had already filmed. It was a film that was made with hardly anything. It cost ten times less than we said. It's not that we lied, but in the announced budget, you take into account anticipated post-production costs. In this film, filming cost about a tenth total of the budget, and costs outside of that about nine tenths. Obviously, the crew were paid for filming and editing. So, you can see what a cheap film it was. I filmed the dates, I wrote them myself in green ink, and the heroine should have stayed a bit longer in Biarritz, where there were a few more days. Then I did shorten it a bit. For example, the day of the sunset wasn't the same as the one where she walks on the beach, the day of the discussion at the café was not the same one as she met the Swedish girl. They were the only things I changed. For the rest, I cut some shots that we filmed on a day when she walked on the beach and it rained. We thought we'd give it a go, but it didn't add anything. Oh, another shot too where she's alone on a bench. But the sequence where she's alone in Biarritz seemed enough to me as it was. The sequences with dialogue are all in their entirety. Obviously there was some waste, but not more than two or three times the amount filmed, which is really hardly anything.

Q: You said you were a bit thrown by *The Green Ray*, but you filmed *The Adventures of Reinette and Mirabelle* before *The Green Ray* was edited.
ER: I was a bit confused yes, by the success of the film. Before, when I was filming *Reinette and Mirabelle*, I wasn't confused. I wanted to reassure myself that we could have the same experience. I had really enjoyed making *The Green Ray*, but I didn't know then that it was going to be a critical and even a commercial success. But I felt that it was a film that had succeeded on its own terms, anyway, and I wanted to carry on in the same vein, with the same principles.

Q: You directed another film, *My Girlfriend's Boyfriend*, before *Reinette and Mirabelle* was released.

ER: I made another kind of film in different conditions. It was a more professional film, made in 35mm. But at the end of the day, the crew wasn't much bigger. There were two more people, that is to say, there were five rather than three. Still it's not the same thing making a scripted film compared to a film with no script and improvisation. Because in a film like *The Green Ray* or even *Reinette and Mirabelle*, you can afford to fail. And of course that's what means that you don't. For example, the sequence we were just talking about, with the beggar, the railway station, the supermarket, and the department store, all that was decided the night before. And I didn't even know if I would be able to do it. For the railway station, I had asked permission, and it just so happens that the SNCF always grant me permission without problems. The problem for them with people filming in stations is that it creates crowds, but as soon as you film with unknown actors, they are very accommodating. What they don't like is people filming with stars. So we film in stations with extraordinary ease. Obviously there were extras playing the beggars in the scene, but they were friends. She could have just gone up to people on the street. But I don't really like doing that, because I respect people's right not to be filmed. If I film a crowd, I make sure it's anonymous, if not I would have to tell people, "You're about to be filmed," and that complicates everything. All the people we see going by are people who weren't aware they were being filmed. However, I nearly didn't get the station shots that day. It was last September, and the weather, as the forecast had predicted, was magnificent. But in the Paris region the start of the day was cloudy. Now, Montparnasse station has poor, neon lighting; it's also lit by natural light from large windows, but like all public windows they are very dirty. When there isn't much sun outside, we really are at limits of good enough light exposure. We nearly had to give up. Finally, the sun came out a bit and we were able to film. The scene was possible. But the camera was still hired for another day, in case we had to start again the next day. So, I said to myself, since we had the camera for another day, we could do something else, we could do a supermarket. So between 4 PM and 7 PM my assistant and I found a shop that would allow us to film the next day. You can see how things get decided. That said, the story was decided, but the settings weren't, and I had thought I would film that section later.

Whereas in a film that's scripted, with stories that follow on from each other, it's not possible. You have to have a more precise schedule, and if you can't film a scene one day, it's a bit stressful because you have to follow the schedule. That's what I did in the latest film. On the other hand, some of these ideas were used in my next film, that was filmed in a New Town, where I filmed in the street, and in 35mm. (But 35mm cameras aren't much more awkward than 16mm.) And I filmed the street a lot more (that's to say the people who are there, the urban fabric, the crowd) than I did in the previous two. And this use of the camera, that we could call post New Wave, which consists of going beyond what we were able to do in the 1960s, I think it's the best representation of the streets of all my films, including *The Sign of Leo*, where I hid myself a bit more. Now, I don't hide myself, it's more open.

Q: That's a constant thread in your second series. In *The Aviator's Wife* there are street scenes where you don't seem hidden at all.
ER: Yes. I carry on being faithful to that, and I think it's possible to go further. Perhaps I might return to the studio, as with *Perceval*. I know that in the seventies, I didn't want to film in the streets anymore. That's why I made *Perceval* and *La Marquise d'O....* it could be that once again, I won't want to film in this way. But at the moment, the desire is still there and I've gone to the limits of what I want to do, even with my latest film.

Q: At the same time, does that way of filming that moves away from the "interlude" films, if we can call them that, and the first series, become a kind of moral evolution? We feel like we are moving towards something more pragmatic, more instinctive, than that which happened in the *Moral Tales*; the characters are less calculating, there isn't a bet on someone else's destiny...
ER: Perhaps. But at the same time you could say it's a lot more superficial. To be honest with you, when I was making *Reinette and Mirabelle*, I thought "this could be café-theatre," and I think what got rid of that element was precisely that it was filmed in the street, in reality. For the final episode, I nevertheless took the risk of filming something that didn't have the advantages of the earlier episodes, that's to say the presence of reality. It was a lot more theatrical: it takes place in a precise area, it's based purely on speech, there's very little mise-en-scene, and people stay resolutely in their places. There I'm returning perhaps to *Perceval*.

Q: A very interesting thing about your career is the way in which, especially in the last series, you have moved towards filming with simple methods, small crews, which gives you, and this is something I'd like to discuss, a greater freedom, as you don't have to bear the weight of the cinema industry.

ER: I said to myself: "Perhaps there are some people you really don't need when you're filming." First of all, during *Perceval*, we had to make some deep cuts. I had a certain amount of money, and the sets were extremely expensive, as were the costumes—more expensive than they should have been, in my opinion—so we had very little money left for the shoot. We had to make some sacrifices. So I got rid of the continuity advisor. Up until that point, I'd always vaguely had someone looking after continuity, though never really a professional continuity advisor. I don't need them. I don't want to disparage continuity advisors, but just because I didn't use one, that hasn't led to any continuity errors in my films, and you can easily get rid of that job. . . . Then I got rid of the assistant director . . . after all, you're never better served than by yourself . . . and I realized that the first assistant really only makes sense if there's a second assistant director to manage. . . . The continuity advisor has to discuss things with the assistants: that's the role of the continuity advisor. So in that case, you might as well get rid of them all. Why have assistants? As for production matters, I thought that one person could manage and when I had two, there were always misunderstandings and errors in coordination. So, there, I have one person to help me, for example, when we are filming on location with organizing meals, to sweeten the police when we're parked—in that case, you're better off with a woman . . .

Q: That's administration . . .

ER: Yes, you can call that administration. What's more, we can use the feminine form "intendance" for an administrator, but there isn't a feminine form for a producer. What remains is the technical side, everything that is to do with the actual physical making of the film, which is very important. So, I get rid of things, and I rely on myself. Why not? Up until then, I had a standard technical crew, apart from grips because I had very little in the way of technical equipment and very little electricity. In *Perceval*, there were a lot of them, but after that I haven't needed them—the operators themselves place their projectors in the right place, now that they are lighter, and plug in the wires, which is not of an extraordinary difficulty. Of course, it takes time, but it's not really lost time. I have three people who work on the image, and two for sound, who seem pretty much indispensable. You need three people working on cinematography, even if one person looks after both framing and lighting; they will need to be helped either with lighting or to operate the camera itself, and you need someone to change the film reels, so that's three people. As for sound, you need a boom operator, if you want good results, and even if you're using lapel microphones you need to place them correctly and it goes more quickly if there are two people.

But I wanted to go further. I wanted to know if you could reduce all this to one person. That's what I did in *The Green Ray* and *Reinette and Mirabelle* where one person worked on the cinematography and another on the sound. I took beginners, two girls who up until then had worked as assistants, and had never, I think, had the responsibility of completing this work alone and who were, I have to say, absolutely fantastic, really remarkable. What happens when there is only one person? There are some constraints, such as when you want to analyze the work so far and see how you're doing, but my general assistant could step in and help with that. When you're filming in 16mm and at the beach, there's less to be done anyway, and I could step in as well. I could have done the framing as well, because it's not inconceivable that the director should do it, but I'm not very gifted for that, so I leave the responsibility for framing to the cinematographer. Even when there are zooms, she organizes it as she wishes. It is difficult to intervene with that anyway, to be there at her shoulder asking her to move forwards or backwards. All you can do is agree on some general principles. And that was perhaps more difficult. It demands a lot of work, all the time, for the person who is looking after the lighting, the framing, the equipment, the film—there is no respite on set. And as for sound, it is even more difficult: holding the boom while keeping the Nagra recorder around your neck is very difficult, particularly for women because the Nagra is very heavy. In those situations, there are things you can't do; you can't change your mind while you're shooting. But at the end of the day, that isn't really important. What is more difficult from the technical point of view for sound, in *The Green Ray*—a problem that wouldn't really have been resolved by the presence of another person, though—is the placing and position of the boom when people are improvising: they can even speak at the same time, and that can cause problems (my producer wrote an article about this for *Cahiers du cinéma*). In *The Green Ray*, everything was done using a boom microphone because of the clothes. We thought, especially in Biarritz where everyone would be in swimming costumes, that it would be difficult to use lapel microphones, and especially the micro transmitters. Generally, there were a lot of people, and at certain moments there could be four or five people talking at once, and that required a fairly complicated equipment set-up. So we chose the boom, and on the whole I find it satisfactory and the defects, if you consider them defects (certain words are a bit lost), are not only not really noticeable, but accentuate the impression of reality. I find it perfect. In *The Adventures of Reinette and Mirabelle* we used a different system: lapel microphones and micro transmitters—all in public—in the countryside all the time, apart from inside; at Montparnasse, we used micro transmitters. So that's the technology. As for morality, you can do this, I wouldn't say for every film, but you can make a film with just two people, one for the cinematography and one for sound.

Q: You're going to say that I'm being pedantic, but there is a slight continuity error at the end of *The Green Ray*, in St Jean de Luz when Delphine is sitting at the café with the young carpenter: the glass of beer.
ER: You're right, but I thought it couldn't be seen. We realized, and the glass of beer bothered us. But we edited it in such a way that we got around it. However, you sensed it anyway, and you're right. I wouldn't say that there are never any continuity errors in my films, especially in films like that. But for *The Green Ray* and the way in which the film was shot, I don't see why I would need a continuity advisor. Yes, he or she could have told us about the glass. And other mistakes as well, but those were without consequence because we didn't use the shot. There was a shot where the actress was cold—it was in fact very cold—and so she put on a pair of trousers although she had been wearing shorts, thinking that it wouldn't show. It was when she was sitting at the café, and she thought her legs were out of shot. Now, there was a slightly wider angle shot where you can slightly see underneath the table. . . . But I think it's better that I take the risk of a few mistakes rather than adding an extra person to the crew, which wasn't even possible in this case.

Q: Do you get more pleasure working in these conditions?
ER: Yes, to the point where I'm asking myself if I could work in the usual conditions of the cinema industry. What's great is cutting out the middle men, because what is painful for me is having to explain something to someone who will then have to go and explain it to somebody else. Whereas here, I explain directly to my actors and my crew, and it's relaxing. *The Green Ray* and *Reinette and Mirabelle* are both "amateur" films: one is a holiday film, and the other a weekend film. These are films that left me emotionally intact. That wasn't the same with the last one, I don't really know why, as there weren't many people. Things just piled

up on top of each other. The only thing that was tiring with *Reinette and Mirabelle* was shooting the "blue hour" sequence. Because it was the middle of summer, we had to get up at 3 AM and to top it off, it was very cold (it's always cold on shoots, even in the middle of summer), but that was all. Often on shoots there's a lot of tension and stress, and some directors like this and make use of it. I would say that sometimes my films lack tension. And when you want to film dramatic scenes, that can make it difficult. But when you're alone, there's no tension and filming is a pleasure.

Q: Is this why we get the impression that you are renewing your links with comedy, an influence we felt in *Place de l'Etoile* and *The Sign of Leo*, but that declined with the *Moral Tales*? You are amusing yourself more as you seek to amuse. I'm thinking about the black cat that crosses the screen from left to right in *The Green Ray* . . .
ER: I call these films comedies so of course I would recognize their comic nature. But are they comedies above all? I don't know, and I wouldn't want to reduce them to that, because that would be shallow. But—even if I was in comic mode for *Reinette and Mirabelle* and I want to stay there—I couldn't always be comic either.

Q: *Pauline at the Beach* has the perfect farcical construction, the characters are alone at the end as they were at the start . . .
ER: That's the whole question of happy or unhappy endings. In the first *Comedies and Proverbs*—I've often said it's an homage to Marcel Carné— my films finish as they begin. The people find themselves back where they started. Why not? It has a slightly bitter, disenchanted, ironic feel. Now—because I've put *The Green Ray* into the *Comedies and Proverbs*—I didn't have to, but it's done now—I wanted to finish my comedies in a more open, optimistic way. Instead of coming back to the point of departure, the character has made some progress, which is positive: this is what happens in *The Green Ray*. Perhaps there's an element of discovery in *My Girlfriend's Boyfriend* too, where we don't come back to the setting and situation of the start. For *Reinette and Mirabelle*, I had the idea of a series. But everything depends on the actresses and my inspiration. I don't know if I will make some new adventures with *Reinette and Mirabelle*. I want to, but for the time being, it's uncertain. But anyway they're little stories where the ending depends on others. When one character discovers that the other is a waiter at the café, she is disappointed—or rather, her hopes are dashed. But that's only one of the stories. In another,

she succeeds. I can take one ending or another. In comedy, anything is allowed.

Q: Unfortunately, the recording we received of *Reinette and Mirabelle* was a PAL version, so we saw the film in black and white.
ER: I know what that's like, because I made a black and white copy for editing and I had to watch the film like that. So it was rather wonderful when I saw it in color. It's a film where color plays a really important role.

Q: Color is always important.
ER: I could say that I really am from the color age. I read recently that Franju, talking about *Les Yeux sans visage* in a journal interview said, "I see in black and white." There were a lot of filmmakers from that generation who saw in black and white, for whom color was something monstrous. And I've even heard younger filmmakers say, "I'd love to make a black and white film." Well I wouldn't want to at all! I made my first films in black and white through necessity, because there really wasn't color stock at the time. That was the case with *The Sign of Leo*. But the only film I wanted to make in black and white—strangely, because by this time color was becoming the norm—was *My Night at Maud's*.

Q: In returning, I think, to the old technique of filming on a black and white set.
ER: The interiors, the set, yes, that was effectively black and white. But that decision was really to do with Clermont-Ferrand and the vision I had of it. Clermont-Ferrand is a black town, and this black would have seemed yellowish or violet on color stock. I also wanted a certain Jansenist quality to the image, a simplicity. I didn't want people to get lost in the detail of color. In this film, the smallest advertising billboard or traffic signal could have bothered the audience. But it was a very particular case. In other words, the ideal reading for me of *My Night at Maud's* is that it is a color film where everything is either black or white. The people were dressed in black and white, the walls were in black and white, so, if we had made it in color, the film would still have been black and white. Furthermore, in *Full Moon in Paris*, there are some shots that are black and white, but that are on color stock, and it's not the same thing as a black and white film. I think that black and white filmed in color gives a rather extraordinary impression. But for me, in this case, black and white are colors.

Well, so much for *My Night at Maud's*. In my other films, color is very important. My films' scripts, when they have one, because for *The Green Ray* there wasn't one, have a cover that matches their color. In general, it's not a single color. *The Aviator's Wife* was green and blue; *A Good Marriage* pink and chestnut; *Pauline at the Beach* a very light blue, white, and red; *Full Moon in Paris*, grey. Normally, there would also be bands of different colors, but here I cut out a small picture of a moon I found on one of those grocery boxes. I didn't find an adequate cover for the latest film, *My Girlfriend's Boyfriend*, because Cergy is a town of bricks, but its colors are green and blue, those of the lake and the forest. I needed a pale pink background out of which emerged blue and green—moreover, it's a film where green and blue are very important. For *The Green Ray*, the colors are orange and green—I had a small notebook for practical remarks that was green with an orange band—but the colors you see most often in the film are, of course, green—the green of the countryside—the green-blue of the sea, and red. In *Reinette and Mirabelle*, there's a lot of red as well. But you'll have the surprise of seeing the colors.

Interview with Eric Rohmer

Gérard Legrand and François Thomas / 1990

From *Positif*, March 1990. Reprinted by permission; translated from the French by FH.

Question: You have just begun a new cycle, the *Tales of the Four Seasons*. When did you know that the *Comedies and Proverbs* would finish, with the film *My Girlfriend's Boyfriend* as it happens?
Eric Rohmer: I'm going to start by saying it's not necessarily finished. I might well have another idea for a film that seems "proverbial" to me, that I'll decorate with a proverb and add to the series. It was more difficult with the *Moral Tales* because I announced six of them from the start, but with *Comedies and Proverbs* there's nothing to stop me making another.

In reality, *My Girlfriend's Boyfriend* is an inaugural film, that happened to get filmed at the end of the series so far. It was imagining this subject, admittedly in a rather vague and confused way, that gave me the idea for a series that would be called *Comedies and Proverbs* and in which I would integrate some old themes and some old stories that I had started a very long time ago. It wasn't the first story I'd invented, but the first one that I wanted to integrate into a larger series, even though then I didn't know which proverb to give to the film. I had a story which seemed very proverbial, but no proverb, and in fact I only found it in extremis. I didn't deliberately set out to create it, but if there is a common denominator in the *Comedies and Proverbs*, it's at its clearest in *My Girlfriend's Boyfriend*. At the beginning (when I was writing the stories, all with provisional titles), the first schema was called Permutations. This was obviously the story of a permutation, because the lover of one friend becomes the lover of the other and vice versa. I don't think we really find that level of permutation in the other *Comedies and Proverbs*, I don't think so, but perhaps it's there in the background. But it wasn't really the permutation that interested me in and of itself so much as its theatrical and comic potential. After having written *My Girlfriend's Boyfriend* I saw *Twelfth Night* by Shakespeare where there's a sort of confusion and quid pro quo that's very close to *My Girlfriend's Boyfriend*. It's a familiar theme in comedies. So the common denominator really is finding comic situations. With the *Tales of the Four Seasons*, there will be both comic and novelistic situations, I don't know yet, but the two might come together, but the unity won't be in the situations. For the time being, the only unity is going to be climatic.

Q: This preoccupation with the weather, given that you're filming on location, will come down to a choice of lighting and setting.
ER: I like each of my films to have distinctive locations. I think my films have a certain thematic resemblance, which is even greater because I group them into series, but within these series, I stress the difference of settings, more than most directors perhaps. Often, the location is determined first. I could even recognize one of my films by its color, because each film has its own particular color. Here the distinction is very clear, there won't only be a distinction of places but also through seasons. Here, for springtime, the dominant colors are green and white . . .

Q: Did the idea of a *Tale of the Four Seasons* precede the idea of *The Tale of Springtime* or was it the other way round?
ER: The idea of the set came first and *A Tale of Springtime* took its place in that. The seasons have always interested me—I've already said that my films are meteorological, they take account of the weather outside, and my films are situated in fairly precise and fairly varied seasons. I've already used all the seasons, although spring is rather rare. The only moment of springtime I've had so far is at the end of *Love in the Afternoon*. It's not that marked in the film, but at the end you have springtime rather than winter.

Q: Have you written all four scripts already or are you taking the films one by one?
ER: I'm taking them one by one, but one always has ideas, I know what I'm going to do. When I made the *Moral Tales*, I had a fairly precise idea about what I was going to do, because at that time I had difficulties making films, so ideas had accumulated, and I had a certain provision. I announced the titles of the *Moral Tales* in advance. As far as the *Comedies and Proverbs* are concerned, I didn't have all the titles, and concerning the *Four Seasons*, obviously I have the titles, but I don't have all the

subjects in a precise manner. This time, in contrast to the *Moral Tales*, I'm not proposing a common theme, in fact I'm looking for thematic contrasts, trying to proceed by differences rather than resemblance. But in the end, the contrasts can build up and from these differences some resemblance can grow. At the fourth tale, you might be able to perceive some similarities that I don't have any idea about at the moment.

Q: There's a certain visual disparity—in picture quality, in format—in the *Comedies and Proverbs*, to the point that you hesitated to include *The Green Ray*, whose appearance is closer to that of *The Adventures of Reinette and Mirabelle*, that also made use of a certain amount of improvisation. Will the *Tales of the Four Seasons* be visually homogenous?
ER: Carried along by the movement of the *Comedies and Proverbs*, I did put *The Green Ray* into the series, but, between us, nothing is preventing me from changing everything. All these titles, all these groupings, are useful pretexts, but I'm not forced to respect them and I have great freedom with them. All I can say is that *The Green Ray* is a perfect Summer's Tale.

Concerning the *Four Seasons*, I am looking for diversity, and perhaps I will even vary the formats. It would be amazing to have something that looks very precise and very similar. You can manage it within one film, but in a work of art whose construction takes several years it's not possible or even desirable because the viewer is looking for a certain variety. I allow myself some freedom and incoherence. I think diversity is more interesting than unity to the extent that there will always be some unity because a director/auteur has his particular themes and ways of making a film. I know that this diversity won't take me too far, and that there are subjects I would never tackle.

Q: In *Tale of Springtime*, it's the first time since *My Night at Maud's* that there's a big philosophical debate. In *My Night at Maud's*, the Jansenist problematic is really at the heart of the film, one could even say that it is the subject of the film. What relationship is there—pleading the case for the spectator who doesn't know about this is advance—between Kant and the behavior of these characters?
ER: I think a relationship does exist. At the beginning, when I wanted to make my character a philosophy teacher, I didn't think I would use pure reason, but practical reason, meaning there would be a relationship between the moral attitude of this character and Kantian moral reasoning. But that seemed rather hackneyed to me, and I found it wasn't really

a film based on a moral attitude as such. This story wasn't one of action, about a conflict between freedom and duty, it was something else. It was really about different degrees of thinking. From the start, Natacha says to Jeanne, "You're someone who attributes a lot of importance to thought," Jeanne replies, "Yes, I do, but not because I teach philosophy." We can see this film is really the story of Jeanne's thought processes, about everything—her life with her boyfriend, a boyfriend that we never see, about what Natacha might think about her—and at the end Igor asks her, "What are you thinking?" That's why, when they have the philosophical discussion, they talk about thinking, in its pure form, transcendental thought, not simply empirical thought. So now, why Kant and not another philosopher? First of all, I chose a philosophy that inspires me. For example, Freud doesn't inspire me, and he doesn't inspire Jeanne either because she doesn't explain psychoanalysis to her pupils. It's ontology which interests me, which corresponds with my tastes. I've written very little theory, when I was a cinema critic I didn't make references to Kant or any other philosopher, well, hardly, but it underlay everything. What André Bazin called my theory of cinema is underpinned by what we could call transcendental idealism.

Q: The film is a sort of reprise of the proverb that starts *The Aviator's Wife*, "One can't think of nothing," because the heroine is always thinking of something.
ER: It's a theme I like. In *The Aviator's Wife* I expressed it in a naïve fashion, by people who weren't intellectual, and here I've taken up the theme again. As my films advance, it's obvious that themes will get repeated and developed, I think that's normal. The area in which one evolves becomes increasingly narrow, themes that seemed secondary become more important, and I'm going to carry on developing things that I believed to be exhausted.

Q: To what extent did Anne Teyssèdre and other actors in the film participate in the construction of their characters?
ER: As strange as it might seem, I didn't have the philosophy teacher at the start. I met Anne Teyssèdre when my story was still very vague. We were talking one day about roles she had played, in particular on television where she tends to play active women, such as pilots, when she said, "I'd love to play a philosophy teacher, I even have a philosophy degree." We spoke a little bit about philosophy, and I said, "Why not?" I would

never have dared to do it if I didn't have someone who was well versed in the ideas. Having said that, I wrote the role entirely myself. The actors didn't collaborate on the dialogue, in contrast to other films where there was some collaboration.

Q: How did you choose Hugues Quester? It's unexpected to see him in one of your films, yet at the same time he seems to play the Fabrice Luchini role.
ER: Yes, he could be a similar type. He could also resemble Trintignant in *My Night at Maud's*. I like his romantic side. I thought of him when I put Kleist's *Catherine von Heilbronn* on the stage, but he wasn't free, so casting him alongside Pascal Greggory didn't happen, but it was a possibility. In *A Tale of Springtime* I found a role for him, which was quite different for him because he had played teenagers for quite a long time. I saw him again recently in a Jacques Demy film, *Parking*, which isn't that old, but he looks so young. For once he got to play a father.

Q: His character is touching because he is a failed romantic. He would like to be able to behave romantically but his lifestyle doesn't allow it.
ER: Yes, that's true.

Q: It seems that in your work, even within the same film, there are actors who are very natural and flowing, and then others who have a more jerky and staccato style. It's very clear for example in *My Girlfriend's Boyfriend* with on the one hand Sophie Renoir and Eric Veillard, and the other Emmanuelle Chaulet and François-Eric Gendron whose gestures are far more "structured," you can follow the different stages of an arm movement or the shift in the gaze. We find this opposition in *A Tale of Springtime* with Anne Teyssèdre on one side and Hugues Questor on the other, who pushes this structured nature of the gesture to an extreme from his first appearance . . .
ER: I didn't see it like that, but I know there are oppositions between my actors. I like oppositions between my characters within a film. I've always been rather shocked by the resemblance between actors in the cinema. People think that directors are experts in physiognomy but I'm not really, and in lots of films—I'm not talking only about war films where everyone is in uniform—I muddle up characters. Some directors favor a certain physical type, especially a certain female type, in their films. Often different women in a film resemble each other. In contrast, I've

always sought out strong oppositions, with the men too. I don't want to find a unity of tone with my actors, I put actors together who should be difficult to use at the same time because of differences in their style.

Q: You spoke earlier about the visual common denominators in the film linked to nature: green and white. In the interiors there are also green details (when Natacha looks in the mirror at the end of the film she is in green next to a green vase), but there are other registers too, such as blue. Does this appeal to blue correspond to a certain coldness?

ER: I think in films you need a certain unified palette, but not one that is too unified, and that's what distinguishes cinema from theatre. In theatre you can find a perfect harmony, something extremely harmonious, whereas cinema you have to have incidental colors. If everything is too perfect, with no discordance, it becomes too artificial. So I introduced some colors, and there are others that are there by chance. I was attracted to cold colors, which seems right to me for springtime. I don't use much yellow in my films but I like it in small doses, and there you have some fairly cold yellows, the flowers but also Jeanne's blouse that was bought specially. Blue is part of this cold harmony: green and blue. It's a color I like and that works well with others. But I didn't plan this film's colors that carefully, there are others where I did more. For example, *Pauline at the Beach* I absolutely wanted red and blue, and I forbid green and yellow. At the time, the fashionable color was black and my actors were starting to wear it, but I rejected black, and khaki. Often I'll use the actors' wardrobes, but when it doesn't match exactly what I have in mind, we buy things. As for *A Tale of Springtime*, that big conversation in the countryside one evening, for example, Hugues Questor is in a blue shirt that we took ages to find. We tried other shirts but because of the color of the sofa we needed a cold color. At the start, like everyone, I was wary of flowers, but I changed my mind while I was preparing the film. The owner of the house we were filming in told me we could repaint if we wanted, and that she was fed up with the floral wallpaper, so I thought we could get rid of that, and the floral chairs, because generally I like single blocks of color. And then I realized that the flowers worked well, because they provided a visual rhyme with the flowers outside—that was the same reason for bringing flowers into the flat—and I kept the sofa as it was. Warm tones did not work at all with the slightly pink flowers of the sofa pattern. Anne Teyssèdre couldn't wear yellow, and Hugues Questor couldn't wear a garnet shirt he had that was beautiful. So in this case, blue was required because of a different color that had imposed itself on me, that I could have got rid of but finally decided to keep.

Q: For the first time in a while, and with music playing a concrete role in the story, you used a pre-existing musical score in *A Tale of Springtime* (a Beethoven sonata) over some of the images in your film.
ER: Yes, but all the same, the music wasn't the background to dialogue. You might consider it a lazy indulgence on my part, but on the other hand, I might well use music in the same way in another of my *Tales of the Four Seasons*, by which I mean music that is extra-diegetic. It won't be a specially composed score, but for the first time you will hear music and speech mixed together in one of my films.

So why did I use Beethoven in this way? Well, partly because I'm free to do so, by which I mean I have a certain critical position regarding music in film, but this doesn't mean I can't break the rules, everything depends on how you break your rules. I haven't put music over the credit sequence itself, I placed it as a small quote in a particularly "empty" part of the film, just at the very end of the credit sequence and over the first scene, a place where it doesn't interrupt the action. At the end, it reappears in a more emphatic way, and perhaps in a more traditional way as well, as it plays over the final credits, but it is not only music for the credits. Let's say that the music is there to help the film, I call Beethoven to my rescue. I thought the end was a little too bitter. My heroine returns to a place she has left because she felt uncomfortable there and she didn't like it, and at the same time it had to be happy, it had to somehow express the interior happiness of someone returning to a place even if they don't like it. I could have shown it softened by light, but that would have been cheating. I could have used flowers as well, but there were some practical difficulties with making these flowers stand out enough. A bouquet opening takes time, we would have needed an ellipsis, but the entrance into this dark apartment was important. The bitterness was in the image, but I wanted something beyond that, a sort of uplifting feeling beyond the rather sordid aspect of these images in which I had imprisoned her. So, although generally I try to avoid it, music came to my rescue, but I didn't have another solution. You could imagine that this music is music that this character hums to herself, that is in her head. Jeanne probably prefers Beethoven to Schumann. When Natacha plays the piano, she listens to Schumann, but now she is no longer thinking about Natacha, the Beethoven returns. I wouldn't have used this music if music hadn't already been important in the film and it wasn't music that the characters know well and like. I wouldn't have put it in a film where the characters preferred rock to classical music.

Q: What role does Jean-Louis Valéro play for you? He wrote the score for the blues for the evening in Montmorency and he has added extremely discreet musical moments for all your films since *The Aviator's Wife*.
ER: He's a man who has done some very interesting things. As for my films, let's say he helps me. It would be really hard for me to ask someone who wasn't a friend. For *My Girlfriend's Boyfriend* for example I asked him to write music we don't notice: I could never have asked that of someone I don't know. He teases me about it, but there is very little music in *My Girlfriend's Boyfriend* and we don't notice it.

Q: We notice the music in *The Green Ray*.
ER: Yes, in *The Green Ray*, I suggested the theme to him, asking him to write a fugue for the end. For *Reinette and Mirabelle* I gave him a schema and I said, "I want music that goes simply from middle C to high C and back again, that's all. I want there to be an obsessive, repetitive quality." He replied, "Why don't we make it like morse code?" So, one of the Cs is the long pip, the other the short one, and we used them to spell out the title of the film, and the beginning and end credit sequences spell out the title of the film in morse code. We could certainly call that meaningful music! What's funny is that I was the one with the musical idea, and he was the one who made it more literary.

To reply to you more completely, let's say that I don't want to be reliant on a musician. Music is so important to the feeling of a film that I'd rather use banal or bad music than one that I don't understand. I'm not someone who would show a film to a musician and say "Does it inspire you? What are you going to do with it?" I can't. So there are two solutions. Either, not being a musician myself but sometimes having some ideas, I propose a theme—for what it's worth—to a musician, and he helps me. Or I ask for help from a musician such as Beethoven or Mozart, as we often did during the New Wave. The first person who really used a lot of classical music was Melville (I don't know if it was Melville or Cocteau's idea) in *Les Enfants Terribles*. It had a massive impact, because it was the first time someone had dared—the general belief was you should use music specially composed for the film. Godard went very far when he made *Prénom Carmen* based on Beethoven's Quartets; perhaps it would have made Beethoven turn in his grave but it was done in a very intelligent way. He's someone who knows the quartets well and was very sensitive to them (and he used them before, in *Une femme mariée* and *Deux ou trois choses que je sais d'elle*). Personally, I would be loath to use music that was so special to me. But it doesn't seem to me too sacrilegious to use these tiny fragments of Beethoven.

So that's my position as far as music is concerned. Obviously, if everyone thought like me, there were be no film music composers! But I just can't bear to give my film to a musician, to allow a musician to enter into the world of my film.

Q: You said you put Beethoven's rondo in a "hollow" part of the film. It's significant in terms of the film's structure, which starts with a silent prologue that lasts ten minutes and also finishes without sound. After a succession of false starts, after people who seem important disappear offscreen, and secondary characters become more important, the action is really set in motion with the arrival of the character played by Hugues Questor.

ER: It's rather an episodic film. I tell one story, and then another, and right up until the end, new stories are told. We don't really know everything right until the end. Even when Igor arrives the film starts without really starting because a lot of information only arrives later. So you could think the film is one long exposition. There isn't the classical division between introduction, development, and conclusion; each bit of the action builds on another, much more than usual, including in my other films. From the point of view of telling the story I was trying something a bit different, I know it might seem a bit over the top but that's what interested me in it. It goes a bit against the spectators' expectations, but I took it as far as it could go because I thought it would increase rather than diminish their interest, as long as you follow carefully from the start, because the start is rather slow, more than in my other films. I don't like getting too quickly into a subject. I could have finished sooner—once the necklace is discovered, everything goes very quickly—but from the point of view of the image and a kind of dynamism on the screen, we couldn't finish in the bedroom, we had to get out, and go elsewhere. That's also why there's some music, to signal that it's over . . .

Q: In fact, there are really two films: there's one about Hugues Questor, which could be called My Friend's Father, which starts later and finishes sooner.

ER: There are two different stories which are superimposed, Igor's failed seduction of Jeanne and the story of the necklace, and these two stories contain each other, run along parallel lines, and then finally one overtakes the other. The spectator is perhaps rather overwhelmed, but I want to show them that what seemed trivial, the small thing they weren't interested in is at the end of the day, very important. It seems that the necklace is a pretext for talking about the father but then in fact it's the necklace that's at the heart of the story. This story is the relationship between Jeanne and Natacha. For Jeanne, her relationship with Natacha is more interesting than her relationship with Igor, which is a kind of game. That's the difference from the *Moral Tales*, where I privilege relations between men and women. Here I think I'm on a very different path from both the *Moral Tales* and the *Comedies and Proverbs*.

Q: We could say that when both Eve and Natacha leave the house, Jeanne and Igor find themselves in a Moral Tale for twenty minutes.
ER: Yes, that's right. They're playing at being in a Moral Tale, but they aren't really.

Another reason—I'm going back to an earlier point now—that I don't like going too fast at the start, it's that I like a lot of things to be learnt through hearing conversations, not to be delivered too quickly. I prefer not to take advantage of cinema's ability to go anywhere, but to restrict myself to a certain time and place, even if it means lots of things that are necessary to understand the story are evoked in speech. For example, I could have put in scenes with Jeanne's boyfriend, or others in her philosophy class, but I cut them out. When I write a story it is often through elimination, and the result of these eliminations is that the dialogue gets richer. For the time being I don't see how with this system I could invent stories that don't have any text. It's part of my way of doing things at the moment, but there wasn't much text for *The Sign of Leo*. There was something else in its place, there was a spatio-temporal continuity which created the sort of unity I now find in other ways.

Eric Rohmer: Coincidences

Olivier Curchod / 1992

From *Positif*, February 1992. Reprinted by permission; translated from the French by FH.

Olivier Curchod: The title of this second *Tale of the Four Seasons* coincides with that of a play by Shakespeare whose final scene you show as part of a play that your heroine goes to see. Did this Shakespearean reference pre-exist the conception of the film or did it find its place in a pre-existing plot?

Eric Rohmer: Well, you know that some of my *Comedies and Proverbs* were in gestation when I was making the *Moral Tales*, even if I wasn't really thinking about them: in the same way, certain *Tales of the Four Seasons* were conceived of when I was making the *Comedies and Proverbs*. I like to proceed, in a purely formal fashion, through antithesis in my films: for *A Winter's Tale*, I had the vague idea of a story that was completely opposite to that of *A Tale of Springtime* (after one man and three women, we would have one woman and three men), but also of *The Green Ray* where a woman doesn't manage to find a man, whereas here she can't choose between three men. And then, in the early eighties, I saw Shakespeare's *A Winter's Tale* on television, performed by the BBC, and I had the confused memory of the return of a loved woman—in reality, it's the resurrection of the queen, or at least the animation of a statue. Rewatching the cassette on which I'd recorded the play, I was struck by how much emotion emerges from that scene. That was when I had the idea that there would be the return of a man who had been loved, and that I would call, through reference to Shakespeare, *A Winter's Tale*. From the moment I had *A Winter's Tale*, I thought of making a series that would be called *Tales of the Four Seasons*. So, I thought of *A Winter's Tale* before I thought of *A Tale of Springtime*, but I didn't talk about it at the time because I don't like to talk about films which aren't yet made.

OC: So is the reason why you set the film in Nevers because of St. Bernadette's reliquary being there?
ER: No, that's a pure miracle, the miracle of Nevers if I can say that! While I was preparing the film, I met someone by chance who knew Nevers well, and I told him the story: he told me I could find people in Nevers who would help me, and he found me the hairdresser's and the apartment straight away. Once I was in Nevers, I owed it myself to make an allusion to St. Bernadette given my subject and the sentence in the film where it's said that Loïc believes in miracles at Lourdes. The visit to the convent of Saint-Gilard [where St. Bernadette's relics are—translator's note] led to me to twist my usual mania for geographical exactitude: people who know Nevers well will see that Félicie and Maxence's walk is all in a zigzag because the convent is far away from all the other places. But the dramatic progression of the sequence prevented me from putting the visit to the convent at the start or the end of the walk, which would have been more logical.

The choice of Nevers is due to a fortuitous meeting, what I would call a "miraculous coincidence," and that happens a lot in my films.

OC: The dialogues in the film reinforce the possible similarities between Félicie and St. Bernadette: both have Greek noses, both have visions, and both sacrifice their lives for their convictions. There's also something of Rousseau in Félicie's character—she likes what's natural and reproaches Loïc for living his life through books.
ER: Yes, but a lot of people are like that. Remember that in *La Collectionneuse* the hero is reading *Confessions*.

OC: You like your characters to be trapped in the words that they use. So Maxence, after having told Félicie that you don't use the phrase "stare raving mad" [*sotte à lier*] but "stark raving mad" [*folle à lier*], reproaches her for being mad when she tells him she is moving back to Paris; Loïc and Charles both accuse her of the same thing. And Félicie refuses to live with a man that she doesn't love "madly."
ER: My characters can be wise or "mad." It's never madness as such, but a sort of exaltation, a spiritual fervour, the refusal of a flat reality, sometimes even a Don Quixotesque madness. I think Félicie has this kind of gentle madness.

OC: Maxence, Loïc, and even Félicie are both touching and unsympathetic, annoying and endearing.
ER: That's my Aristotelian side! Characters in a tragedy must be neither totally good nor totally bad, neither totally guilty nor totally innocent. For example, the great Hollywood westerns respected this law of classic dramaturgy. When I used to go to the cinema everyday, films showed rich, complex characters. Today, as far as I can tell (because I don't go to the cinema very often), characters are thinner and simpler. I don't want to follow that fashion.

OC: Your *Tales of the Four Seasons*, like the *Comedies and Proverbs*, have new principal actors in each film who are little known by the public.
ER: I don't try to present unknown faces, but I don't want to film with actors whose public image is too worn out, usually because they have been made into media stars. I need my characters to be totally credible, which would be impossible if they were played by stars as the public would then see the actor behind the character. It's also more exciting and more invigorating for me to work with new people who still have something to prove and find an interesting character to play for the first time and that can give a lot of themselves to it. I like this kind of virginal quality the actors have. In general this is more the case for women than for men. My actresses have often played fewer roles than my actors: it's not to do with age, there are more roles for men whilst a young actress can be pushed aside and finish her career very quickly. I have no problem finding new faces, even if they have been seen elsewhere, in adverts or TV series for example. So Charlotte Véry who plays Félicie had been on a TV show on Channel 5, where she had short hair, for example—no-one could recognize her, which was better for her anyway.

OC: At what stage in your working process do actors become involved?
ER: Generally, my scripts get written in two main stages. First of all there is the general idea of the story and I don't think about a precise actor. Even in the case of *The Green Ray*, which relied on improvisation, I didn't think of Marie Rivière straight away. As my ideas become clearer, but before the plot line is completely finished and all the scenes determined (so well before the dialogues are written), I choose one of the actors—and usually a woman. I need to think about her in order to write, even if she doesn't collaborate with the screenplay, as happened for *The Green Ray* and perhaps *La Collectionneuse*. I need to know the actor personally, to see her in the role. Sometimes I'm inspired by what she's told me,

even some of her phrases. But the overall role of the actor in deciding the character is very difficult for me to determine and I can't really talk about it with you.

OC: It's the first time a little girl has played an important role in the plot of one of your films, and in some scenes.
ER: There have been some children before, but it's not the same thing. In fact, I've suffered for really only showing one generation in the *Comedies and Proverbs*, without parents or grandchildren, or at least very few. In the *Tales of the Four Seasons*, I've enriched the picture: there are two generations in *A Tale of Springtime*, and here there are three.

OC: The portrait of this little girl is very truthful. Did she improvise at all?
ER: Strictly speaking, there is no improvisation in this film. No doubt we changed small parts of dialogue during rehearsal but it was basically written. On the other hand, sometimes the little girl said things I wasn't expecting, but I prefer not to tell you what they were. I once heard a director say that children are much more at ease if they have a text which is far removed from their life than if they have to show themselves as they really are. He was absolutely right. The problem is that when there is no improvisation, children tend to over play the text, playing let's pretend. For Elise, I was looking for a mix of these positions. Pure improvisation, with its chaotic qualities, wasn't suitable, because we had to follow a certain direction; and because children don't really understand improvisation. Children are logical, they don't like mixing up reality and pretence, that's the problem. I hope that I've obtained something truthful, that doesn't seem acted. What I like in my films is that that which appears written is improvised, and what seems improvised has been written. But I'm not going to let the cat out of the bag.

OC: After *A Tale of Springtime* where the characters discussed Kantian philosophy, *A Winter's Tale* stages conversations about reincarnation and Pascal's wager; now you've already approached this subject in *My Night at Maud's*.
ER: I would like each of my Season Tales to address or at least illustrate a different philosophical problem, but I don't know if I'll manage it. In *A Tale of Springtime*, it was thought, and here it's immortality. The return to the question of the wager was very deliberate, and in fact it's the third time I've spoken about it. The figure three is very important: twice

is repetition, but a third time suggests its permanence. In my play *Trio en mi bémol* I didn't directly quote Pascal but I made an allusion to the wager when Pascal Greggory tells Jessica Forde, "I don't want to tell you the sentence I want you to say to me because if you say it to me of your own volition, you would give me such immense pleasure that I would prefer to live in the hope of that moment, even if it is very unlikely that it will happen."

These long conversations also have a dramatic value, it's how the story is formed. So for example the dinner at Loïc's might seem to simply serve as an illustration of opposition between a girl who isn't very educated and the "intellectuals" who have a conversation that bores her; but suddenly Félicie intervenes, and it's her intervention that brings the conversation to the point that is the subject of the film: she isn't just linked to Charles for life, she is linked to Charles through the existence of another life. Without having particularly searched for this effect, what I really like about that scene is that what seems superfluous suddenly becomes essential.

OC: Faced with such scenes, the audience might just laugh.
ER: People often tell me that people laugh at such and such a scene in my films, but it depends on the audience and it's very difficult to explain. If *A Winter's Tale* makes you laugh, that's great, and if it makes you cry, that's great too, and if you move from laughter to tears, that's even better. I think you only have a comic sense if you have a tragic sense too; all scenes from tragedy could play as comedy: *Oedipus Rex*, with its quid pro quo, could be a comedy and that's true of all the great dramatists, Racine, Corneille, or Shakespeare. But when I'm describing either habits or my characters, I'm not aiming at caricature, to ridicule an intellectual or to make a rather uneducated girl seem ignorant. The comedy has to be seen by the characters themselves: when Loïc is being a pedant, when Félicie says something silly or makes grammatical mistakes, they have to have a sense of their own ridiculousness—they know how to brave it out and make the most of it. So I think my situations are comic rather than what my characters do. Anyway I definitely don't want to place myself above my characters and mock them. Perhaps that's the public's attitude, but that comes from habits formed from what they see generally, and certainly not from me.

OC: From another point-of-view, you're continually misleading the spectator as to the content of the plot: after an enigmatic prologue, we think that the film is the story of a girl hesitating between two men (rather in the manner of the *Comedies and Proverbs*), then that she's fixed on one (as in *Moral Tales*), and then there's a highly improbable final resolution (which recalls *The Green Ray*).

ER: Yes, I was quite aware of this as I was writing; I wanted the spectator to feel a bit lost in the story, to not be sure where it was going, and then there's a sudden shift which leads to the joy at the end. I deliberately kept the spectator in the dark. I think it's the art of story-telling that keeps the spectator guessing—what I would call my "suspense," in reference to Hitchcockian suspense. (When I show students Hitchcock films they ask what relation there is between our films—I think this is the only influence he had on me.) It's part of the game I play in my films. All film viewers or readers of books like to guess the story and feel that at the end they've guessed what was going to happen. Now, I think I'm like that, and my viewers are like me—I don't seek out difficulty, but I don't want to flatter my audience or simplify their task. This is a very important at a time when people say that the public isn't capable of following a complex plot any more—it's another reason to make sure my stories are well constructed.

OC: *A Winter's Tale*'s structure is a bit like a play, with a prologue, three acts, and a long epilogue.

ER: My New Wave colleagues and I had a strong grounding in classical literature—we wrote essays on French literature. But we didn't speak enough about our shared love of music. Rivette had a pronounced taste for music, Godard loved Beethoven's Quartets that we used to listen to together. Even though we never played any music it was vital to our sense of composition. Godard is a great composer—even if he was never able to or wanted to tell a story. In my work, this sense of composition creates dramatic tension.

OC: Your dramatic composition respects classical rules such as plausibility. How do you reconcile this with Charles's "miraculous" reappearance in *A Winter's Tale*?

ER: But miracles aren't implausible! It's not impossible, from either a psychological or a material point-of-view, that you would bump into someone on a bus that you hadn't seen for ages. It's rare, that's all. I find it far more improbable when you bump into someone just outside your house who lives in a completely different part of Paris and say "hello" completely naturally, as if Paris was a small village—and you see that a lot in films. Charles's reappearance in my film is not implausible, it's a coincidence.

I wanted to begin this question of plausibility with the story about the lost letters that Félicie tells. I can tell you, I checked everything: There is indeed a Victor Hugo street in both Levallois and Courbevoie, and they are both in the process of being demolished. So I sent a letter myself to the address in Courbevoie, and it was returned by the post office. I sent another in the name of the actress poste restante and that was returned too. So not only is what happened likely, it's true!

OC: Indeed. But by writing this denouement, did you think about the danger that the spectator will find it unbelievable?
ER: You know I wrote this film so easily and rapidly that I didn't have time to ask myself those kinds of questions. I sometimes ask myself if finishing with the return of Charles was a good idea—I could also have finished in the middle, as with *A Tale of Springtime*, or have Félicie stay with Loïc, or have another man come along. But then the story would have become more banal, or would have become more like one of the *Comedies and Proverbs*. Now, I wanted a melodramatic schema, if you like, something more like a saga, and the reference to Shakespeare encouraged me and brought in this fairy-tale aspect. So this ending fitted into those ideas, and I pushed it through a sort of necessity. And too bad if people reproach me for it.

OC: In fact, in the scene in the Shakespeare play that you show, before Paulina animates the statue, she declares to the audience: "Then all stand still;/Oh: those that think it is unlawful business/I am about, let them depart." That says it all . . .
ER: The extract from the play serves as a commentary on my film's story: Paulina also says that if you were told this story, "you would call it an old fairytale." Some people might think that this is too distancing. It's true, I took an intellectual approach. I'm not totally naive, but I wanted a certain naivety to come through without people thinking I was being too crafty—that's the word used for Hitchcock.

OC: Paulina also encourages others to believe in her—"It is required/ You do awake your faith."
ER: That's a coincidence as well because when I was writing the script I'd forgotten those lines.

OC: You looked after the mise-en-scène of the play yourself.

ER: Yes, and I wanted to translate the lines too. You know I translated Catherine von Heilbronn myself from the German, but I didn't learn English at school and so I was less comfortable with the Shakespeare. When I found Legouis' translation, I didn't think I could do any better so I kept it.

OC: The representation of *A Winter's Tale* is very different in look from the rest of the film.

ER: Yes, because it's a play and I wanted its theatrical aspect to stand out. I asked the actors to respect the pacing of the verse and the marked Alexandrines: I was very happy because they played the scene in a very measured way, without pushing the text too much, with gestures that worked very well for the camera framing. The feeling of rupture with the rest of the film is also explained by the fact that I didn't use the same cinematographer and that we filmed with two cameras, without cutting. I wanted the presence of the camera to be felt, as if you were watching a news report on a play on television, whereas normally I prefer the camera to be invisible so that you're closer to the characters. So in editing I deliberately chose moments that maybe normally you'd leave out, transition shots, re-framings, where the camera moves from one character to another and you're not sure who's speaking. I found it very beautiful. The theatricality came, if I dare say it, from this extreme "cinemacality."

OC: Upon leaving the theatre, Loïc says he doesn't understand why the queen comes back at the end of the play: is it because she never died (the rational explanation), or is it some magical powers of Paulina? Félicie replies that he hasn't understood at all—it's because she had faith! I want to ask you the same question. Why does Charles come back? Is it by chance, by magic, or because Félicie discovers faith?

ER: No, it's not magic, I don't think. Chance? All I can say is that personally I can't tell you. If I make films, it's to ask a question rather than give a response. I think most viewers will experience the film as I do. Those who aren't like me, I'm not saying they won't like it, but they'll like it in a different way. But it will be received best, as in my opinion it should be received, by those who ask themselves this question and don't really know at the end if Charles's return is fortuitous, or if there is let's say "something else" other than chance in their meeting.

OC: The scene in the bus is very difficult because it's what we've been building up to.
ER: I had lots of very difficult scenes in this film, particularly linked to the weather. In some places we were filming in mid-winter and we couldn't get a full day's filming. Because I was interested in the seasons, for *A Winter's Tale* we had to have snow: now there was very little snow last winter. One day, at 10:15 they told me snow was falling, at 10:30 we were filming, and by 10:45 the snow had disappeared!

For the scene in the bus, we couldn't film it just on a normal bus in Paris. We rehearsed for two days just taking the bus as normal passengers, and I filmed the actors with a small video camera, without being noticed. I was able to set up a very precise storyboard for the scene, then we hired a bus and filmed using extras. The filming of the scene was very quick, but its conception took two to three years. I thought about it a lot and sketched out many different ideas. And it wasn't until that scene was really perfected that I was able to develop the rest of the story. I always start at the end, that's what decides what comes before.

OC: The film has lots of scenes set in public transport. Félicie spends her time criss-crossing Paris. How did you determine this very precise geography?
ER: These aren't aimless wanderings, Félicie is always going somewhere. My story was a story of places—it was important to situate them. Félicie is in one place, Charles in another, and they don't see each other. I wanted to show someone alone in the crowd in a big city looking for someone else in this crowd from which they could emerge at any moment. Now the crowd is very dense on public transport and it is easier to meet there. I also wanted to show, in a way that suited my subject, Paris during the holidays: I think I did but probably not enough. The choice of locations posed a rather insoluble problem: I wanted realistic locations, I wanted locations that would suit "A Christmas Tale," but also rather grim suburban locales which I liked a lot because there weren't these Christmas lights.

OC: *A Winter's Tale* represents the reality of daily life. Your series in this way make me think of Balzac and his "Scenes from daily life"...
ER: Yes, I like the reference to Balzac, I prefer it to Marivaux that people often evoke when they talk about my films though he didn't inspire

me as much. I'm as sensitive to sociological plausibility as I am psychological plausibility. I try to vary the locale where my characters live, so I could just as easily show chic hairdressers in a posh part of Paris as a little library in the suburb where Félicie lives. Perhaps it's not as varied as Balzac, but which contemporary filmmaker or novelist would be able to achieve that?

OC: Balzac undertook enquiries in order to paint reality.

ER: The cinema allows us to undertake these kinds of enquiries. Each actor belongs to a certain type, a different social type, and I often borrow their social status from my actors. For example, if one of my characters paints or plays the piano, the actor will too, and if one of my actors speaks in a very polished, classical French, I'll give her a different social status than if her French is more working class. Places allow us to detect the reality of how things are as well, better than a novelist or a theatre director can evoke, when they have to recreate everything. In my film, the hairdressers we see in the salon really are hairdressers. At the library, there is a librarian, even if the readers are in fact film students because it's always complex getting permission to film in official buildings and we had to use extras. For Félicie's family life we used a modest milieu and we were able to improvise around that.

OC: As with most of your films, *A Winter's Tale* doesn't credit anyone for costume or set design.

ER: I like looking after the sets myself. For this film, I did some research and we organized the places where we were filming. For Félicie's mother's apartment, I kept the place exactly as the person who lives there has it because she was so like the character I wanted to show. We just moved a painting that got in the way when we were framing. For Elise's bedroom, my assistant and my production director both helped me, because it's such a feminine space. She found the objects we put on the shelves, and the drawings on the wall are really by the little girl. For Loïc's house, I wanted it to feel like the interior of a rented home, so we kept the personality of the lounge in the house we hired, but we took what was there off the walls and replaced it with posters of paintings by Egon Schiele, Delauney, Kandinsky, and a poster of August Macke that I found in a bookshop in Beaubourg. We also bought shelves, but I got rid of all the knick knacks because in the house of a man who reads, I wanted there to be only books on his shelves. We took some books from my office, and we used books that were in the attic and the cellar in the house we were renting. In the apartment in Nevers on the other hand, we tidied up all the shelves, we only kept the porcelain which allowed us to cut to the museum the next day.

I also think that costume is very important because they play a considerable role on screen in determining color. I bought Félicie's parka myself because I wanted exactly that kind of drab brown shade. The other actors are almost all in black, and the little girl's hat is red.

OC: These colors are all the more noticeable because the film was shot in 16mm, which makes it quite grainy. Only the prologue and the theatre performance are an exception.
ER: For the Shakespeare play, it's because there was more light. And, according to critics, the title *A Winter's Tale* doesn't mean that the play takes place in winter, but rather that it's a tale that gets told in the winter in the evenings. The prologue was filmed a year and half before the rest of the film and the summer film stock, being a bit less sensitive, feels different. If I hadn't written the screenplay so quickly we would only have filmed the rest this year, as I initially considered, and the difference would have been more pronounced. In general, I wanted *A Winter's Tale* to have muted colors in a dreary location, in total contrast to *Full Moon in Paris* where the cinematography was shiny and bright and the colors were lively and almost metallic, colors from the world of advertising which suited the milieu and the fashion designers who were my subject.

OC: You're traditionally a bit mistrustful of what we might call "film music." Now *A Winter's Tale* starts with a series of silent shots accentuated by some pretty piano music in complete contrast to your principles: this musical theme gets taken up by violin that we hear in the cathedral in Nevers and in the flute sequence which announces the queen's resurrection in the Shakespeare play.
ER: The music in the prologue may seem strange because there's no music afterwards. I wanted to make the prologue in a different style from my other films with an aesthetic that recalls holiday photographs: I took photographs for these scenes and by placing them together we reconstructed the prologue so that it resembles a pop video. This music is an artifice of the cinema that normally I reject, but here it works because we jump artificially from one time period to another without taking into account the real temporal duration. Because this kind of editing is exceptional in my films, the music could be too! When I allowed myself to stray from my narrow ideas about how to use music in films, I'm also

being ironic about myself. Because really where does the music come from that we hear in films? When the theme of the start is heard again in Nevers it could be a symbol of Félicie's thoughts. It's the fable aspect that allows that, I introduced this music at magical moments in the film. In *Love in the Afternoon* you have the same thing—the hero dreams at a café terrace that he has the magical power to seduce women. It's silent, we see him in front of the café accosting Françoise Fabien—"Madame, would you come with me?"—"Yes, with pleasure," and in this magical moment we hear music from the Swiss composer Arié Dzierlakta who then worked with Resnais. In *The Green Ray*, there's another magical moment. Every time the heroine sees a green object, we hear the music: ta-tim ta ta . . .

OC: When you made *A Tale of Springtime*, you said that your next film, which we now know is *A Winter's Tale*, would be a reaction against it.
ER: Perhaps not a reaction, but in opposition, certainly. You know for me opposition is a kind of inspiration. Spring is opposed to winter (or perhaps to autumn—but I wanted to start with winter). You have the opposition of color—after a "white" film, a "black" film. It's also opposed through the number of characters: a man and three women then a woman and three men; and an opposition of philosophical themes. In *A Tale of Springtime*, there's a Kantian agnostic irony, and here there's a Swedenborgian spiritualism. I search out variety, a variety of locations, of characters, perhaps that's why when I use the same actor I never give them the principal role twice in a row. But having said that, when you write stories there's no point in searching out variety at any cost. A director who isn't an auteur and who uses very different themes from one film to another can allow himself or herself to work with the same actors, nourishing them with different material; we've seen it with Gary Cooper, Gabin, and Fernandel. But the oppositions that are in my films resemble the oppositions you find in great musical symphonies (minor/major; quick/slow), allowing the return of recurrent themes. There are these returns in the *Moral Tales* and the *Comedies and Proverbs*, and this will be true for *The Tales of the Four Seasons* as well. But the number of themes an auteur has is very limited. He is a prisoner of the structures into which he has voluntarily shut himself and outside of which he can't create anything. I find myself in such a world—which began with the *Moral Tales*, perhaps even *The Sign of Leo*. Not only do I not have reason to leave, but I don't want to and I must not. I try to find new combinations in my "personal computer" and I don't think I've exhausted them yet.

All the great creators, whether of the novel, the theatre, the cinema, used a limited number of themes. All Balzac's novels, which seem so varied, are machinations where someone tries to appropriate someone else's power. It's not the plot which makes Balzac's variety, but the settings he uses for the action. He can allow some of his characters to reappear by using them in a different way; this is part of an extraordinary inventive energy, that is seductive but which is very difficult to achieve in the cinema, because there is such an identification between the actor and the character that you would have to use the same actor and that would be very complicated. Now, the simple inversion of a motif, such as a musical motif, allows me to be creative: it allows me to take a new direction, to revisit an old motif that I thought was useless, to give it a new life in a way. So in *A Winter's Tale* Pascal's wager came to me so naturally and spontaneously I didn't push it away. This is a really obvious example, but there are other elements which when they reappear are so transformed you hardly notice them. This combination, which proceeds through oppositions and convergences can sometimes draw on elements from outside my world and appropriate them, but I don't know in advance if I'll be able to use them or not, some things which seem interesting are finally unusable, and others which seem nothing will become a catalyst that kick starts the whole process. Opposition is almost a mechanical method of inspiration for me. Inspiration can only come if you prepare for it and you seek it out. At the same time, inspiration is also a gift from heaven, or a gift of the Muses if you like. In this sense, you don't look for inspiration, you find it.

OC: Your next two films will be called *An Autumn Tale* and *A Summer's Tale* I suppose?
ER: I am going to reply differently to your question: the next two films in the *Tales of the Four Seasons* will be called *An Autumn Tale* and *A Summer's Tale*.

The Amateur: An Interview with Eric Rohmer

Antoine de Baecque and Thierry Jousse / 1993

From *Cahiers du cinéma*, February 23, 1993. Translated from the French by FH.

Watching *The Tree, the Mayor and the Mediatheque*, one understands that Rohmer is continuing his journey towards simplicity. To get there, he needs a method, which is that of a filmmaker who has definitively broken away from the cult of professionalism. This interview is a defence and an illustration of a light economy, 16mm film, and filming as a family affair.

Q: Let's start with a concrete question.
ER: Yes, let's.

Q: Traditionally, a film crew is perceived, usually correctly, as a group of invaders when they arrive on location. How did you work to not give that impression when you arrived at the small village in the Vendée where you filmed *The Tree, the Mayor and the Mediatheque*?
ER: I am always furious when, wanting to film somewhere, the owners of the property refuse, frightened by the damage from earlier film crews. In general, when a crew has filmed, the location resembles a battlefield. On the contrary, I make it a point of honor to respect the location. No breakages, no disappearances, and a discreet crew, even if there are more of them than on the last film. In the case of *The Tree, the Mayor and the Mediatheque*, it was some friends who lent me a place, in particular the chateau where the crew slept, ate, and filmed. We came as friends, respecting the place. As for street scenes, whether in Paris or in a village, our role is to be the "invisible man." Furthermore, in the chateau there were eight bedrooms, including the owner's, to accommodate everybody,

crew and cast, so everybody. The actors had to take it in turns, according to their other jobs, and there were never more than two at a time in the Vendée. As for the technicians, there were three of them, two for image and sound, and Françoise Etchegaray for all the rest, from the lighting to general management.... In this case, I don't know if we can really talk about a crew, more a little gang where everyone, me included of course, had to take it in turns to make sure everything was working, whether to hold a projector or to cook. In general, anyway, I make sure I work with resourceful people who are able to look after themselves while filming, while editing, while sound editing. On *The Tree, the Mayor and the Mediatheque*, for example, it was the same sound engineer, Pascal Ribier, who filmed, edited, and undertook postproduction, as the film went on. That makes the group very responsible. This group of four, which I had already used for *The Green Ray* and *Reinette and Mirabelle*, is completely achievable. It satisfies me completely and I'm very at ease for sound and image recording. I never do complicated things, but everything I do is done well.

Q: Is it the subject matter of *The Tree, the Mayor and the Mediatheque* which made you want to work in this way, or is it the other way around, and the method caused a particular approach to the story?
ER: I had a point of departure, which was the location and my four actors, Arielle Dombasle, Pascal Greggory, Fabrice Luchini, and Clémentine Amouroux. Then I decided to write the dialogue as we filmed, having in my head the idea of working absolutely in the conditions of an amateur. A more written story and a more "professional" shooting script would have been artificial in this environment where the point was, as the end of the day, to get people to talk. I wanted to avoid clichés, which would have been dangerous for a film whose themes could be seen as clichéd: politics, the countryside, themes furthermore which I don't know well, at least not directly, and that I master less well than my usual subjects. Politics is something I know through the intermediary of newspapers and television, i.e., through a certain number of clichés, and these were clichés I didn't want to reproduce, even if I was going to have to film them as well. This film, through its subject and its setting, was therefore better if it was more amateur than professional. It was a clearly made political and aesthetic choice.

Q: The script was written as you filmed...
ER: Lots of people have told me that the story seems well constructed,

very elaborated. However, the script was written bit by bit, sometimes right at the last minute. I always had the idea of using intertitles, which means you don't have to tell the whole story through images and allows you to jump over scenes that are there just for information. On the other hand, I didn't really know what would be written on them. . . . When I started the film, at the beginning of March 1992, I still hadn't written the different dialogues. I simply had a text which described each sequence. For *The Green Ray*, I didn't have anything at all, because the actors were playing themselves. Here I couldn't use the same principle, because Pascal Greggory isn't a politician, and François-Marie Banier isn't a newspaper editor. I had to give them some text, even if they also brought a lot to the role. I wrote this text individually for each actor, like a sort of personal ID card, with indications of what kind of dialogue there should be and references to certain discourses.

Q: So there are some improvisations . . .
ER: Yes, effectively. Notably Clémentine Amouroux when she's interviewing people from the village. She wrote the questions, and she had complete freedom in carrying out the interviews. And she did very well. On the other hand, the visit to the architect's office is also improvised. Without doubt it's the scene I'm happiest with, not only because people speak well but also because they move without too many problems. Arielle Dombasle and Pascal Greggory have a remarkable sense of framing.

Q: How far did you push the improvisation? Did the architect go as far as designing the plans for a fictional media center, the one in the film?
ER: In fact, it was the architect himself who gave me the idea for a media center. He went to the location in the Vendée. I explained my film to him, the idea that the mayor wanted to build something in the field, behind the tree. He proposed a mediathèque to me—it was a word I didn't even know—designed it, and had to defend the project in front of Arielle Dombasle and Pascal Greggory in the scene filmed in his office. It was his way of really becoming involved in the film, to make it a real competition, with real plans, a real scale model, a real place, real constraints, even if it was all fictional.

Q: Let's continue with this theme. When the villagers were being interviewed by Clémentine Amouroux did they think that a media center was really going to be built?
ER: There are two ways of considering the villagers. You can consider

them as characters in the film, and when they talk about culture or the media center, you have to assume they know the mayor's projects, and therefore the fiction of the film. You can also consider them as real inhabitants, who talk about their relationship to culture in general and the problems of their village in particular. In fact, the inhabitants weren't told about the story of the film, and responded to Clémentine Amouroux as if she were a real journalist who was writing a story along the lines of "the cultural needs of the rural milieu" . . . They all replied in relation to the reality of the village, not the fiction of the film that they didn't know. But I like this little mismatch. I see it as a proof of the interference between the reality of a village and the story I invented with the help of my actors and the architect.

Q: There is another discourse in the film that's unusual for you, that's to say a purely political discourse, for example Pascal Greggory during his interview with Clémentine Amouroux. How did you write these texts, that are close to the political discourse we hear on television, and yet still very much yours?
ER: I would call that political doublespeak [*langue de bois*], even if it was very worked on for the film. I didn't want to fall into parody. It was rather: how would a young politician believe in the waffle that he's reeling off? It's a matter of belief, so it's interesting for the cinema. Technically, I operated through impregnation rather than collage, the impregnation by the ambient political discourse, the media's discourse. I certainly took some very precise phrases from Chevènement and a lot from what the real mayor of the village said, but on the whole it's a kind of restitution of a type of language.

Q: There are also other discourses which follow Greggory's political discourse, such as Luchini's theatrical discourse and the on-the-spot reactions from the inhabitants. It's quite unusual to have such a mix of registers in your films.
ER: It was a risk I wanted to take by mixing actors and non-actors. I think it's easier for me in this amateur kind of film, all the more so because I asked my actors to play as naturally as possible. I've always done that. I'd like that what is felt in my films is written, and that what seems written is improvised, that's always what I'm looking for. That's why I framed the eyewitness accounts from the villagers with those of Greggory and Luchini. I didn't want a slightly artificial succession of accounts, but a real imbrication, that involves the actors as much as the villagers.

Q: Your lens could be turned the other way: you make a story, a fiction, from the villagers, but you are also making a documentary about a politician, or even Fabrice Luchini himself . . .

ER: Fabrice Luchini is a very strange actor. You often think he's improvising, that he's making up his own phrases, in his own way, almost at the limit providing us with a permanent self-portrait, but nevertheless he needs strong initial constraints, a text that can't really be strayed from at all. On *Full Moon in Paris*, I gave him text that was only slightly written, texts that were far from being sacred, and he couldn't manage at all. So, to really "be" Luchini, he asked me to write the text more, to further constrain him. It's the same in *The Tree, the Mayor and the Mediatheque* . . . everything is written, but in this sense, as you say, it's almost a documentary on Luchini's working methods. It's my text, including his interview with the journalist, which seems very free, but Fabrice is never as good as when he has a text.

Q: We'd like to come back to the question of television. You've worked a lot in television, you have talked about its virtues of "freshness," but this is one of the first times we've had the impression that one of your films has integrated it, made the "televisual manner" one of the motors of the story, the impression that certain people's language and their ways of behaving come directly from television.

ER: *The Tree, the Mayor and the Mediatheque* is a film that is contemporaneous with television. My information comes at least partly from television. But my characters also appear on the screen in a way they couldn't on television. For example, I recorded certain political debates on the television, I studied them, but I deliberately distanced myself from them during filming. My way of filming is very different. First of all, technically, because I refuse to shoot in shot-reverse-shot with several cameras. Next, spatially, because the relationship between characters and their environment will never happen on a set but through a stronger, more realist inscription in space. Finally, television always films through a greed for information, while I am looking for something else, not in the order of knowledge but finding a certain truth about each character. Moreover, in the film I cut one of the interviews, probably the most informative from the point of view of culture, so that I could keep those where people appear to be themselves through what they say. It's this appropriateness to the ontological that is the mark of cinema, and that television, through its eagerness for spectacle, for information, for key discourses, doesn't manage to capture. What I like best in the film is the farmer who only replies with "yes" or "no," without discussion, always out of sync with the question; he has a certain way of being, a certain truth about the countryside, distrustful of those city dwellers who want him to speak. That's fascinating.

Q: This method of superseding television is important in your films . . .
ER: It's something I've wanted to do since *My Night at Maud's*: to transfer part of the televisual experience of my school's programs towards interviews integrated into the film. People said to me at the time: that's television, that's radio, it's not cinema. This practice has always helped me, and I've used it several times, even when it doesn't function as such in the film, with Lazslo Szabo in *Full Moon in Paris* for example. This has led me to pay particular attention to my characters. One of my characters will never say something that is manifestly wrong. They all have a truth, and conflicts arise from several possible truths that may emerge from the same event. I think the right way to view my films, if there has to be one, is to be persuaded in turn by each of my characters, to believe each one, and finally to understand that there is a mystery which holds together several explanations, several stories that are all equally credible. Let's say that I, as the author, while writing, am persuaded in turn by each of my characters.

Q: We felt this ambivalence above all in the temporal organization of *The Tree, the Mayor and the Mediatheque*. We don't really know how long the story takes, there are several ellipses, and the intertitles give the air of a fable. The organization of space is very rigorous, but time is far more uncertain.
ER: It's true that time doesn't have a realistic duration in this film. The chronology is fairly muddled, and one can't date the different moments of the film. The first lesson the primary school teacher gives on the use of the "si" clause is timeless, functioning as exegesis, but fully integrated into the film. In the same way, the sequence where Arielle Dombasle and Pascal Greggory walk together goes beyond verisimilitude, what generally I don't allow myself to do but in this case introduced the idea of fable or tale: the mayor and the novelist's costumes change in the cut from one shot to another. There is an immediate indeterminacy which, in this fairly codified space, that of a countryside walk, gives the flow of time a feeling of the fantastical. It was the opposite of *A Winter's Tale*, where everything was very precisely dated, to the very day. The two experiments have been convincing, and the public hasn't been confused. They are

able to orient the two films: *A Winter's Tale* as a social chronicle, *The Tree, the Mayor and the Mediatheque* as a philosophical fable.

Q: In a preface written recently for Balzac's *La Rabouilleuse* [*The Black Sheep*], you talk very precisely about the novelist's use of time, that it is more vertical than horizontal, more concerned with harmony than melody. Would you apply this organizational principal to your latest film?
ER: I hadn't thought about it. Perhaps . . .

Q: This way of playing with several points of view, making them reply at one end of the film to the other . . .
ER: I must say that I wrote the preface to *La Rabouilleuse* just before making this film. I like Balzac, but people don't normally notice it in my films: I'm pleased you've noticed it. It caught me a bit unawares, and I've surely been more balzacian in this film. It's a script I wrote after having re-read most of Balzac, in particular his *Etudes philosophiques* that I didn't know before.

Q: In this sense, we could say that it's less contemporary matters that's led you to deal so directly with politics, than your strong relationship with and recent re-reading of Balzac. After all, the mayor is a very balzacian character, as are the relationships between the characters in the film. It's a sort of *Scenes de la vie de province* as seen by Eric Rohmer . . .
ER: That's not at all impossible. But I didn't think about this. The subject came spontaneously, naturally. Perhaps what should be said that what came naturally was a resurgence, possibly unconsciously, of those readings and that balzacian universe that is very familiar to me. To be honest with you, my reading of Balzac, and the preface to *La Rabouilleuse* are very clearly polemical from my point of view: against Barthes's work in *S/Z*, against a semiotic reading of Balzac, to settle my personal argument with structuralism, including with *Cahiers* from the structuralist era, what's more (laughter). I wanted to explain Balzac through an ontological reading, inherited from my theoretical reading of Bazin, and not a semiotic one.

Q: How is this reading of Balzac embodied by your characters?
ER: In their manner of "playing," I think. We said a while ago that actors that act, non-actors that act as well, and the real people who don't act, have the same attention and the same space to express themselves in my films. That means there is no stylization in the act. In my cinema—and

I don't think this is the only kind of cinema that is possible—there is no artistic transposition from actor to character, I try to show the actor as he or she is in life, even if for that, as with Luchini, they need a written or even very literary text. On the other hand, I've noticed that a lot of directors have a tendency to want to stylize the acting, to push the actor towards playing. What interests me are the actors' spontaneous gestures, although it doesn't stop my cinema having a certain style. Furthermore, I would point out to you that in most of the films made by my New Wave contemporaries, we find this way of acting, in opposition to the very theatrical style we find at the moment. I don't think that my actors act very differently from those in a film by Godard or Rivette, for example, although our filmic worlds have very little in common. In the world of French cinema, there is a very clear dividing line: on the one hand, a very theatrical, stylized presentation of the actor, and on the other a deconstruction of his acting, allowing us to see something else, the personality itself.

Q: In *The Tree, the Mayor and the Mediatheque*, your actors speak "naturally" about politics or philosophy. How can you hold together these things which seem so contradictory: the naturalness of the acting with the stilted soundbites of politicians or the abstractions of philosophical principles?

ER: It's not the content that matters here, it's the way of saying it, the gestures if you like. Whether someone is talking about politics, philosophy, or love, the first thing I look for is authentic gestures. I don't like actors using deliberate gestures, that simplify expressions in contrast to life's richness, on the other hand I study unconscious, natural gestures very carefully, such as scratching your back while talking about philosophy, or crossing or uncrossing your legs, or any other example. You'll have noticed that all my actors, whether it's Arielle Dombasle or Fabrice Luchini, move well and have a natural sense of gesture. I don't like gestures that act like a language that comes from actors who overdominate their bodies, but I like gestures that escape conscious control and thus, quite simply, lead us to the truth about a person. Bresson tried to fight this gestural language through a hierarchy and the non-gesture; I try to fight against it through the overuse of gesture, the disturbing or unconscious gestures that arise spontaneously. Unlike most directors, I never tell my actors what gestures to perform, but I try to capture their own gestures and record them almost without them realizing, against their will. If an actor becomes aware of their gestures, we have to abandon everything. I prefer it when an actor is so taken with their text that they have spontaneous gestures. Physically they are very interesting gestures, as well. When I'm choosing actors, I talk with them and see how they move their hands. And that's why I prefer filming in a 1/33 ratio, the format of my last film, with a 16mm camera with an almost square frame, because that allows me to show off an actor's gestures more effectively.

Q: Let's talk very precisely about these technical details and finance: what choices did you make in these areas?

ER: I bought a second-hand 16mm television camera, and I decided to make a low budget amateur film, which also corresponded to a desire to make a film differently from those one usually sees. For example, take our current prejudice against 16mm: that its image is less crisp than 35mm, and that spectators will be bothered by the fuzziness of 16mm. It's true 16mm is less clear. Personally, however, I don't like the crispness of 35mm, that hyperreal look where objects stand out with staggering clarity, sometimes even better than faces. 35mm hardens everything, especially faces, that then you have to soften with make-up. 16mm is a lot kinder on faces, which allows you to avoid make-up; it also has greater depth-of-field. At the end of the day, it is more pictorial, has fewer sharp contrasts, and is much better at respecting color balance.

Q: Your 16mm image is closer to an ontology, a recording of the world, than a 35mm image that moves from the real towards "the world of cinema," towards a hyperrealism that has become synonymous with the cinematic...

ER: Yes, exactly. 16mm is more realist. I noticed something during the color-correction of my last film. At this moment, technicians are tempted to correct an overpowering pink tint, a magenta, a pink tint that bodies have when they are recorded on film, which gives color to the face. I realized that my characters were pinker than those in other films, which gives them life and renders them more sympathetic, undoubtedly because I respect this natural facial tone which comes from the world, this pale color that 16mm records much better than the sharp contrasts of 35mm. If you like, this is the difference between the ontological recording that I undertake and the hyperrealist recomposition of the world you get in most films, the presence of flesh tones, as in *French Cancan* by Renoir, which for me is the model of a "flesh-colored film."

Q: For us, your latest film is closer still to Renoir's *Petit Theatre*...

ER: I have great admiration for this film, especially for the sequence with the electric shoe-shine machine. To carry on with our conversation about the artifice of color, I've always thought politicians on television were wrong to plaster themselves with a layer of face cream, which always makes them look either too brown or too pale and distances them from reality, or at any case from my own personal sympathy. You never feel the movement of the skin, which for me at least, is one of my basic criteria for sympathy with either an actor or an orator.

Q: In some ways, the more cinema moves towards hyperrealism, the more you are moving towards a poverty, or at least a simplicity of the image.
ER: That's one of the virtues of amateurism. It's almost as if each of my spectators could make their own film themselves. It's my way of inviting them into my world: 16mm image, few characters, no camera movements, almost like a "family film," like a home movie nearly. Why not? Let's talk about my last film for television, *Jeux de société*: it finishes in praise of the amateur, and amateur theatre. Amateur cinema is undoubtedly the kind which pleases me most these days. At the start of the film, I draw up a simple contract with my cinematographer: to light the scenes, they have two simple 800-watt bulbs, a small halogen tube, an aluminium reflector sheet, and that's all. It's the virtues of economy and invention that I like above all. It's the same thing for camera movement, where my practice matches a certain philosophy of the cinema. This philosophy comes from Cocteau: "To film a galloping horse using a tracking shot is to film a still horse." I like the camera to be impassive, just as I like the narrator to be absent, and I only use panoramic movements to increase space, which is another way of staying objective.

Q: How do you situate this amateurism in relation to French cinema?
ER: I'm proud to assert my amateurism and I take responsibility for its consequences. I wouldn't say I deliberately refused CNC approval for my latest film, but I approved of it! That doesn't mean I consider myself marginal, because if I want to mark out my position as an amateur I don't see the interest of doing it under that particular banner. When I was at *Cahiers*, I was much more of an extremist: you had to break the system, championing the amateur over the avant-garde. I criticized the CNC and the system for funding by advancing funds for being stifling institutions, that serviced a profession that operated as a closed shop, that dealt with projects from outside very unfairly, that prevented them from

being finished. I almost didn't get to make *My Night at Maud's* because of this system, if I hadn't had Truffaut's help. . . . Both the CNC and myself have changed since. The French system is a lot more supple these days, liberated from the weight of very conservative unions such as they have in America, and far more open to projects from young filmmakers. As for me, I constructed a small system for myself, the production company Les Films du Losange, which allowed me to avoid commissions and advances from the CNC, and to work in my own way, as an amateur. It's no longer a revolt, but more an independent method of working, by yourself and for yourself. And every one of my films comes in on budget. So I don't need subsidies. If I get them, all the better, but it's not vital for me. Let's say that the commission wasn't very fair to not give me anything for my last film, for technical reasons (I didn't employ enough union technicians), but I didn't make a fuss.

Q: Watching your latest films, it seems that this influence of amateurism is growing. After *Full Moon in Paris* which was undoubtedly your most professional film, with a fairly large crew, there's been *The Green Ray*, *The Adventures of Reinette and Mirabelle*, and *The Tree, the Mayor and the Mediatheque*. These are all films that are outside of the framework of the *Comedies and Proverbs* or *The Tales of the Four Seasons*.
ER: These 16mm films you're discussing were originally conceived as being intermediaries between the series, even if *The Green Ray* is part of the *Comedies and Proverbs*, something I regret a bit now.

Q: But aren't these intermediaries becoming a major theme in your work? There is even a kind of contamination between these films and your series: *A Winter's Tale* seems drawn towards this amateur strain, through its filming, its small crew . . .
ER: *A Winter's Tale* was filmed in Super 16mm, because it was winter and we needed a grey tone, and also because of ease: we were shooting in a lot of different locations (streets, buses, crowds, cars, in the suburbs, in Paris, in Nevers, in small flats, and at the theatre). In this way, we could integrate it into the 16mm intermediaries, but I'd like to leave this idea to one side, because it will really take on its full meaning when the four seasons series is completed. These series films are much more closely scripted. The 16mm intermediary films are much freer: the script doesn't impose as much and the role of the actors is more decisive. It's almost a portrait of the actors and the film is made for them. To give you an example, the only constraint I had for *The Tree, the Mayor and the Mediatheque* was my

decision to film some of the scenes in the chateau and some in the park. The rest, that's to say the story, came from my desire to work around the chateau, that is to say in the village. The actors could take over from each other, and could be replaced if needs be. I was really very free.

Q: So, if you really want to uphold this distinction, we could say, jokingly, that your *Tales* have become your intermediaries, and your 16mm intermediaries your series . . .
ER: It's true that the intermediaries have become more frequent. Since 1986 and *The Green Ray*, they have been one film in two. And they do have a tendency to rub off on my more written *Tales*. If only my colleagues knew how relaxing it is to make a film with only a few people . . . . While most film makers make bigger and bigger films as they advance in their careers, I'm making lighter and lighter films. It's in that spirit that you need to understand your question. On the one hand, when one is the auteur of one's films, as I am, there is a danger of getting stuck in a system that is too coherent and repetitive. That's why I want to vary my styles, characters, and above all my locations. That's why I vary the locations as much as the seasons in *Tales of the Four Seasons*. In the same way, I rarely use the same actors within a series, which allows the stories to vary a bit. And sometimes, more rarely, I make a history film, a very disorienting and very different genre.

Q: Are you following contemporary documentaries, a "genre" that is undergoing a real renewal at the moment?
ER: I watch a lot of television where there are a lot of documentaries. And I should underline here my total support for Arte. I learn a lot from documentary, especially in terms of how to organize a story. Paradoxically for me, documentaries also contain ideas for fiction.

Q: But this method of integrating documentary into your films, to examine streets as streets, the countryside as the countryside, is also a pamphlet against a cinema that wants to be "cinema," the hyperreal cinema we were talking about earlier . . .
ER: I very rarely, if ever, make cinema against something. I don't think that those of us from the New Wave can make our way of filming hegemonic. Anyway, I think it's good that there are good films that have more popular roots and have big success.

Q: Recently, French cinema's biggest successes haven't been films from

popular culture, though, but those from Culture with a capital C: *Cyrano de Bergerac*, *Tous les matins du monde*, *L'Amant* . . .
ER: Those sorts of films don't interest me at all. When I talk about French popular cinema, I'm thinking about cinema with its roots in the café-theatre, which I find a lot healthier. When I was a critic it was Charbonnaux, Joffé, now it's *Les Envahisseurs* [The Invaders].

Q: You mean *Les Visiteurs* . . .
ER: Oh, yes, yes. I won't go and see that film, but I think it's good such films exist. It's not my cup of tea, but I support those films. Not only from a commercial point of view. There are great things in the café-theatre, whereas there is nothing to take from the pseudo-cultural. Truffaut defended popular cinema, and the café-theatre it was derived from, and from this point of view the weekly magazine *Arts* was very interesting. During the 1950s, *Arts* attacked "the cinema of quality" ferociously, and praised Carbonnaux's *Les Corsaires de Bois de Boulogne*, or Joffé's *Courte tete* or *Les Hussards*, as did Truffaut. I think what links this kind of cinema and that of the New Wave is an absence of a cult of form. In each case, the desire is to film things as simply as possible. In the other tradition, of the "cinema of quality," today called "cultural cinema," there is always some kind of intermediary that swells or that bloats the film: the desire for a "beautiful image," a cultural script, a social problem. That's the whole history of French cinema. When it first appeared, there were three cultures: academic culture, such as painters exhibited in the Salons, the Comédie française, and the writers of the Académie française; an avant-garde culture, such as the Fauvists, the Cubists, Debussy, and Stravinsky; and popular culture, such as dance music, the tango, boulevard theatre, the café-concert, and cinema itself. There were very different audiences, that sometimes met, and I think the history of cinema is a history of alliances between either academic culture or avant-garde culture and the cinema, that was nevertheless originally popular. In the first alliance, we get the cinema of quality, and in the second the New Wave.

Q: This alliance was formed in the 1950s, in your writings in *Cahiers* and *Arts*.
ER: I don't like the word "compromise" but I do think, consciously or not, there was a kind of pact, it was very conscious for Truffaut, and the pact was as follows: the avant-garde culture will give up an emphasis on form, on beautiful images, an inheritance of a fantastical world from silent, avant-garde cinema influenced by Surrealism, but it will

gain realism, or at least stories that take place in a contemporary France and a method of filming that comes from popular cinema, whether it be French or American. A sense of the avant-garde remains, at least as far as the cinema refuses to be openly commercial, remains a cinema of auteurs, and the New Wave gained a live aesthetic, an anti-academism, and indeed, a certain audience. People have said that the New Wave emptied cinemas, but this allowed it to keep a certain loyal knot of spectators for auteurs that emerged from this way of thinking. This is very unique, compared to other countries: in France, an "intermediary" audience was created, between the general public and the specialists of modern art, that allowed filmmakers such as Chabrol, Truffaut, and myself to pursue our cinema.

Q: To return to your latest film, can we not see it as an act of defiance against academic culture, the culture of media centers and the Ministry for Culture, who try to impose their vision of culture, to renew the links between academic and popular culture? The conclusion of your film, that is to say the failure of the media center and the final return to folk songs is a kind of statement on the impossibility of that alliance nowadays: popular culture has beaten cultural academism . . .
ER: It's true that that could be a possible reading. . . . Yes, it's a little bit that. The demagogues' problem is that they want to impose culture, because that implies that there is a correct culture, and one that is wrong. While in fact there are different cultures for different audiences. A media center in the countryside, as if that were a universal need, revolts me, even if my film, I'll say again, is not a film against something.

Q: That revolt against a universal culture that wants to impose itself on the countryside, against a cultural modernism that wishes to interrupt tradition, even if it is expressed through fiction, is that not your way of being a citizen, of advancing a political discourse?
ER: It's more an intervention in the combat of the city, almost in the Greek sense of the term. In my films, I've always remained behind the fiction, I don't take sides, or choose one character over another. In my interviews, I'm sometimes more explicit. I remember that in *Cahiers*, in 1969, I gave a profession of faith in the ontology of the image, even if it wasn't really known at the time. For me, an artist should be preoccupied with questions concerning the environment, the beauty of the world, in the countryside as well as in the town, rather than following one particular political line. In 1969, especially for the *Cahiers*, that was a

provocative position, misunderstood, and interpreted as a conservative attitude. Nowadays, I hold some things very dear, but it is very difficult to imagine a film "defending nature and heritage" that isn't a vacuous, sentimental, nostalgic film. I obviously didn't want to make this kind of film, so I had to find a way to have a conversation about nature and architecture in a way that was true to my concerns. I think that an artist is especially attached to these questions of nature and architecture, and perhaps that's his way of being a citizen.

Q: It's a reflection on the landscape, a fable that's also an essay on the relationship between builders and the landscape.
ER: I wanted to show that, whatever the architect did, he was destructive, and to ask myself how much you can dominate a landscape. It's a film about a destructive power that's both extremely strong because it's invested with a godlike, quasi-divine power, and very dangerous because it can only feed off pre-existing landscapes or structures in order to transform and destroy them.

Q: In fact, for you, ecology is primarily a cinematic question, in the sense that the defense of the landscape, the field, and the tree is above all a defense of that which is recorded most strongly on film, and brings us back to the prime question: what is cinema? the ontological force of a place. It's a little like Cousteau defending the submarine depths, that were, for Bazin, the essence of what cinema can show. Recording and showing a landscape is cinema.
ER: Yes, in the sense that cinema records, in the words of Bazin, "the beauty of the real." But I would go further: my love of cinema itself springs from my love of nature. And that's what always lead me towards a Bazinian concept of cinema: the mechanical recording of things is cinema's strength, it's a machine before it's art, whereas painting's strength, primarily art because it is forced to transpose, to describe, to use metaphors, to represent a landscape rather than record it, is a strength of the imagination which bothers me more. I prefer to look at a landscape than see it represented via a painting. It's nature which led me to loving cinema, and that's why I prefer cinema to all the other arts, because, unless you're making "cinematic postcards," it doesn't have a predatory relationship to landscape.

Q: But can't this godlike ambition that architects and painters have, that you fear also be seen as political: the desire to construct a new, better world? What you are promoting is modesty in all things, in architecture as well as politics . . .

ER: Certainly. But politicians are also revising their ambitions and beginning to praise modesty. At the moment everyone is questioning political actions and political discourses, me included. I have to admit that I've no certainty about this. If I had to give my own personal opinion, I'd support the primary school teacher in my film, who has an ecological point of view but who distrusts all the ecologists' political discourse. Well, it's more complicated than that: I'd have a tendency to speak like the primary school teacher, but to listen to the Socialist mayor.

Q: That's exactly Zoë's, the primary school teacher's daughter's, position . . .

ER: It's true that that's probably the position I'm closest to. And that's why the film is not at all pessimistic, or nostalgic, or conservative: it's a child who is expressing a simple truth about the landscape, her desire to keep the trees around her alive. I've always kept faith in the future and trust in the past together. In a certain way, I am very conservative, but the more conservative I am, the more I'm waiting for the future. As far as architecture goes, for example, I defended the Utopian, futuristic projects of the 1960s and 1970s, as in my television program on "the oblique function" in architecture with Paul Virilio and Claude Parents. Everything is a question of context: you have to be conservative in the framework of tradition, for example, in Paris, but one has to be resolutely futurist in Utopian settings, such as in the New Towns, where everything can be allowed.

Interview with Eric Rohmer

Aurélien Ferenzi / 2001

From *Senses of Cinema*, no. 16 (September–October 2001). Copyright 2001 by Senses of Cinema, Inc. and the contributors. Reproduced by permission.

AF: How did the idea of *The Lady and the Duke* come to you?
ER: While on holiday about ten years ago, I came across a digest of the memoirs of Grace Elliott in a history magazine. This English lady had been the mistress of the Duke of Orleans, King Louis XVI's cousin, and had written an account of her life during the French Revolution. The article mentioned that her town house was still standing at such-and-such a number on Rue Miromesnil. I have always been interested in places and was particularly struck by the idea that this house could still be seen at a certain address. That gave me the idea of making a film that would be set in that particular spot in Paris and would play on the relationship between the peaceful apartment, which served Grace as a kind of hideout, and the rest of the city in the throes of revolutionary turmoil. Strangely enough, I found out later that the article in the history magazine was wrong: the house on Rue Miromesnil had been built after the Revolution, so Grace Elliott couldn't have lived there! But without that mistake, I'm not sure the article would have sparked off the idea in me.

AF: The portrayal of Paris was the driving force behind the film.
ER: Yes, and I had to find a way of depicting historical Paris. I'm often frustrated when I watch period pieces set in Paris. People always tend to go off and film in Le Mans, Uzes, or other towns with well-preserved historic neighborhoods. I can always tell it's not Paris, which has its own specific architecture. I didn't want that, nor did I want to make do with filming the same handful of old carriage doorways that always feature in period films. I wanted to show a big city with big open spaces like Place Louis XIV (now Place de la Concorde), which was a focal point of the

Revolution, and the parts of town that Grace Elliott mentions in her memoir: Boulevard Saint-Martin, Rue Saint-Honoré, down which she is taken on her way to the Surveillance Committee, and so on. When she says she walked all the way to Meudon via the Invalides, she had to cross the Seine somewhere!

AF: So what was the solution you came up with?
ER: I had shot two period films before: *The Marquise of O* (1975) in real locations and *Perceval le Gallois* (1978) entirely in the studio. I knew that neither of these methods would give an authentic portrayal of Paris. So I had the idea of inserting real-life characters into scenic backgrounds that I would have specially painted, based on the layout of the city at that time. Inserting characters into sets is one of the oldest tricks in the filmmaker's book. Melies was probably the first to do it. But ten years ago, when I first started thinking about the project, digital technology was still in its infancy. If the characters and scenery had been composited on film, each new layer would have incurred a loss of picture quality. Kinescoping, i.e., transferring from video to 35mm film, wasn't very satisfactory either in those days. Now both of these techniques have been perfected.

AF: How did you have the scenic backgrounds made?
ER: They were painted by Jean-Baptiste Marot. We designed them together in the appropriate period style and according to the requirements of the mise en scene. Hervé Grandsart did the preliminary documentary research. We worked from pictures and engravings, but also from street maps of the period. The interiors are not real locations. They were all built in an adjoining studio by the set designer, Antoine Fontaine, and the rigger, Jérome Pouvaret. To me, this work was not just a matter of being meticulous, it was about striving for an authenticity that underpins the whole film. At heart, I wasn't especially intent on making a film about the Revolution. I don't much like being pegged as an eighteenth-century buff! Even though I've sometimes been compared to Marivaux, it isn't my favorite century.

AF: Was your approach comparable to the way you made *Perceval*: using pictures from the period to depict the period itself?
ER: Yes. I don't much care for photographic reality. In this film, I depict the Revolution as people would have seen it at the time. And I try to make the characters more like the reality you find in paintings. The

opening scenes of the film are pictures, and I'd be pleased if the uninformed spectator thought they were period paintings and was surprised when they suddenly come to life.

AF: One is also reminded of your work in educational television.
ER: I didn't make this film for any political reasons. I don't use it to defend any party, royalist or anti-royalist. On the other hand, I would like to help cultivate a taste for history in audiences, both old and young. I have heard it said that France is the country that publishes the largest number of history magazines, whereas the English-speaking world has more taste for historical novels. There is a huge potential interest in history in France, but period films have often been rather lax about historical exactitude. In fact, my scrupulousness is the reason why I have only made three period films. I pay close attention to the language of a period and it's very difficult to write dialogue in the words of a different era. It keeps the characters from expressing themselves. If I used my own style to write a story in the past, it would be a pastiche. It wouldn't be any good. Here, Grace Elliott's story gave me a very sound basis, right down to the dialogue.

AF: Did you watch other historical films again before starting on *The Lady and the Duke*?
ER: I watched three period pictures: D. W. Griffith's *Orphans of the Storm* (1921) (which is set during the French Revolution), Abel Gance's *Napoleon* (1927), and Jean Renoir's *La Marseillaise* (1937). All three films are admirable for different reasons. For example, for a long time Renoir was praised for making his characters speak as they did in the 1930s and not bothering about eighteenth-century speech. That's a myth, unless we believe that the language of the 1930s was closer to the eighteenth century than our own! Griffith made me realize something else: I was wondering how to film the exteriors, i.e., how to insert the characters into the scenery. Would I film sequence shots or reverse angle shots, which would make the process even more complicated to set up? Seeing *Orphans of the Storm* again, I realized that most of the time, its strength is that each shot is static. So I took static shots, and closer shots with a second camera.

AF: Were you always sure that the characters could be keyed in as you wanted?
ER: We ran tests. We had to know how the characters would fit into the

scenery, so we filmed a test with extras going through a doorway and it worked. We sometimes had to adapt a little, especially when the set was deeper than the length of the studio. For instance, the view down Rue Saint-Honoré had to be two hundred meters long, while the sound stage was only forty meters wide. We had to shoot that sequence in several parts with cutaway shots in between. It was a constraint, of course. I normally decide how to shoot each scene as I come to it, whereas here I had to design the shots very precisely beforehand. But the advantage is that the result is truer than if I had edited it altogether from little bits of houses and roofs framed from odd angles to cut out the TV aerials. That wouldn't have interested me. I like to show the scenery as it is. On the set, I often hear people say "We'll cheat it." I don't like cheating. I like to take reality the way it is, even if it's a reality I created through painting, like here. Truth comes from the painting, not the editing. You could say I'm faithful to Bazin's teachings, even if he was too hidebound regarding depth of field and the sequence shot. And I do think that resorting to a highly visible artifice gives me truth.

AF: To return to the story itself, what appealed to you in Grace Elliott's memoirs?
ER: My researcher found me a complete copy of the text, which had been published several times in France. Grace Elliott was born in 1760 and died in 1823. Her journal begins on 14 July 1789 and ends just before she was let out of prison, after the fall of Robespierre. Over and above its undeniable historical interest (it contains a few minor errors in dates, but most of it has the ring of truth), there is something striking about it, as though it had already been written as a script, with scenes, sequences, and even dialogue. It has a very different tone from the other journals I have read. Memoir-writers mostly tend to write about themselves, their fears and hopes, but Grace Elliott includes herself in the picture, though always maintaining a certain detachment and distance. We see her acting and moving around, but the other characters also live in a very powerful way, especially the Duke of Orleans, of whom we have very few first-hand reports.

AF: Was it her loyalty to her commitments that touched you?
ER: No, it was more her British stiff upper lip: a certain modesty and self-control, a completely unaffected way of talking about herself and, above all, a way of looking at events that makes her the heroine of a novel. Perhaps this is how it happens when History overturns the lives

of individuals. Few other historical characters have ever seemed so close to us, and so moving. I can only talk about my intentions, not about the result, but the details of her private life that appear in the book, which I kept in the film, create an effect of reality. For example, I'm thinking about the moment when Orleans looks at his watch. We're in the present, in the moment. That's what makes it filmic. The past is the tense of the novel; the present is the tense of cinema.

AF: You were also interested in the light the characters shed on the events of the Revolution.
ER: What interests me is their lack of fanaticism. Grace stands up for the King but she is not an extremist. She doesn't want to leave France. She has Republican friends such as Orleans and Biron. She is probably actually less of a royalist than she says, given that she wrote her book in anti-Revolutionary England. As for Orleans, he is often shown in a totally negative light, but there is a mystery, an ambiguity, a duality about him that interests me. He was vindictive and he didn't like Louis XVI, but he was also sincerely attracted to new ideas. I have added some details drawn from his own correspondence and the testimony of his son, Louis-Philippe.

AF: The audience might be inclined to condemn the killing of the King, as Grace does.
ER: I think that at the time, everyone wanted the King dead for fear of appearing reactionary. It was the trend then, rather as it is the trend nowadays to claim to be an environmentalist. I wanted to make my film with Grace Elliott's story, not against it. If anyone wants to pass judgment on historical grounds, they should judge the book on which the film was based, not the film itself.

AF: How did you choose the actors?
ER: By intuition, as always. I audition one person, he or she reads the lines, and that's it! I had difficulty casting the Englishwoman. A casting director known to Margaret Menegoz sent me photos of actresses and an audio tape of their voices. The only tape I liked was of an actress who said she knew Grace Elliott's book and wanted to play her. Her voice appealed to me before her photo did, and when I met her, I found the actress even more attractive than her picture! As for Jean-Claude Dreyfus, I didn't think of him at first, but I was looking for a strong personality. I needed somebody big and stout, even if he didn't physically resemble the Duke

of Orleans all that closely. I am very pleased with the cast. My directing of actors, as usual, went no further than giving them technical instructions. Feelings are the actor's business. All I did was tell them to enunciate clearly so that they would be understood. They didn't let me down.

AF: Do you think the film will surprise audiences used to your *Comedies and Proverbs* and *Tales of Four Seasons*?
ER: No, and besides, whenever I have made slightly different films, be they historical or political, like *The Tree, the Mayor and the Media Centre* (1992), the audience has followed. I wouldn't want to limit myself to overly psychological topics or romantic comedies, even if that's where I feel most personally involved. I like to get out from time to time.

Interview with Eric Rohmer: Does Cinematography Have an Artistic Function?

Priska Morrissey / 2004

From *Rohmer et les Autres*, ed. Noël Herpe (Rennes: Presses Universitaires de Rennes, 2007), 185–200. Reprinted by permission; translated from the French by FH.

In this interview, Eric Rohmer discusses his ideas concerning the collaboration between the director and his cinematographer. Considering the question of who authors the image and his long collaboration with Nestor Almendros, his work with Renato Berta and Diane Baratier, the filmmaker reveals some of the key principles of his aesthetic of light (how to render color, the relationship between background and foreground, windows and shadows, the problem of the changeable sky, etc.). We find some "New Wave" characteristics in his attitude towards light, that is to say both a rejection of standard lighting set-ups—actors picked out by key lighting, lighting that favors dramatic shadows—and the application of new principles that favors a supple, logical, and noncumbersome approach to lighting that allows actors freedom of movement.

ER: I'd like to start by discussing terminology. The expression "chef opérateur" [director of photography] amuses me because often this "director of photography" is not a director of anything, he or she is all alone. As for the expression "directeur de la photographie," I know the people I work with find it rather pretentious. In my credit sequences (I always look after everything, including the credit sequence), I never put "un film de" [a film by], I find that ridiculous and commercial. I write, as if for a book and I'm the author of it all:

Eric Rohmer
"Comedies and Proverbs"
The Green Ray

As for the word "réalisation" [direction] I'm rather against it because the realization of the film is the result of all the crew's work, and the director should be called "the director of the process of realization," as they are abroad, where one talks about a film director (even if often this term is used to discuss the direction of actors) . . . because realizing the film isn't just down to him or her. Furthermore, making a film is as much about the conception as it is about realizing it. Once, for a television film where I was forced to use the term "réalisation" in the credits, I insisted that the term was "conception et réalisation." I prefer the term mise-en-scène, but that has rather a theatrical connotation. I would like to use the term "auteur" because I consider myself the author of the film. Author and collaborators . . .

As for sound, there are three jobs: recording, mixing, and now sound editing. For a long time I wasn't really sure what a sound editor did and I'd never used one. Now with computers it's different. Before it was a pasting job, but now it's closer to sound recording. In my films, it's the sound recorder (who is often labelled "the sound engineer," which I find a bit overdone) who looks after the sound editing. So, to summarise: for the image, I won't use "directeur de photo" or "chef opérateur," as that doesn't mean anything to me other than in certain very precise cases. I prefer to say "camera operator." In the credit sequence, I could put camera operator, but I use the term "Image," it's prettier. So, in the credit sequence, for photography, I put:

Image
So-and-so

Finally, the question that was asked at first, and it's a more delicate question than you might think, is: does cinematography have an artistic function? It's obvious that it's technically challenging, but it's also artistic in a way—as are other jobs in the crew: actor, set decorator, musician. All these roles are artistic. On the other hand, electricians and technical crew, because they don't act alone, but are managed by the director of photography, assume purely technical roles. They are often called "workers." For me, they are the "pure technicians." As for me, I often ask myself, particularly concerning the areas where I make the decisions, about the relationship that exists between my work and that of my cinematographers, sound recorders, set decorators, and to a certain extent musicians. Personally, being very egocentric, even while I respect the people who work for me, I don't give them complete freedom. And that's only possible because my crew is very small.

PM: But it seems that in some of your films, such as in *The Green Ray* you gave a wide margin of manoeuvre to your director of photography . . .
ER: Not more than usual. Well, it all depends what you mean by freedom. In this film, there's no work on the light, because almost no scenes are artificially lit. Only two are and I was the one who placed the lights. On the other hand, concerning the frame, the DP did have some control and took some initiatives. But it's difficult to define this in general, you can only talk about specific examples. In a very general manner, when we consider directors who are also auteurs (in France: Bresson, Renoir, Godard, and others and abroad: Fritz Lang, Hitchcock, John Ford . . .) the question is: is there more of a resemblance between the images of these auteurs' films than between the images of films from different directors with the same cinematographer? In other words, is style the preserve of the cinematographer or the director? This doesn't mean that a cinematographer has no style, of course. . . . But is his style as obvious? For example, is the style of the cinematographers Renoir worked with as obvious as Renoir's style?

In the conception of the image, the auteur, or director, has an important role. Some of them create personal and interesting images, others banal images—and the choice of cinematographer won't change that. Lots of cinematographers say to me that what matters is not establishing your own style, but being in service of the director. Well, that's what I understand personally. Others might think that cinema is truly a collective art, but that's not how I conceive it. And when I'm looking for a cinematographer, I don't look at what they've done before (well, I might do . . .), but I'm more interested in their personality and that we get on: I want to make sure they'll understand me and if they'll use the methods I suggest to them.

For example, the first time I met my cinematographer on *The Tree, the Mayor and the Mediatheque*, Diane Baratier, I had already seen several people. It was a film with a very small budget. I said: "The film will probably be filmed outside most of the time, but there will be some interiors. For those, you'll have access to two lights." In general, the cinematographer establishes a list of material they require. . . . I went out and bought two lights. I warned that I wasn't going to spend any more money than that, and that she would have two cardboard sheets that we would unfold, one covered in aluminium foil and the other in white paper, to act as reflective screens: "That's all we'll have. There won't be an assistant and I'll hold up the screens." This was a massive constraint because the quality of the photography depends a lot on the methods you use . . . and she accepted.

Recently I've made a short that we filmed here in this office. There was a discussion with the cinematographer: "Do you think we can film in this room, with so little light and using the minimum budget? The light varies a lot, we'll have to put gelatines on the windows." . . . She said yes, we'll use gelatines . . . but from that moment on I didn't feel as capable as her. It's a very delicate balance getting enough light for faces and for the background, and sometimes cinematographers I've worked with have struggled . . . you need some contrast, but you don't want the faces to become too dark . . . for example, right now in this room, we couldn't film against the light without some artificial lighting.

So, the cinematographer used orange gels—the light outside being blue—and I asked her (I always ask these kinds of questions), "You don't think it will look like it's night time?" and she replied, "No," and I said "OK, I believe you." But that's an act of faith—because it was at the limit! But in fact the result was very successful.

When I made my first film with Diane, we filmed indoors in a room in the chateau and in the classroom. There wasn't enough light in the rooms in the chateau. Now, I like contrast and filming people against the light. It's probably a taste I picked up from my first cinematographer, Nestor Almendros, who loved that effect. So there's a lot of filming against the light in my films, and I show windows. The inside-outside relationship is very important for me, I don't like showing people in apartments without windows. But it's difficult because there are very few ways to compensate for the strength of the outside light. Either you can make it weaker by placing gels, or you can strengthen the interior light through artificial lighting. But we only had two lights (and in fact you're better off with one rather than several).

In the case of the short, we used gels and we did use a small amount of artificial light inside, with one light, of two kilos, of a type known as a "blonde" probably because its bulb is yellow, and we placed it against the wall, to create reflective light (rather than directly under the character which would have been too strong). But for *The Tree, the Mayor and the Mediatheque*, we were in enormous rooms with windows . . . so I was less rigorous than for other films, but that fits with that film's more documentary style: because we didn't have much lighting equipment, I didn't film people in front of windows. . . . People don't realize, but I showed the windows in editing. So from time to time you'll see a shot of a window that doesn't have anything in front of it, but because it's shown very quickly, as a kind of establishing shot, it works. For the remainder, we lit characters and let the background remain darker, which was rather attractive. If we had wanted to show people as you are now, sat in front of a window, we would have needed a lot more light. . . . So, although you might not think so, I do use editing effects, but people don't notice! At that time, my cinematographer had previously only worked as an assistant, and hadn't made any films herself; she listened to what I said to her . . .

PM: You've spoken about having deliberately chosen an all-women crew for *The Green Ray*. What do you think this female crew brought?
ER: In *The Green Ray* you told me that I gave more freedom to my cinematographer. These are films that one could manage to make alone (as for example Claudine Nougaret's husband Robert Depardon has done). But, for a fiction film, with actors, that would seem difficult to me. And then physically I can't do all the jobs. . . . Some directors take care of shot composition themselves . . . personally, I can do this as an amateur but not as a professional. It's not my habit, apart from in small, personal films that I make in Super 8 or 16mm (*Fermière à Montfaucon*, for example, I organized the composition myself, but that was a very light crew with just one camera and a stand . . .). As for sound, I really don't have the strength: you can't look after image and sound at the same time—unless you have sound that looks after itself, through radio microphones . . . for example, I've never been able to hold a boom. It's very tiring, you have to be relaxed and I just don't have that attitude. And you have to have a pretty remarkable sense of where the frame is. I really admire boom operators who just know they have to hold the boom 2cm higher: I can never tell. For *The Green Ray*, I told Claudine Nougaret that I didn't have anyone for the cinematography, and she introduced me to Sophie Maintigneux whom I didn't know.

As for lighting, there wasn't really a problem. I had two bulbs and a slightly stronger 800-watt tube, and my reflective sheets. We understood each other really well, I can't remember anymore how we organized the lighting, but as I was the one who had the kit, I must have participated. On the other hand, she was definitely in charge of the camera. When we were filming, I asked myself, "Should I tell her what to film, should I give her some indications, or should I leave her alone?" I decided to leave her alone. And she did something I didn't expect . . . fairly systematic camera movements. Instead of leaving a character when they stopped speaking, and moving rapidly to the next, she took a rather slow panoramic shot according to a very personal rhythm—and I really liked it, it made the film seem less amateurish: instead of moving too quickly from one character to the next she used both travelling shots and a front and back zoom. I only intervened once, which was rather risky but it worked. It's the scene where Marie Rivière is talking to the two boys and the Swedish girl. I could see that Marie was starting to cry, while Sophie was pulling back with the zoom. I can't remember how I did it (I didn't want to disturb her), did I make a sign, did I tap her on the shoulder? . . . but anyway, she stopped pulling back and moved forward, because it was very important to stay with the person who was crying. But apart from that scene, I didn't intervene.

Sophie was very at ease with zooms and travelling shots. On the other hand, some cinematographers are less so, and in that case, I won't ask them to do something that they wouldn't want to do themselves.

In fact, the whole question of human relations is very important in all of this. You have to understand the person. In the same way that the cinematographer has to understand the needs of the director, so the director has to understand the cinematographer and play to their strengths. At the same time, as generally in life, you have to rub along: I've always had good relations with the people I work with.

In my very first films, it was other amateurs who looked after the camera: I've lost touch with them all apart from Rivette who worked as my cinematographer on one of my films. He did very well! The first professional cinematographer I worked with was Nicolas Hayer on *The Sign of Leo*. He had already made some very famous films, like Jean Cocteau's *Orphée*. Melville suggested him to me; he had already made two or three films with him. Melville particularly worked with Henri Decaë—who was also the cinematographer on *The 400 Blows* and *Le Beau Serge*, but never on one of my films.

Melville told me that Hayer was very charming, and told me about his theories which seduced me: that lighting had to be *logical*. I realized, and what's more, thanks to him, that lots of cinematographers didn't use lighting logically at all: by which I mean that if you're in a room with a window, you don't sense that light comes from the window—you don't know where the light comes from. It happens that in some films (and I'm talking about great cinematographers such as Claude Renoir or Eugen Schuftan) you can see shadows on the exterior window frame—which is ridiculous, unless it's very dark outside and very light inside! Hayer thought that it was better to have rather a dark face (perhaps not as much as in real life) and then you didn't need to have such strong lights, perhaps you could just have one lamp. He preferred to use reflected and indirect light. The way that cinematographers worked in that period was as follows: I light from the ceiling, with lots of projectors, and I find a path in which the actor is really well lit. The cinematographer had to know what the actor was going to do, and would pick them out in a brightly lit path, to the extent that a good film actor would be aware of this light.

With the New Wave, we wanted more freedom, and to be able to put our actors where we wanted, so we wanted a much more diffuse and reflected light. For exteriors, Hayer used reflectors for sunlight or electronic light, which were great sheets of zinc. These are things that people notice in the street—you can't make a documentary-style film with these tools—but he liked that kind of light.

PM: I imagine that it was your taste for the cinematography in Melville's films that made you want to work with him . . .
ER: Yes, I liked the look of Meville's films, and I found Hayer's cinematography remarkable. In particular, his blacks were beautiful. At that time, films had a greyish quality I didn't like. Even if he worked with reflective light, and didn't use many lamps, Hayer created a slightly hard image, that returns to cinema's sources.

PM: You said that it was thanks to him you recognized certainly "illogical" lighting schemas that were the norm for films at that time: do you think that realization came from cinematographers?
ER: It came from the cinematographers but I think the directors were responsible too. Well, I know that we, that is to say Rivette, Godard, and myself (Truffaut perhaps a little less) discussed this question a lot. The big issue was especially shooting against the light. We thought that French cinema looked too smooth and flat and that it didn't reflect reality. Godard liked images with very strong shadows. He's continued in that vein. . . . Did we influence our cinematographers? I think Melville was important for that. He interfered with lots of things, and he must have influenced people like Decaë, who was the first to make films in that style, with Chabrol and Truffaut. Then that was also the case with

Raoul Coutard who didn't really share Godard's ideas. Godard pushed him a bit, and forced him to take images that cinematographers at the time said were impossible. In particular, he made him film Belmondo passing in front of a window which made him appear completely dark or absorbed by the light. What did Godard do? In editing, he cut the shot in the middle, and he invented the freedom of cutting mid-shot.

We'd already noticed all this—but without doubt Nestor Almendros developed them. . . . He only lit indirectly, with limited means, small pieces of paper that he put in front of the projector, as in *My Night at Maud's*; and in the end, his images weren't very different from Hayer's: softer and more diffuse, but with some sharpness.

Hayer said, "Actresses don't like me because my lighting doesn't flatter them, it's a logical light that isn't arranged to suit skin and faces . . . ." As far as the relationship between actors and Almendros, it's rather difficult to describe. I remember when we were filming *Pauline at the Beach*, he said, "I like filming with you because you film with beautiful people." I replied, "But you've worked in America, with the biggest American stars!" But, he thought that their skin wasn't beautiful, they had to be made-up, and he didn't like make-up at all. Hayer didn't like it, nor did Nestor. In all the films I made with Nestor, there was never any make-up . . . and I realized that with other cinematographers, I was more or less obliged to use some make-up. If not, they feel ill at ease. But I prefer to go without, and I think the lack of make-up gives my films a truth which is felt by the viewer, even if he or she doesn't consciously realize it. I saw *A Summer's Tale* again the other day: there's no make-up, and you can tell. Whereas in lots of films, there's make-up and it's artificial and "cinematic" . . .

PM: Do you do photographic tests with your actors?
ER: I don't use much technical equipment, and I tend to throw myself into filming as well. . . . But I always use people with beautiful skin. That's why they don't need make-up. Another thing which matters to me (which isn't strictly speaking part of cinematography but which is also linked) is what you call the presence of the actors. Some actors are transparent, they don't impress themselves on the image: others are photogenic, not when they are immobile, but in movement. I call that presence; it's a term which comes from the theatre . . . so the tests I use are always amateur, with me in charge of the photography. I know that once or twice I've photographed actors and been disappointed because they've been less good that they are in reality. But I tend to just sense

these things. When I see someone in my office, I can tell how they'll be in front of the camera, in particular through their gestures: I notice if they have beautiful gestures or not, if they're a bit stiff . . . after I've photographed, I will do screen tests sometimes as well—but often just with a small, amateur camera, outdoors. In general, if I've decided to film with them, it's positive, but also (as with *Claire's Knee* or *Love in the Afternoon*) I might do a screen test with a cinematographer, that gets sent to the lab. That's a more professional screen test because we've already started filming. I've done some for more recent films, for the *Tales of the Four Seasons*: spring, winter, summer. As I knew the actresses for autumn, so the tests were for the locations rather than the actresses themselves . . .

With Nestor, I used this reflective light. He didn't like hanging lights from the ceiling, which would also have been very complicated in the locations where we were shooting. He generally used lights on stands, with white surfaces behind them to act as reflectors, but gradually this kind of lighting became more common and appeared on American appliances; soft lights whose light source was already located towards the back and that had a reflective surface at the back. We used these soft lights for the last film I made with him, *Pauline at the Beach*.

For *La Marquise d'O*, we weren't able to use daylight. All the costume films I've made have been more difficult from a technical point of view. The day when Nestor and I visited the castle where we were filming the sun shone through the windows and he said, "This light is magnificent, we won't need artificial light." But I replied, "Yes, but at the moment it's one or two in the afternoon. By three o'clock the sun will have gone." He said, "Well, we must light from the outside" and so from that moment on I decided to construct some scaffolding. We were on the ground floor, but the garden was lower than the court and we were filming towards the garden . . . so we used this scaffolding to light through having lights from outside the windows. Some days we used gels and sometimes we didn't, I can't really remember now how it all worked.

As for *Perceval*, I was a bit disconcerted. We shot in an old-fashioned studio, where the lights came from the ceiling and you needed to use gangways, that were also very high up, to get to them. We needed a horde of electricians. And these lights only lit small areas. There was an electrical arc. . . . Nestor was uncomfortable too—especially as the film was set in the Middle Ages, we didn't want people to be able to sense electricity, we wanted the lighting to be like miniatures, with a flat, direct feel . . . we hesitated . . . Nestor had just made a film with Truffaut where the photography was very different with high contrast, *La Chambre vert/*

The Green Room: it took him some time to get used to this new system but the final result is pretty successful.

For *The Lady and the Duke*, Diane also used a team of electricians and had to light from above: but today it is a lot simpler than it used to be. There was a gangway but only for the very back of outdoor-style shots. In *Triple Agent*, there was less light—but it still mainly came from above— I have to say that when the lighting works like this, I don't look after everything. The only instruction I give is to keep the light fairly diffuse and to avoid shadows. But how you achieve that, I don't know. And I'm impatient and I don't like it when it takes a long time to set up the lighting, I get bored. I prefer it when lighting is achieved with very little. But I have to say that the result isn't that different and I like the cinematography as much in *The Lady and the Duke* as in *Triple Agent*.

PM: How do you conceive the lighting for your historical films?
ER: For lighting historical films, we have some models. For *La Marquise d'O*, we have those Romantic German paintings that helped us a lot, with their fairly chiaroscuro light; it's fairly easy to imitate. As for the Middle Ages, it's more difficult to locate where the look comes from, because it's from the set as much as the photography . . . but it was the same thing—avoid shadows. For *The Lady and the Duke*, the works of that era's painters (in particular genre painters such as Boilly, Robert, Greuze, who is much better than he is generally given credit for) are close to photography, which makes them very easy to reproduce.

As for *Triple Agent*, I did think about filming it in black-and-white; but it wasn't very interesting imitating the style of that era—which I lived through and which perhaps therefore seemed more modern to me— in other words, I saw it in color. Having black-and-white photography seemed primitive to me, and it added nothing. I thought it was better to make the film in color: the contrast between the color images and the archive footage instead of being shocking, would be interesting, it would give the image a certain dynamism, a sort of a variety . . . and I chose a highly colored set and palette, imitating the colors of the period (for the clothing as much as the set). I realized when a bit later I went to the Vuillard exhibition (a painter I know of but hadn't thought about) that there was a certain link between the feel of my film and his paintings. . . . But in this film I didn't have any particular ambitions for the photography.

PM: Did the idea of inspiring yourself from photographs from the period (with their multiple shadows and beams of light) cross your mind?

ER: No, I didn't attempt this. It would be very difficult if not impossible nowadays, because the film stock has changed. Precisely because photography already existed then, it was important not to try and imitate it, whereas painting . . . to see a scene from the eighteenth century in black-and-white . . . it's a feeling that I have: I'm from the era of color and not black-and-white. I know a lot of filmmakers loved black-and-white, but I've always been attracted to color from the start, even if I made certain films in black-and-white such as *My Night at Maud's*. First of all, at that time, we were just leaving black-and-white behind. I had a lot of ideas about that and talked about them with Nestor. Secondly: color film stock wasn't that sensitive and as I wanted to film at night, I thought it would be better in black-and-white. Thirdly, I don't know, I just saw it in black-and-white! I saw that Clermont-Ferrand, where the houses are black, would be more beautiful in black-and-white and it would have bothered me to see red traffic signs and red traffic lights in the middle of all that black. And then there was the theme of snow. . . . I had to struggle for it because one of my producers, Pierre Braunberger, really wanted us to film in color. I resisted and it was one of my most commercially successful films. On the other hand, *La Collectionneuse*, which I made before hand, could only ever have existed in color.

In *My Night at Maud's*, the idea of placing light sources into the frame came from me. First of all because a lot happened in the evening, and putting light in the frame gave it more life and made it more interesting. I had thought about showing light sources in *The Girl from the Monceau Bakery* and *Suzanne's Career*. I like the contrasts that creates and I like windows . . .

PM: You haven't said if having an all female-crew creates a particular sensibility?

ER: I don't know, I might have said that at one time . . . with Diane, it's a little by chance. My editor knew Diane's mother who made documentaries and spoke to her about her daughter. Before, I'd worked with Nestor, Bernard Lutic, and Renato Berta, who is an excellent cinematographer and who makes beautiful images. But he is more traditional: he likes people wearing make-up, he lights from above, which means you notice his photography, it's different from my other films. . . . On the other hand, Luc Pagès, who I worked with next, suggested different methods from those Nestor used but which came back to nearly the same thing . . . his soft light was obtained from using neon tubes. That meant using rather cumbersome equipment. The light wasn't very warm, the source was very close to people—whereas Nestor would have placed projectors against the wall at a certain distance.

PM: Did he place projectors towards the ceiling?
ER: No, very rarely, because he didn't like that look—he was right as well—light shouldn't come from above. That was what he criticized in traditional lighting, it creates shadows. He preferred lower lighting, about 2m or 2m50 . . .

PM: Were the working methods as different with Berta as well? He talked in an article about how lighting was built up step-by-step, from suggestions and disagreements . . .
ER: I remember that once, I thought about what Nestor would have done in his place: he was bothered by a fairly low ceiling, because he wanted to place his lamps fairly high. He lit by pinpointing objects . . . and I wasn't always happy with that, so yes, we had discussions. . . . I trusted Nestor more. That was for composition as well as lighting. Nestor didn't work with anyone else for shot composition. Nor did Berta. But with Berta, I told him, "I don't want the crew to talk to the actors, to tell them, 'put your hand there.' The actor has to be completely free, he mustn't think about all that." I was very firm about that. As soon as he began to talk to the actors, I said, "No, no, we have to find another solution." Anyway, the actor will place his hand in a certain way in rehearsal—and then change it—you can't organize the shot lighting from that point-of-view. There's a funny story about that. When we were filming *La Marquise d'O*, Nestor saw a small bit of elbow in the frame and said to Edith Clever, "If you could just move yourself a little bit, we won't see you and it will be very beautiful . . ." and she replied, "Well maybe I'll just remove myself from the film entirely and then it will be even more beautiful!"

PM: How did you meet Renato Berta?
ER: I would have liked to have carried on working with Nestor but he left for the States. So I had to find someone. People mentioned Berta, and perhaps I saw some films he'd worked on. He's really charming, I got on very well with him. Then I filmed with Sophie Maintigneux . . . and then for *My Girlfriend's Boyfriend*, I asked Nestor's assistant from *La Marquise d'O*: I discussed it a bit with her, and I realized she didn't think at all about cinematography the way Nestor and I did. . . . So I worked with Lutic again. But Lutic didn't do shot composition himself, he worked with someone. After that I was on the set of a film that Pascal Ribier was

working on, and I met Luc Pagès who was working with him. I asked him to come and film the television program I was working on, *Jeux de société*, and he did an excellent job. Then I used him for *A Tale of Springtime* and *A Winter's Tale*. But then he wanted to get involved in direction, so he left, and I wanted to make a film in very simple conditions. I met Diane Baratier and as I was very happy with her work . . .

For *Rendezvous in Paris*, I had a budget but the conditions were pretty difficult. We made *A Summer's Tale* and *A Winter's Tale* together and a certain number of shorts. . . . She was excellent. She has made quite a few films! She even managed the historical films really well, although she really wasn't used to that kind of production.

PM: In an interview, you explained that you rarely use close-ups because you don't like having a two-camera set-up. But you can insert a close-up when you only have once camera, but you have to consider it on its own terms, perhaps with different lighting and a certain immobility . . .
ER: Yes, when you want to introduce a close-up and match it with a wider shot, you have to make your close-up as still as possible to help continuity. On the other hand, with two cameras, it works, but it makes for a more complicated crew. I used the two-camera system for some scenes in *The Lady and the Duke*. For example, when the two women are in Place de la Concorde, the close-up was filmed with a second camera. We matched it in with the background and the extremely agitated nature of the scene.

PM: Does giving your actors more freedom mean as a matter of course you have a less meticulous and constructed lighting arrangement?
ER: I think so, yes. . . . I don't know how far back you have to go, to the silent era no doubt, to find shots with really subtle lighting arrangements. But generally these days I think we look for lighting that favors, that suits actors. Here is a general problem: what should we give preference to? The actor or the setting? There are certain people like Hayer, Almendros, or Berta (who, while he was very different from Nestor, still had this taste for logical lighting) who don't necessarily favor the actor . . . . There are also those who like using short focal lengths, which doesn't really suit people very well. But, in contrast to general thinking on this point, people aren't always flattered by longer focal lengths either. Some people suit short focal lengths, it's quite strange. For example, Haydée Politoff and Charlotte Véry are often better shot in closer focus (not too close!) than the longer lengths which wash them out . . . so I don't have

any remorse about using short focal lengths. In contemporary films, the camera is often very close to the actors, the camera moves all the time and the mise-en-scène disappears. I prefer to show the relationship between the setting and the characters.

PM: Do you prefer your cinematographer to organize shot composition too?
ER: These are two activities which can be distinct, or undertaken by the same person. If it's the same person, there are advantages: the cinematographer has a global vision of the image, there's a unity—but it's also very difficult, he has to work all the time and doesn't have a moment's rest. Whereas if you're just looking after framing, you have time to breathe, while the director of photography sets up his lighting. . . . Nestor or Diane just didn't stop working. Diane's always behind the camera. Framing is exhausting and demands an extraordinary level of attention.

PM: Is the cinematographer present when you're choosing the props and the costumes? Do they at least give a technical opinion on how the colors will photograph?
ER: In my opinion, all these technical issues are increasingly insignificant, because film stock is increasingly capable of rendering color in all its nuances. At the time of black-and-white cinema, the transcription of color was unreliable. For example with orthochromatic film, the red was very dark and the blue very light. Then there was panchromatic film where the green was very dirty. When you were filming landscapes you had to use filters to overcome that horrible green. When I made films in black-and-white I banished the color green. . . . For *My Night at Maud's*, I dressed my actors in black and white clothing. Even if we had filmed in color, the film would have been black and white! The white was too white as well. We had to soften it. Even in *La Marquise d'O*, Nestor tinted the white linen by soaking it in tea . . .

Nowadays, white photographs much better, we use white with impunity in my later films. . . . I could never have used this green sofa in a black-and-white film, it would have looked dark and ugly.

For *Perceval*, there was no consultation between Nestor and the set designer. They didn't meet. The set designer had some really interesting ideas, but he wasn't very communicative, he didn't really speak about them. It was very strange. At the same time, Nestor used to say, "For the cinematography, the choice of costume is more important than the lighting." He really thought it was important. I often ask the cinematographer what he or she think of such and such a color—but for the overall palette in general, the choice of the type of color, I have very specific ideas, especially in my contemporary films. For example, *The Aviator's Wife* is founded on the trio blue-green-yellow: the green came because Marie Rivière's room had green wallpaper. The person who lent it to me said, "But this wallpaper is dreadful!" but I found on the contrary that this green was very photogenic. And then there was all the green of the Buttes-Chaumont. The other young girl had a light blue jumper that worked very well with all this green. And she had a mac with a yellow lining and a little yellow appeared from time to time. And then there was a homeopathic dose of red: she wore a small red necklace. All these colors were chosen by me.

At the same time, in the period when were filming *My Girlfriend's Boyfriend*, very bright colors were in fashion: oranges and greens . . . and the actors were dressed in those colors, which worked very well with the New Town. In *The Green Ray*, Marie Rivière wore a red jacket which gave a certain unity to this documentary-style film, and contrasted with the colors of the sea. In the same way, in *A Good Marriage*, we find autumnal tints; faded pinks and browns . . . whereas in *Full Moon in Paris*, there are very lively colors again, and on the wall a reproduction of a painting by Mondrian, with primary colors: reds, blues, greens. . . . These are issues I find very interesting.

For historical films on the other hand, I don't work alone. I have a set designer and a costume supervisor. I have to say that often the costume designer is more important than the set designer, because costumes take up more room in the image and sometimes, the costume designer has more ideas. In *La Marquise d'O*, there wasn't a set designer—well, I fell out with him because he had stupid ideas that didn't make any sense. He had no idea of the style of the period, which was very serious. On the other hand the costume designer, Moidele Bickel, helped me find the curtains for the set. It was a very plain design, we put paintings from the period on the wall which covered the empty surfaces, and she had some really good ideas for the curtains.

In *The Lady and the Duke*, everything began with the costumes. The set decorator chose the colors of the walls from the colors of the clothing—that had to suit the actors and be in colors from the period. But the costume was first.

On the other hand, in *Triple Agent*, the same person chose the costumes and organized the set, and the costumes were designed to suit the wallpaper. . . . Things weren't that awkward because for each period there is a synthesis between décor and costume. This time as well, I made certain choices . . . the costume designer suggested colors I didn't like, and so I chose different ones—that suited the actress better as well.

For me, film has a realist basis. You mustn't be able to sense the artifice, colors mustn't appear too harmonious and decorative, as they can at the theatre. On the contrary, there should be some dissonance, colors that don't go with others, especially when you are filming on the street. So you have to be quite modest: sometimes, ideas have come to me from painters. For example, in *Pauline at the Beach* there's a reference to Matisse—but that came to me when everything was in place. I was walking past a shop which sold reproductions of paintings, I saw a Matisse reproduction and I said to myself, "Hey, someone today at the seaside could wear those colors . . ." and we chose those colors.

Another example: Pascal Greggory would like to have been in black and I refused, I thought we should eliminate black. So I suggest that he wore the stripy sailor top which worked really well with the idea of the sea and the atmosphere of the film. . . . So I took some time choosing the colors.

In *A Tale of Springtime* (it was the fashion at the time, but it suited the film), all the girls had corsages with flowers: it was an unusual choice for me, but there I did it systematically. In *A Winter's Tale* people wear drab colors, brown and chestnut. In *A Summer's Tale*, each girl wore colors that suited her, so it's quite varied. . . . On the one hand, you don't want complete aesthetic unity, but on the other hand you don't want colors that are too striking that could be distracting. Certain colors are dangerous, such as red . . .

PM: But you use red a lot . . .
ER: Yes, but it's a color you have to use with care. In *Triple Agent* we used soft colors: these are easy colors that work well together, that won't distract the audience. It's more complicated when we weren't in Paris, and I wanted flowers. I was bit upset not to be able to choose them myself, and my props buyer bought them in a color I didn't like—and the flowers were very important! They were a reddish-orange. Red is an unstable color and can look different in final prints than in reality, so you have to be careful. There's a certain moment in the film when you can see white flowers on the terrace, and I really like that. Then there are these red flowers, and I did use them but slightly against my own will . . . I don't really like them. I think they're too violent for the scene. I would have preferred white flowers! In general, I don't use props buyers. In the

cinema, every item is essential so you need to have a props buyer who will create items to order, but for flowers, you can't know in advance. In *Love in the Afternoon*, I had a props buyer and I asked him to find me a green shower curtain. It was a film with a lot of green. He brought back a shower curtain that was a really violent green. What did I do? I got up a bit earlier the next morning, I went to BHV [a French department store which specializes in homeware—translator's note]: yes, all the greens were ugly but I found a translucent shower curtain and I thought that was fine, so I took it. If someone's carrying out your request, they would never pick out translucent rather than green . . . but I know what I want, and I can change my mind.

A similar thing happened with the choice of sofa. I wanted to put some material over a sofa that was really ugly, but I couldn't find the fabric. So instead of a beige, I finally opted for a blue or a grey that worked. . . .That's why you have to look after everything. It's when you delegate that it becomes complicated. In *The Aviator's Wife*, I put an aquarium in the bedroom—I wanted some goldfish. Someone who worked in the office at the Films du Losange offered to go and buy one and he brought back the wrong color—it was too pale! I wanted a really red fish but I didn't have the time to go out and buy one.

PM: You are also very reliant on the weather; talking about working in studios, you've said "I prefer to struggle with the weather and take my time."

ER: Yes, I may well have said that, but at the moment I'm working in a studio: in depends on different periods of my life and my films. There are of course enormous contingencies when you work outside but that doesn't bother me. If I had been Marcel Carné, I ask what I would have done. Carné was preparing a film just after the war that Anouk Aimée was slated to star in. He went to Belle Ile and the weather was terrible, and the film wasn't made. At that time, in black-and-white, perhaps it wouldn't have been very pleasing but I think that today, in color, it would be possible to film in the mist . . . and perhaps it would have added something.

Something like that happened to me during *A Tale of Springtime* when the young girl says: "In Fontainebleau forest, there's a place where you have the impression that it's the Amazon, you climb up on a rock and you can see the entire forest." They climb the rock and there's mist. And she cries, "Oh, it's misty, and it's even better." In the same way, each time there's rain in my films, I haven't sought it out, but I use it. I hate artificial rain, it looks so false, like someone taking a shower in the bathroom!

I used this and the surprise element of rain in *Four Adventures of Reinette and Mirabelle*. One of the girls asks a farmer if it's going to rain. "No, it won't rain," he replies. The leave and it starts to rain, it's quite funny.

In *The Aviator's Wife* it's the same: we had just finished filming, or perhaps having lunch, and anyway, the sky clouded over. I said, "We're going to film in the rain," and we managed to get the rain just as it was starting, and it was really successful. It was possible because we were such a small crew, and everyone was available. With a bigger crew, it would have been a lot more complicated. I film things in the right order, in continuity, so it was that very morning that the pilot, played by Mathieu Carrière, is asked by Marie Rivière if the weather is going to be nice, and he replies, "Yes, it will be sunny apart from a shower at the end of the afternoon," and I could keep that because I filmed it just beforehand. I hadn't foreseen it, you can't forsee everything.

PM: But there are some limits to this—you need to have continuity and to be able to match your shots. So for example on *Claire's Knee* Nestor Almendros wanted to carry on filming in the shade but the sun had moved, so he was forced to use tarpaulin to keep the shadows. . . . You have to work hard to keep sunshine or shade . . .
ER: Yes, there are some difficulties, but they're rare. I'm usually flexible enough to cope with these restraints . . . but yes, sometimes we have to make adjustments. I remember a scene in *Love in the Afternoon* in a café when the sun arrived, we had to stop because it bothered me. It was the same in *Full Moon in Paris*. We were filming in the winter, and winter sun can be very strong, it shone into the apartment and we had to stop. In fact, sun is more troublesome than grey weather, both indoors and outdoors. Imagine filming today—if there were no clouds, it would completely change the lighting. The grey background would suddenly become luminous.

PM: At what stage in the film production process do you decide on your cinematographer?
ER: Relatively late. Cinematographers are never free anyway, they're always busy. Sometimes I'll do some pre-production work with a cinematographer. It depends on the film. For the *Comedies and Proverbs* I went

by myself with the actors to the locations where we supposed to be filming, with an 8mm camera. And then I showed what I'd done to the cinematographer. For *A Winter's Tale* I had a nondigital video camera, I made a few small tests but the cinematographer was with me. For *A Summer's Tale* I went to Brittany with Diane. For *Triple Agent* I shot everything in the office and in Charlotte Véry's apartment because the apartment in the film is hers. Then I showed Diane my locations on video: she really like the editing, the way in which it was filmed. . . . I rehearsed everything with the actors. As for *La Cambrure* I wasn't there half the time, I was ill. It's the only time that's happened to me. But I gave Diane my tests and the results of the location scouting, and she followed exactly what I'd done.

PM: At the start of our conversation, you told me that you sometimes place the lights yourself.
ER: Yes, for example in *The Tree, the Mayor and the Mediatheque* I helped with lighting placement: I also held the reflector, the cardboard sheet that helps with lighting—it's usually for the films on Super 8 or 16mm that I'll place the lights . . . and for my latest short, I only had one light, and then another small one above the camera that allowed us to film faces without any shadow. However, the cinematographer must be able to look after all that themselves. It's his or her work, and they'll do it better than me. For purely technical work, it's very rare for me to intervene. I have some idea about what needs to be done, but I only interfere in very particular situations.

Interview with Eric Rohmer: Video Is Becoming Increasingly Significant

Noël Herpe and Cyril Neyrat / 2004

From *Rohmer et les Autres*, ed. Noël Herpe (Rennes: Presses Universitaires de Rennes, 2007), 201–4. Reprinted by permission; translated from the French by FH.

ER: I haven't really been to the cinema for a few years; I've gotten used to video cassettes and now to DVDs. . . . I don't admit this very often, because I think it could shock people who love the cinema. . . . You couldn't really say I'm reactionary about this, I'd say I was rather avant-garde! Video is now becoming increasingly significant. The video format is more faithful to my original vision of my films than the cinematic version because of the aspect ratio. I shoot in 1.33 format, but it will be screened in 1.66. There are no longer any screens with facilities to project in 1.33 format.

Q: So why start with a 1.33 format?
ER: Because, quite simply, with 1.33 I have more space. People talk about the big screen, when they should talk about the narrow screen! In order to have a wide screen as the image appears on a camera, you have to cut off the top and the bottom of the frame. Now, I need those parts of the screen: I've always wanted to show what's above people's heads, and I also like to show hands. I don't like telling actors to raise their hands, because it's completely unnatural. I like to show the table. . . . There are so many things I like showing, and I can't because of the current format! Nor am I at ease with the wider formats, such as 1.85 or CinemaScope. . . . When CinemaScope first appeared [in the 1950s—translator's note], I defended it, along with the majority of my colleagues at the *Cahiers du cinéma*; but recently I wrote a critique for *Cahiers* of that original article, defending not a square screen but ratio aspects such as 4/3 and 1.33—because too

wide a screen favors laziness on the part of young filmmakers, and stops inventive shot compositions. . . . There is a monotony in widescreen, and far more resources in a more traditional screen format.

Q: Has your experience on television influenced you in this desire to work with a restricted screen?
ER: Yes, a lot. I used rostrum cameras on stands to pick out certain parts of documents, with the result I thought a lot about framing. As the documents were being filmed, I had to make various movements which were really useful exercises for me. If I manage to find the correct frame fairly easily, it's with the help of my directors of photography—whether that was with Nestor Almendros or now Diane Baratier, or those I worked with in between. . . . I also like my cinematographers to be in charge of both framing and lighting—which is quite demanding, it's very absorbing work and they don't get much respite. But Nestor liked that, and Diane likes it, and I do as well! Nowadays, there is something new, it's called a combo and it allows you to see the image on a small video screen, so you can check the framing precisely. Especially as I can't walk so easily now and need to stay sitting down, I often position myself by this combo: it makes everything easier. You used to have that anxiety: "Have I framed this properly, will it work?" You don't have that anymore, you know where you're going.

Q: You're further away from the actors too.
ER: When you're filming, you're far away from the actors, but it doesn't mean you're not in a good position, because you're exactly where the camera is! Whereas before, it was more difficult, you had to put yourself behind the camera, with the risk of getting in lots of people's way. . . . It's not that useful to be close to the actors; I prefer being close to them in rehearsal.

Q: How many takes do you shoot?
ER: There are different sorts of take: those where I ask to start again, because I think we can do better; those where the cinematographer asks us to start again; and those that the actor wants to try again. . . . My actors on *Triple Agent* were very demanding of themselves, wanting to retake scenes that I thought were very good! With the cinematographer, it's more awkward—often it's a technical issue. I never shoot many takes, and often, the first take is best. You don't really realize it at the time, which is rather trying. When I shot using celluloid, I only developed one

shot, in order to save money: now that I can watch everything on video, I can see all the takes. For *Triple Agent*, I chose the takes that seemed the best to me—and then watching back again on video, I saw that the first takes that I had left to one side were, at the end of the day, the most successful . . . there I'm sure that I'm right! So, when editing, I developed certain takes that I hadn't chosen at the time. All that to say that often the first take is the best, and that's true regardless of how much experience your actors have. . . . It's not always true, which is why you need more than one take—but you shouldn't ignore the first take! It's often the best.

Q: Are you more worried about actors stumbling over or stuttering on a word or that they respect the whole text?
ER: Sometimes I correct those stumbles while editing, you don't even realize. . . . As for the text itself, there are several kinds of actors: those who respect it scrupulously, and those who systematically change it: I accept both kinds. . . . In modern films, often they will change word order, so a phrase such as "ça, c'est intéressant" becomes "c'est intéressant, ça," what really is the difference? They add in "ahs" and "oh wells" and so on. And I let that happen, it adds life to the text! I only intervene if I really disagree. But for *Triple Agent*, the text was spoken exactly as it was written: for the actress, it was a foreign language, and she couldn't improvise in French: and for the actor, it was a text he had prepared in a certain accent, so it was the same issue.

Q: Do your rehearsals concentrate on the articulation of a certain phrase, or do you engage in more general direction?
ER: In principle, I'm not someone who actively directs my actors, although sometimes I have certain demands: and when we have a script read-through (which were rather rare for this film, as Katerina Didaskalou only arrived on the eve of shooting), I pay great attention to articulation: it's my text and I want it to be heard. . . . I sometimes feel that some directors don't care about the text, and they cover it up with music, or they drop the volume of the voice so it's more like sighing or babbling! I like people to speak clearly—and it's natural, because I place my actors at a distance from each other, and there's no reason for them to speak in low voices: even in the hotel bedroom in *Triple Agent*, he's far away from her. If I ever start over during a take, it's usually for a word that has become incomprehensible: in particular, there are words that are essential and that are sometimes pronounced rather hesitantly—such as

names for example—I've sometimes asked for a retake because of that. But before shooting, I film the whole of the scene, or even the sequence, on DV, with either myself or my cinematographer holding the camera. . . . I don't say anything to the actors, I just say "Go on, say your lines." If I think it's going badly, I stop them, but often, it goes very well. For example in *Triple Agent*, the great scene in the green house, when he admits "I'm a triple spy," well I filmed that without saying anything to the actors, only telling them where to move (one of you here, the other one of you here), suggesting how they could get from one place to another; the scene where he decides to go to Russia to care for her is the same: it was filmed in a very precise manner, even if it was a bit more complicated, with a digital camera, and then we knew exactly how to block the scene.

Q: So does the digital filming help you with editing, with understanding how to communicate the space to the viewer?
ER: I don't edit myself: at the same time, I have made some little shorts, unsigned, that I really enjoy editing . . . and I pride myself on being the one who organizes shot composition. But I do that after having told the actors to perform without editing: and it's during filming that, together with the cinematographer, we find the correct angles. I've never found that difficult, it's always come very naturally.

Q: Before digital, did you do this with a video camera?
ER: Yes, for me it's the same thing really . . . but I did it on Super 8 as well, from *Perceval* up until *A Winter's Tale*. Then I started to use video, then digital from *An Autumn Tale* onwards.

Q: So how did you record sound when you were using Super 8, if you were also checking the actors' elocution?
ER: It wasn't really to check elocution, but more to plan the blocking of the sequence, to know where to put the actors, to organize the sequence.

Q: Did you ever film the rehearsals that took place before the shooting?
ER: It depended on the films: for films with a set location, I could undertake this kind of detailed planning . . . for example, for *An Autumn Tale*, I went to the locations three months before shooting began, at the end of Spring: I filmed without any actors, with other people or even myself in the frame, just to see how it would work. But on the other hand, for *Triple Agent*, where the actress arrived at the last minute, I only filmed

rehearsals right before shooting: at the end of the day, if we finished up a little early, we would rehearse what we were filming the next day.

Q: When you publish your scripts, do you edit them?
ER: In general, my scripts don't indicate any kind of instructions concerning mise-en-scene or cinematography . . . often to the extent that they are reduced to dialogue. . . . Perhaps that's one of the reasons I've been refused advanced loans from the CNC! I find that is much more agreeable to read: I don't like it when there are lots of numbers and directions . . . and I rarely put anything that is a matter of mise-en-scene rather than plot: "I will be there at such and such a time, hello, goodbye, etc." unless it is said in a very particular way. So for example in *Triple Agent*, when someone says "Bonjour, Piotr Alexandrovitch," that gives us the Russian character of the film: in that case, I write it out in bold.

Q: Is your choice to return to History—and in the case of *Triple Agent*, a history that occurred during your lifetime—born of a feeling that you've exhausted your ability to talk about the contemporary period?
ER: It's happened twice in my life: after the *Moral Tales*, when I made *La Marquise d'O* and *Perceval*, and after the *Comedies and Proverbs* and *Tales of the 4 Seasons*, with *The Lady and the Duke* and *Triple Agent*. . . . Am I going to continue in this vein or return to a more contemporary subject matter? I don't really know, I'm at an age where I can't really know what's going to happen! Having said that, nowadays, given the loss of some of my physical strength, it's easier for me to film in studios than the way I used to—in the Parisian streets, in mountains, at the beach . . . in any case, there are difficulties in both approaches—I don't like having a big crew (which was the case for *Triple Agent*, certainly less than *The Lady and the Duke*), but I no longer have the capacity to film using only three people, which is pretty exhausting.

I'm a Filmmaker, Not a Historian

Philippe Fauvel and Noël Herpe / 2007

From *Positif*, September 2007. Interview conducted July 3, 2007. Reprinted by permission; translated from the French by FH.

Question: How did you discover *L'Astrée*?
Eric Rohmer: In general, I find things by myself: I had the idea to film *Perceval* when I was teaching thirteen-year-old school children; I discovered *La Marquise d'O* when teaching Kleist's novella, which wasn't even translated into French. When I taught French in secondary schools, *L'Astrée* was two pages from a school text book written by Chevalier and Audiat (the precursor of Lagarde and Michard): it didn't interest me particularly! What's more, you can't really find the book anymore, other than in small segments. But it just so happened that Pierre Zucca, a filmmaker whose films I like very much, pitched a script loosely based on *L'Astrée* to my production company, Les Films du Losange. He had changed quite a lot, some names, and some characters such as Adamas had been cut out. It was in a different spirit.

Q: Was it in modern costume?
ER: No, it was in period costume: he had been inspired by the same engravings as me, the only ones that are really good, the ones by Michel Lasne, which he showed me. He introduced the project to Films du Losange. Margaret Menegoz said she wouldn't be able to find the money to do it, and she sent it on to Daniel Toscan at Plantier, who also said he didn't have the money. It was at around this point that Pierre died. I thought it was a shame that the film hadn't been made, the subject interested me, and I said to his wife that perhaps I would be able to film it myself. But that wasn't possible for two reasons: as it was written, it would have been difficult for him to find a producer; and I didn't see myself filming a story when the script had been written by someone

else, even someone I admired as much as Zucca. Above all, I discovered that Honoré d'Urfé is a great author, not minor, ridiculous, or old-fashioned: he has been read by entire generations, from Mme de Sévigné to Rousseau, who said a lot of good things about him! Also, it's cinematic: when you open the books, it seems as if there's not any dialogue because there are no paragraphs, but the dialogue is excellent and really lively. So I wanted to film *L'Astrée* without taking into account Zucca's adaptation; there is no relationship between his adaptation and mine; the only phrase they share is "Make sure you are never seen by me again, unless I order it of you," which comes from the book—he didn't take any others.

Q: But you took a very particular structure by tying everything around the love affairs of Astrée and Celadon.
ER: Yes, that's why I called it *The Romance of Astrée and Celadon*: I wasn't claiming that is was the book *L'Astrée*, which is a far bigger work: it's six volumes in folio. Wanting to dedicate myself to the film, I didn't want to lose myself in that. Apart from a few peripheral episodes, I simply read everything concerning Astrée and Celadon. Not knowing if I would make the film or not, I didn't buy the Swiss edition which cost the trifling sum of four thousand francs! And I wouldn't have known where to put it. I went to the library and photocopied everything to do with Astrée and Celadon, and that's what I made the film from.

Q: You also moved certain episodes around, such as Hylas's verbal joust.
ER: I made a fairly serious change which certain admirers of Urfé might reproach me for, and he might be turning in his grave! But the reason is to do with the necessities of cinema; financial needs (there are fewer characters), and the balance of the film, which isn't the same as a novel, especially when the novel is very long. Concerning Astrée and Celadon's affair, some very interesting things are said at the start by Lycidas, and then by Sylvestre. But it would have been complicated to introduce him, and would have lengthened the film, and then we would have had to introduce another character, Diane, Sylvestre's platonic lover, who is interesting but quite secondary. So I made Lycidas say what is said by Sylvestre in the book, also because I really didn't want to lose Lycidas, who is played by an excellent actor. Also, when Hylas talks about love, he takes Phillis as his example, who is Lycidas's lover and Astrée's confidante. Following that logic, she has to be accompanied by Lycidas, so he can't disappear into the background. That's why there's that betrayal of the text: Lycidas takes on Sylvestre's words.

Q: You changed the end as well.
ER: Well, there I had no scruples, as d'Urfé didn't write it. It seems really interesting to me, and it isn't on the page. In the book, the scene where Celadon, disguised as a girl, sleeps in the girls' bedroom, happens two nights in a row: the moment when Alexis is about to admit that she is Celadon, a servant comes in, and we move to a different episode and everything is different. I preferred to finish using Astrée's sentence which marks her power over the proceedings: "I command you to be seen, Celadon!" That was my invention, I extrapolated a bit.

Q: In the credit sequence, you say how impossible it was to reconstruct the Forez area as it would have been.
ER: Yes, we took three years to find a location: we couldn't film in the Forez region, the river Lignon has partially dried up. We had to find a wild river. I find it difficult to travel now; it was my producer Françoise Etchegaray who found the valley of Soule, where everything is still more or less wild. The roads are far off, and there is nothing modern. So I divided the story in relation to two rivers. First, there is the Lignon and its gorges, which Urfé doesn't mention but which are really beautiful where I filmed and which were important to show. At the start, I thought about showing Celadon throwing himself into the water, without having found a river where that was possible. Either the waters were deep but stagnant, or there were torrents (like in the Ardèche, which I know a bit) with rocks just below the surface; you could get carried away by the eddies, hit your head against one of the rocks, but you couldn't deliberately set out to drown by diving in! So I thought that finding his hat floating on the surface would be as powerful as seeing him dive in the water. As for the chateau belonging to the nymphs, I didn't find that in the Soule valley, but at Chaumont-sur-Loire. I know the castle's curator, Jean-Paul Pigeat, and he helped me with organizing filming (I was also able to film in the neighbouring chateau at Fougères-sur-Bièvre, which belongs to Adamas in the film). "What is there as a river there?" I asked a boat-keeper, explaining my idea to him: I wanted a place situated between an island and the banks of the Loire, where there would be a small enough amount of water to give the impression of a small river. "But why don't you simply want a river?" he asked. "I don't know any." "But there's the Beuvron, which flows into the sea a few miles east of Chaumont." No-one had thought of it! But all along this river there's a vague path, a sheep path that must have been built in the nineteenth century, with ash trees all along it, it's very beautiful. That's where the nymphs

discover Celadon. And, just to show you how much cinema can cheat (even though I don't really like doing this), it's not on this river bank that Celadon washes up (this river doesn't have any banks), but on a very pretty sand back of the Loire.

Q: This diverse range of places joins a diverse range of times: we are simultaneously in ancient Gaul and towards the end of the Renaissance.
ER: In my period films, I'm very attached to historical verisimilitude. But I couldn't be more authentic, because the engravings that illustrate *L'Astrée* show people from antiquity in front of a Renaissance chateau! So I did the same thing, although at the start there is a French folk dance known as a bourrée where they wear seventeenth-century costumes (I just couldn't see it in antique dress) and with music from that era. In the book, it's also a seventeenth-century ball—I've simply followed the author's directions.

Q: What about the songs?
ER: The songs were composed by my longterm collaborator Jean-Louis Valéro, who I asked to do more than usual. He added music to some of the verses: "Here my beautiful sun sets. . . ." He also composed the credit sequence music. I wanted an original tune because music from that period is difficult to use, very stylized and formal. There is however a great musician from that time, Monteverdi, and I asked Valéro to write in the spirit of that period.

Q: Did you use a lot of historical research?
ER: Less than I did for the Middle Ages in *Perceval*, or German postclassicism in *La Marquise d'O*. I'm slightly ashamed to admit it, but I didn't read very much (apart from a thesis I glanced over at the Bibliothèque nationale); if I read too much, I was afraid that my script ideas would change. It seemed well structured to me and sufficient in itself. I'm a filmmaker, not a historian: I wanted to allow myself to interpret history in my way, without advisors. So that's how I work, apart from for details: when I write adaptations, it's between me and that author, Chrétien de Troyes and me, Kleist and me, d'Urfé and me. I don't want anyone else, even if others might reproach me.

Q: But in each of your "historical" films, you've worked with a costume designer.
ER: In my contemporary films, I don't have a costume designer because

I feel I'm capable of doing it myself: usually, I go with actors to buy clothes, I check the length of the dresses. . . . But here, it's different. I'm not competent and I asked Pierre-Jean Larroque to help. He had already worked on *The Lady and the Duke* and *Triple Agent*. I had made a particular symbolic use of ribbons: in the book, when he is separated from Astrée, Celadon takes a ribbon from her which he keeps as a souvenir, and he drowns with it. But it was complicated, so I transposed the motif by asking the nymphs to play with ribbons in this scene; it gives it great elegance.

Q: Were you inspired by seventeent-century pastoral painting?
ER: Yes and no. When I chose the banks of the river Beuvron, I was delighted to discover the beautiful ash trees that looked like the trees one sees on engravings from the period, and I rejected a lot of the countryside in the Forez region because now there are lots of conifers, while there were no pine trees at all in paintings from that period—they have leafy trees that resemble oaks or chestnuts. It wasn't easy to find those where we filmed. For the painting that Celadon sees upon waking from his fainting fit, I chose a canvas by Simon Vouet. The second painting is of Love and Psyche and is attributed to Vouet, but these are not the paintings cited by d'Urfé. It doesn't really matter because they're not vital to the story, mine are closer. There are other paintings in the temple, we had to make them especially, not without difficulty in trying to match d'Urfé's description of two lovers with intertwined bows; I managed with the help of a painter, who made a very pretty painting from his ideas. He also painted a picture of Astrée with her sheep. There's also the picture that Adamas comments on which represents the judgement of Paris. In the book, this episode is recounted by Astrée: I didn't want to film it because I don't like flashbacks, because of the age of the actors. I think it's more interesting to suggest it through a painting that the adults see: it's the work of a little known painter, Jacques Blanchard, a copy of Ruben's Judgement of Paris.

Q: Your pictorial quotations were explicit in *La Marquise d'O . . .* or *Perceval*; here, they're more diffuse.
ER: Yes, it's more inspired by engravings from the period. The costume designer took his models from Lasne, according to his taste and that of the actors. But there was no particular desire to imitate. The only thing I really respected was the language, the writing, the style—what the characters say was written by d'Urfé. For *La Marquise d'O* and *Perceval*, these

stories were faithful to one period. It's more difficult to be faithful to *L'Astrée*, because what are you being faithful to? Antiquity itself? Or the seventeenth-century version of Antiquity? You had to act more freely.

Q: Did you film using direct sound?
ER: In general, when you're making a period film, you use post-synchronization, which I don't like (although one of my favorite films, *La Collectionneuse*, was entirely post-synchronized). I've always preferred direct sound. I managed to use this for *L'Astrée* and I'm proud of it.

Q: There's an intimacy and a warmth in the voices.
ER: How can we distinguish a good from a bad sound? I think sound is bad in all films, apart from mine! Let's say I'm very demanding. I have a fault which is also a quality, the same one as Buñuel: he was really deaf, and you can hear people in his films really well; I'm losing my hearing as well, so I need people to speak clearly. And language from that era is articulated more clearly than nowadays.

Q: You insist on clear articulation from your actors.
ER: Yes, we rehearse the text a lot. To cast my actors, I make them read from classical theatre such as Racine, Corneille, Molière . . . and I listen. I want them to be as careful with the prose as the verses. I am the opposite of those drama teachers who say, "Be natural, don't exaggerate!" When there's a lot of information, you have to emphasize nouns and verbs.

Q: Were the actors naturally at ease?
ER: Some of my actors aren't French. Stéphanie Crayencour is Belgian, and she doesn't have the faults of contemporary French speakers. André Gillet isn't Parisian, and Véronique Reymond is Swiss; the French they speak is more beautiful than that of Parisians. My actors in *Astrée* had pictorial gestures, they had the same sense of where the frame was. I never tell my actors how to gesticulate, that happens naturally. Actors are interested in finding their own way of acting, especially when they are young: they find new and surprising things. They knew how to make use of the location; for example Celadon, when he is in front of the hut with Adamas, he butts the stone with his foot, leans over, and taps the ground. He did that himself, if I had told him to do it, it could have appeared artificial.

Q: What production problems did the film have?

ER: If I had been the producer, I wouldn't have done it! Françoise Etchegaray really believed in it, as well as producers at Rezo after they'd read the script. I was always the most sceptical, and I still am. My last film *Triple Agent* didn't appeal to the public. I knew it was a difficult subject, especially if people thought it was an action film, which it really wasn't . . . anyway, no matter, I enjoyed making *Astrée*.

Q: Do you think that these love stories could still speak to young people today?
ER: It enchanted young people in the seventeenth and eighteenth centuries, as a kind of guide. But it uses ideas that don't work as well anymore; people care more about verisimilitude. The way Celadon drowns, is found, and recovers . . . perhaps that doesn't really fit in with modern medical ideas. That love, that determination to respect Astrée's request, I don't know if that's the same today. And we don't really know if the relationships are sexual or chaste (this interests me): in contemporary films, people prefer relationships to be clearer, I think. Between Astrée and Celadon, nothing happens, but it's not chaste either. There are things that seem strange to us in the courtly tradition. For example, in Chrétien de Troyes, *Perceval* sleeps naked in the same bed as Blanchefleur and they hug closely, but nothing more happens. Furthermore, homosexuality doesn't really exist in d'Urfé's work, but there are very sensual caresses between the girls. It was important to me to keep these descriptions, to the extent that I had them spoken, to demonstrate that this came from d'Urfé rather than me. I could have removed all that commentary, but I like the confrontation between text and image. I don't think the image and the text have to be equal, but the text should nourish the image.

Q: The first voice comes in at the moment when Celadon wakes up at the nymphs'.
ER: Yes, because we are getting inside a character, seeing things from his point-of-view. I noticed that d'Urfé was sensitive to light effects, which shows he was in some ways a filmmaker avant la lettre! That moment where Celadon is dazzled by sunlight is wonderful for a filmmaker. There's another moment of being dazzled by light, but I didn't show it in the same way, when Astrée is sleeping in the forest and he leans over her to kiss her: she sits up, sees him in front of the sun, and she is dazzled. I simply suggest the effect, thinking that it was more interesting, given where we were filming, to not create too strong a silhouette.

Q: In this book that you have just described as cinematic, everything is communicated via language.
ER: Yes and no. He was a contemporary of Don Quixote, where language is important, but images as well. There are two lives for Don Quixote, the one in the book and the one in the imagination. I made a television program for schools about this idea, showing how Don Quixote and Sancho Panza have been characterized through the centuries, from Doré and Daumier to Picasso and Dali. *L'Astrée* hasn't had this impact on posterity. The eighteenth-century images in the Swiss edition are dull and insipid. I wanted a film that would restore *L'Astrée*'s vigour. But what really struck me was the importance of form, and what we could call maths, numbers, and figures. When I was a critic, I was a great admirer of directors who were also inventors of form, and where we could identify mathematical figures: Murnau, Hitchcock, even Lang, who I spoke less about but who I admired too. In *L'Astrée* there's a mathematical pattern I didn't respect because I removed certain characters, and the film doesn't use the same figures as the novel. There are some consistencies, such as using the river Lignon, whose name means line, and although there are two Lignon rivers in the film, we follow a movement up and down the river to go to the druid. Another frequent figure at that time was the labyrinth, evoked here by the garden in the form of a spiral. Then there's the circle, which is the temple; and the triangle, which is the three nymphs and other triangular elements in the film. I didn't try to make a construction out of these figures, but they were there, and often I only noticed during editing. You'll say that that's magical and I say yes, the magic of cinema! If you want to dominate everything, it doesn't work. You have to allow some chance in, and some subjects allow that and organize themselves. I'm more and more convinced by this the more films I make.

Q: You have rendered unreal situations through realist means; for example, when Astrée doesn't recognize Celadon in women's clothing.
ER: Generally, my cinema is rather realist: here, I was taking a risk and I wasn't sure. That's why I wanted Astrée and Celadon to be similar sizes. I disguised him by using a whimple so he was less recognizable and we tried to hide his chin as much as possible.

Q: You made use of digital effects, which is very unusual for you, to feminize Celadon's voice.
ER: There were different solutions. One was that the actor raised his voice, which was difficult and could have sounded ridiculous. The

second was to dub a woman's voice, which was my first idea. And the third one, which was working with Ircam. The problem is that when you change the tonality of the voice, you also change the speed. It's very difficult to simply change the timbre of the voice and nothing else. It's very complicated, you take out certain deep frequencies, but if the tonality of the voice is in C#, you can't put it into D#, unless the speed changes.

Q: There's also a sequence where you use double exposure, when Celadon sings and walks.
ER: In general, I don't use double exposures, or even dissolves. But with digital editing, it's easy: so I used this procedure, in the same way I imagined the incrustations for *The Lady and the Duke*. I wanted to show Astrée and Celadon in love, for slightly commercial reasons: if not, I would have had no images of the two of them together, apart from the scene where they argue, and the scene where he's disguised as a woman.

Q: What is *L'Astrée*? Is it platonic, Christian, courtly, baroque, national?
ER: All that at once. It's from the baroque period and there's also links to Shakespeare and Cervantes, through the theme of illusion, that we can also find in Corneille's *L'Illusion comique*. As for d'Urfé's Christianity, that's hard to define. He wasn't only a fervent Catholic, he was also a member of the Ligue Catholique, someone who fought against Protestants, without wishing to recognize Henri IV's authority. At the same time, this Christian religion was mixed in with paganism and the druids. How did paganism and Christianity coexist at this time, and up until the eighteenth century with Rubens? Anyway, the conflict between pagan sensuality and Christian spirituality isn't really exposed as such in my film. One of my problems with Zucca's script was that he put the opposition between Hydras and Sylvandre (who became Lycidas in my film) into the background of the film. In his script, Hydras and Sylvandre represent the battle between flesh and spirit; I think it's more about fidelity and inconstancy. That's the subject: Celadon's fidelity—he is faithful to Astrée despite everything. Physical love is never questioned (even if we think that these characters are at this moment in time engaged rather than married and therefore chaste). There's no Puritanism in this book, maybe that's why it was so successful. This Puritanism would return with Jansenism, but it's absent in this period, in painting as well.

Q: Is there no original sin in this universe?

ER: I don't see where the sin would be. If there's separation, it's because of a misunderstanding. A tragic misunderstanding, like in *Oedipus Rex*.

Q: Can we talk about resonances with Plato?
ER: The character Sylvandre was a follower of a philosopher in the Platonic tradition, Marsile Ficin. There's something more ascetic about him than there is Lycidas, who is more earthy. In the film, I combined the two of them; I kept the characters that were most vivid, Celadon, Astrée, and Lycidas.

Q: It seems that the historical periods that really interest you are those where a certain value system is ending: the end of chivalry, the end of the Ancien Régime, here the end of a certain pre-Christian courtly ideal.
ER: It's a world that's coming to an end but also starting over. Are there ever really endings? That dizzy love of Celadon's has something romantic about it. The first great romantic role was that of Goethe's Werther, who committed suicide. In a way, waiting for Astrée to come back to him, rather than searching her out, Celadon is extending the chivalrous ideal of Perceval: he also wants to be faithful to a promise that he made to follow his mother's advice (which was to not speak), and this fidelity leads him to a mistake (he should have spoken). Reading *L'Astrée*, I knew that was an aspect I liked, this stubborn waiting. It's also similar to Pascal's wager: if Celadon approaches Astrée, he could lose his love; if he doesn't approach her, he risks unhappiness, but, when she approaches him, it's extraordinary.

Q: You're not claiming to evoke an era, but rather the representation of an era, including its representation of itself.
ER: I can't present the truth of an era. All I can do, the same as any filmmaker or fiction writer, is to show how an era represented itself (I prefer this approach, personally), or show how we represent it to ourselves, through interpretation, extrapolation, and embroidery. I've never tried to modernize history.

Q: Are you tempted to leave History for a while?
ER: If only in terms of moving physically from place to place, I don't have the agility I once had. For the time being, I don't have the physical strength to prepare another film; I've stopped really. But these last few days I've quite enjoyed making a little short, which is part of a group of

films I'm not putting my name to, that are meant to be more or less collective . . . but I'm not sure I'll find another subject.

Q: Well, you've also returned to literature with the publication of your novel *Elisabeth* . . .
ER: What happened was that Gallimard got in touch with me asking if I would republish, but I wasn't particularly interested. Then a German publisher asked the same thing, and I was interested to see what a German translation would be like, so I gave permission, but then it was also published in Italian without my permission. Gallimard then asked me again, and I accepted. Rereading it, I really liked certain passages. I show rain better in the book than I do in *Claire's Knee* for example. I see the rain in the film, but in the book I feel it in a more powerful way. In some cases, literature can be more evocative of reality than the cinema. I love the cinema! But it can be abstract where literature is very concrete. In the film, the rain is very much part of the story, and in the book it's there for its own sake. Notably, there's a passage where a girl shelters under some trees: there's more freedom than in the cinema, where often scenes with rain are a failure, without nuances, whereas one can refine it further when writing. I didn't perceive this relation to my films at the time (including the sensitivity to sound, time, and weather), as the *Moral Tales* were inspired by short stories that were very different, completely lacking description and much more founded on feelings and interiority. This novel didn't inspire me at all, despite its cinematic appearance. Anyway, I'm made to be a filmmaker rather than a novelist. This book opened a door that I didn't manage to open in the cinema, but it's not useful for literature as a whole.

Q: Why have you never adapted any of your favorite authors, such as Dostoievsky or Balzac (not counting the episode of the television program *Jeux de société*)?
ER: The scene from *Béatrix* that I adapted isn't at all dramatic, it's made up of quotations. The most interesting things in Balzac's novels are precisely what you can't show in the cinema, all the reflections on his characters' thoughts and on the sociology of the era. These texts will always be superior to anything you can put on the screen. Dostoievsky makes more use of dialogue, so some of his work could be cinematic. However, it's also very difficult because it's so slow. There's the case of de Maupassant, who is perhaps the writer who lends himself best to adaptation. There was one I rewatched recently, which had a lyricism that was far

removed from the book, and that seduced me, not without reservations, at the time it was released (and that I admire now unreservedly): *Une vie* by Alexandre Astruc. To come back to Balzac, he's universal and read by everybody, while *L'Astrée* is a forgotten book (as is *Perceval*, we only know very short sections). My idea was to try and enable people to feel the charm that *L'Astrée* had for the generations that loved it, without modernizing it. I asked the sound engineer if he thought the character's speeches were comprehensible for a modern audience, and he said yes, that it was more comprehensible hearing it spoken than seeing it written. That's what interested me: saying and performing this text in the cinema is to make it more accessible to today's spectators.

Eric Rohmer: Father of the New Wave

Kaleem Aftab / 2008

From the *Independent*, March 21, 2008. Reprinted by permission.

Eric Rohmer has always been the most discreet of film directors. While his contemporaries saunter from film festival to film festival and spend hours in interviews spouting their views on film and life, Rohmer has, by and large, chosen to stay at home. The first indication of his cloaked nature came in 1946 when he chose to release his novel *Elizabeth* under the pseudonym Gilbert Cordier. Even Eric Rohmer is an alias: he was born Jean-Marie Maurice Schérer in 1920.

He came up with his auteur signature (fashioned together in homage to the actor and director Erich von Stroheim and the nineteenth-century English novelist Sax Rohmer) because, he claims, his society family were embarrassed that one of their own would choose cinema as their living.

Whether it's true or not, the story fits in perfectly with Rohmer's aim when starting out as a film critic in postwar France, that cinema should be recognized as "the Seventh Art," as valuable an artistic pursuit as painting and books. The classicism that Rohmer saw in film is clearly evident in his latest work, *The Romance of Astrea and Celadon*, which is inspired by the seventeenth-century novel *Astrée* by Honoré d'Urfé.

Knocking on the door of Rohmer's office in a Paris apartment building, I hardly know what to expect, having been granted the interview on the proviso that it could be cancelled if the filmmaker's ill health demanded. I need not have worried. Despite being gaunt and having skeletal features, he is in good health. Sporting a cravat and a blue pullover, he looks the archetypal French artist. He ushers me into his main office space. The detritus of more than six decades of work seems to be dispersed everywhere. Folders, books, papers, and journals are crammed on every surface, except the chairs where we station ourselves either side of his small wooden desk, positioned far from the window of the oblong room.

As I look across at him, I suddenly have a sense of what it must have been like for the young Jean-Luc Godard and François Truffaut, going to Rohmer cap-in-hand in search of a few pennies. A former literature professor, he was the oldest of the film critics who penned articles for *Cahiers du Cinéma* before going on to direct the films under the banner of the New Wave. Of that group of directors who changed the face of cinema, it is Rohmer who has remained closest to their philosophical roots.

"Well, it's not the nouvelle vague (New Wave) any more, we're all old now," he jokes. "Obviously Truffaut has died, but both Claude Chabrol and Jacques Rivette have made films recently, and Godard, I understand, is in the process of preparing to make a film. If we have the same cinema, or if we have evolved, it's not up to me to say.

"It's true that Godard has probably grown more as a filmmaker but away from the public, while Chabrol has become a more commercial filmmaker. I think we are all loyal, more or less to the same principles that we have had at the time.

"Myself, I keep the same idea of cinema and at the same time I always do films in my own little way: films that are not too expensive. I like shooting, even when I'm in a studio, I like shooting nature, and I give an importance to the poetry of cinematography. It's very much still following the theories that I expounded in my early articles."

Detractors of the auteur, of which there are many, would argue that Rohmer tells the same story in the same style over and over again. There is little in the way of plot and it's hard to decipher the motivations of the protagonists.

Rohmer defends the similarities in his pictures. "It is better to see all my films together as a collection. At the moment they're showing the *Four Seasons* on French television, one part each week, and that is perfect. There is a relationship between all the films and that is where the interest lies.

"Whether you think that my films are good or bad, they have a value to one another that helps with understanding them. The public often tell me that I make films that resemble each other and they are right, but it is normal because I am a complete auteur, that is someone who creates the film, looks at the subject, and at the same time I am also the man who creates the image."

The Romance of Astrea and Celadon is set in fifth-century France in a world of nymphs and druids. A shepherd, Celadon, tries to win back the heart of Astrea, who falsely believes that Celadon has been unfaithful. Along the way Celadon resists the temptation of a beautiful nymph.

Rohmer says of his adaptation: "The book had a lot of success in the seventeenth century. It's one of the first written in a French language that a modern audience can understand. It has a dialogue that is very clear and good and relevant to today. Modern audiences will recognize the characters but not straight away . . . this is normally why my films don't have a big public and cater more to a certain literary audience.

"You can take an English novel from the nineteenth century and they essay many of the situations that I address. I've read a lot of authors of the nineteenth century—Joseph Conrad, Robert Louis Stevenson, Henry James—and these authors have marked me a lot."

At the outset of the film, in a droll intertitle, he makes a playful comment on the fact that the shooting took place in a location far from where the events are depicted in the novel, because idyllic countryside has been replaced by concrete jungles. The director has never owned a car, and rarely takes taxis, although he does point out that this is more to do with the type of films he makes than an attempt to improve on his already impressive green credentials: "I do this to be in touch with everyday life. If you are hidden away in a taxi you're not in contact with reality, and in my films I try to show people in real situations, especially in my films in a contemporary setting. I can't do this if I stay in big hotels and hide from the public. It's why I don't show my face often in the media. People don't recognize me, so I can get on public transport. It also helps when I'm making a film, I can work on location and people don't recognize me or the actors and it allows me to shoot."

The method of shooting with a small crew and using the latest equipment is typical of the eighty-seven-year-old. "I've always been interested in new technology," he asserts. "The first article I ever wrote, even before *Cahiers*, was for a journal called *Revue du Cinéma*. It was on the use of color over black and white. It was at a time when people preferred black and white, but I liked color and also the use of direct-sync sound."

Sad as it is to report, he intimates that *The Romance of Astrea and Celadon* is likely to be his swansong: "I haven't got plans to make another film, it's not easy for me to make films now. These days it takes me much longer to prepare a film than when I was younger."

If this is his last film, it will bring the curtain down on one of the great classical artists of the last half century.

Interview with Eric Rohmer: The Memory of the Figurative

Philippe Fauvel and Noël Herpe / 2010

From *Positif*, April 2010. Reprinted by permission; translated from the French by FH.

Question: In your series of articles that appeared in 1955 (and entitled *Celluloid and Marble*) you argued that painting was the great art of the twentieth century. Why does this artistic expansion seem exceptional to you?

Eric Rohmer: Well, really, it was the great art of the late nineteenth and early twentieth centuries. Because then, renewal was absolute, without comparison in any other artistic domain. Poetry became—not decadent, but a bit thin! It lost its sparkle at the start of the nineteenth century, it feels as if it's searching for a sense of itself and turned on itself a bit. It increasingly lacks inspiration. It's found new forms, but has failed to fully exploit them. As for music, that's starting to divide more and more into a popular music and music for an elite: it's certainly progress, that, thanks to recording, music is available for everybody (even those who can't read a score or play an instrument). But contemporary music is increasingly an enclosed world. No, I think that in the twentieth century, it was painting, even while it was difficult, even while it grew apart from realistic representation, that continued to attract crowds. And that still attracts them! That's why painting is the art of the twentieth century.

Q: You also defended another idea: painting, because of its increasing abstraction, makes us discover the real in a different way: it makes us rediscover it.

ER: It's a paradox! I don't know if I still think that. It had this power at the moment of Impressionism, Fauvism, and perhaps even Cubism. But after that painting has moved away from that kind of role. For example, I don't know if abstract painters such as Kandinsky make us see aspects of the real world, as we ordinarily perceive it; if they have a deep relationship with the world that is under our eyes. I don't think I would go so far in my argument anymore.

Q: How did you discover modern painting?
ER: I discovered it in reproductions: in a town in the Midi where Parisians fled the arriving German army. It was overwhelming, you would have thought that at such a time, only current affairs would interest people! It just so happened that I was passing a bookshop where a drawing by Cocteau was on display. I found it funny. Cocteau was in the area, I saw him from afar. But, he isn't really a painter. . . . But there was also a book of reproductions by a painter who I knew by name. I still hadn't had an opportunity to leaf through this book, and to buy it was far too expensive. It was Van Gogh, and I was delighted! A bit later, when browsing the bookshops in another town, I discovered a book that reproduced Picasso with a preface by the critic Jean Cassou. I read a formula which really struck me: "Picasso is the greatest creator of forms of our era." It was a phrase I used in my book about Hitchcock: "Hitchcock is the greatest creator of forms in the cinema." I don't know today if I would be as carried away by Picasso—but it was a very strong emotion at the time! It pleased me more than classical painting. I admired them a lot: I tried, very badly, to copy Rembrandt or Raphael's watercolors, through a grid, which allowed me some degree of exactness. But Picasso affected me differently! Later again, in a bookshop in the same town (there were quite a lot of art books during the war), I saw, reproduced, the latest Matisses. They inspired extraordinary feelings in me. I asked myself if I preferred Picasso or Matisse: I think at the end of the day I could like them both. Anyway, they knew each other and respected each other, even though their paintings were so different.

Q: You wrote that Matisse's "papier collé" technique could not be appreciated by a child . . . [1]
ER: A child could like them, but not deeply appreciate them. That's why I don't approve of taking children to the Musée Picasso. Yes, they like it, but not having any pictorial training, they can only appreciate it superficially. What justifies Picasso is Raphael. The first mission of the painter is photographic imitation. There is something else in a painting as well as a photograph. But, if art hadn't gone to the very extreme of

that photographic reproduction it achieved in the Renaissance (through the great Italians, Raphael, Veronese, Titian . . . and then a seventeenth century that was already denaturing reality in the works of Rembrandt and Rubens, followed by a mannerist eighteenth century, to be reborn with Delacroix, until the arrival of Manet and modern art); if this great movement of painting hadn't existed, Picasso would not have had the ideas he did. He would have carried on painting like he did when he was fifteen years old, painting highly realistic paintings—that are by the way very beautiful, even if they are not at all original.

Q: But does one really need all that culture to appreciate Picasso?
ER: I don't see how one can appreciate Picasso if one is not cultured! Picasso has always been hated by ignorant people—so you could say the bourgeois. They allowed Expressionism but Picasso was beyond the pale! There is something repugnant in his painting to your average Joe. On the other hand, if Raphael nowadays has been slightly discredited, he was the great painter at the start of the nineteenth century. From the common point-of-view, all painting is appreciated, even the primitives such as Van Eyck or Memling. It's true that these people knew how to paint! Now, it's no longer possible to paint like Raphael, and even less like Titian, Tintoret, or Rembrandt. . . . And that's where the admiration comes from, it's not for their technique, but for their talent. With Picasso, people say "I could have done that," but it's not that easy. Personally what I like in his art, is his almost classical sense of composition, his harmony and musicality. Concerning contemporary art, I have seen examples, both in France and abroad, that were dreadful. I remember a visit to a museum in Prague where there was nothing but horrors, and then, there, in the middle of them, a portrait painted by Cézanne: it was sublime, that's painting! But the rest was nothing.

Q: You're attached to Cubism as well.
ER: Cubism was a fashion, a moment, a passage. . . . Thank God we didn't stay Cubist! What interests me is that Cubism is born from Cézanne, from his division of space through geometric forms. So that, perhaps, to like Cézanne, you have to know Cubism. Cézanne's greatness owes something to the great painters of the end of the Renaissance such as Tintoret or El Greco, but also to those that followed him. It might be pedantic, but I don't think one can love art today without being an historian, without judging it in comparison to works from the past or the future.

Q: But you're not very interested in painting which respects the figurative tradition, even if it distinguishes itself from it: surrealist painting.
ER: Surrealism is fun. Often it's not painting but drawing. There are some talented painters, like Magritte, but it's very limited. There are others who just don't interest me, like Max Ernst. Dali was an intelligent man and very creative; he had resources, but he wasn't a great painter. As for Chagall (even if he was only linked to Surrealism), it's cute. . . . I can't say much else. That said, I'd condemn the painting of the Surrealists less than their poetry—apart from Eluard, whom I like, and sometimes Aragon. No, Surrealism really isn't my thing.

Q: Do you like nonfigurative painters such as de Stael or Pollock?
ER: Nicolas de Stael is the last painter. After him, there is no more painting, it seems to me. He touches me. Pollock, no—and I don't like American painting, apart from Hopper, but it's very minor.

Q: The décor of *La Collectionneuse* has been compared to David Hockney . . .
ER: Why not? You can always trace parallels with a painter. You could also make comparisons with Hockney in *Pauline at the Beach* because of modern elements such as the decking. When one films a swimming pool, one automatically thinks of Hockney because he has painted a lot of them, but for me it isn't such a fundamental picture as those of Matisse or Picasso. There is another painter that I liked, and who wrote interesting articles on art: Paul Klee. However, in contrast to the other painters I have just cited, I only need to see his paintings once. I can't live with them, they are more distant from me—I wouldn't say *foreign*, but *distant*.

Q: And Francis Bacon?
ER: Francis Bacon repels me. And what repels me doesn't interest me. It's awful, and I don't understand how people can like Bacon. Perhaps I'm a bit narrow-minded, but I say it frankly.

Q: But we could say the same thing about Goya. They both paint ugliness.
ER: Yes, but Goya pulls flowers out of the ugliness, as Baudelaire would have written. . . . *Goya's a nightmare full of things unguessed/ Of foeti stewed on nights of witches' revels/ Crones ogle mirrors; children scarcely dressed,/ Adjust their hose to tantalize the devils.* In Goya, there is great beauty, it's a beautiful ugliness. I haven't managed to find that beauty in Bacon.

Perhaps it's because I came across him later, at a time when it was more difficult for me to be sensitive to things that repulsed me to start off with. But even if I were to make an effort, I don't think I could like him. It's as horrible for me as seeing invalids: it's a lack of charity on my part, but, if something is missing from the face, I feel incredibly uneasy.

Q: For you, pictorial beauty comes first from the model.
ER: Painting is born from a desire to imitate reality, from admiration of the model. I think it's still true that Picasso was a great portrait painter: he made classical, admirable portraits, drawings as well as paintings. In the works of Matisse as well, even if it is a lot less photographic, there is a certain sense of resemblance. As for Klee, Kandinsky, or Mondrian, if they threw themselves into pure abstraction, it is after having done figurative painting and realizing that they were doing nothing more modern than their immediate precursors. If one is not able to paint figuratively, like they taught in the old Schools of Fine Art, I don't think one can undertake abstraction. In abstraction, there is always a memory of the figurative. If not it's pure decoration. If a painting has no contact with reality, it no longer exists. And that's what's happened: painting has disappeared, whether it's on walls or an easel; now, we have installations, which don't just have a relationship to reality, but that are themselves a reality.

Notes

1. Papier collé, literally meaning glued paper, is an art historical term referring to a type of collage in which pieces of decorative or printed paper are incorporated into the canvas. Matisse's use of cut-out paper shapes in his work is a refinement of the technique. The term *papier collé* is used in both French and English. Translator's note.

Major Interviews Given by Eric Rohmer

Eric Rohmer was a prolific interviewer and upon the release of his films was often interviewed in major newspapers in France—included in this book is an interview with *Libération* upon the release of *Pauline at the Beach*. The list below is an account of his interviews in French with major journals devoted to cinema, and some interviews given in books and on television, and the most important English language interviews that Rohmer gave. Asterisked interviews are reproduced in this book.

Interviews in French
Where English language translations are available, details are given.

Cahiers du Cinéma interviews
172 (1965): Jean-Claude Biette, Jacques Bontemps, and Jean-Louis Comolli, "Entretien avec Eric Rohmer: l'ancien et le nouveau"

219 (1970): Pascal Bonitzer, Jean-Louis Comolli, Serge Daney, and Jean Narboni, "Nouvel Entretien avec Eric Rohmer" [available in English translation, "New Interview with Eric Rohmer," translated by Daniel Fairfax in *Senses of Cinema* no. 54 (2010)]

323-324 (1981): Pascal Bonitzer and Serge Daney, "Entretien avec Eric Rohmer"

346 (1983): Pascal Bonitzer and Michel Chion, "Entretien avec Eric Rohmer"

357 (1984): Jean Narboni, "Entretien avec Eric Rohmer: le temps de la critique" [available in English translation "The Critical Years: Interview with Eric Rohmer," translated by Carol Volk in Eric Rohmer, *The Taste for Beauty* (Cambridge University Press: 1989), 1-18]

371-372 (1985): Florence Mauro, "Secret de la laboratoire: entretien avec Eric Rohmer"

392 (1987): Alain Philippon and Serge Toubiana, "Le cinéma au risqué de l'imperfection: entretien avec Eric Rohmer"

430 (1990): Antoine de Beacque, Thierry Jousse, and Serge Toubiana, "Entretien avec Eric Rohmer"

452 (1992): Amila Danton, Laurence Giavarini, and Camille Taboulay, "Entretien avec Eric Rohmer"

*467–468 (1993): Antoine de Beacque and Thierry Jousse, "L'amateur: entretien avec Eric Rohmer"

490 (1995): Stéphane Bouquet and Thierry Jousse, "Le puzzle d'Eric Rohmer: de T comme 'travelling' à C comme 'couleurs'"

503 (1996): Cédric Anger, Emmanuel Burdeau, and Serge Toubiana, "Entretien avec Eric Rohmer"

527 (1998): Antoine de Beacque and Jean-Marc Lalanne, "Entretien avec Eric Rohmer: l'oeil du maître"

559 (2001): Patrice Blouin, Stéphane Bouquet, and Charles Tesson, "Entretien avec Eric Rohmer: je voulais que la réalité devienne tableau"

582 (2003): Jean-Michel Frodon, "Entretien avec Eric Rohmer: le cinéma est un art de refus"

588 (2004): Emmanuel Burdeau and Jean-Michel Frodon, "Entretien avec Eric Rohmer sur *Triple Agent*: j'ai tout de suite pensé que l'histoire devait être montée par la parole, pas par les faits"

627 (2007): Jean-Michel Frodon, Laurence Giavarini, and Cyril Neyrat, "Entretien avec Eric Rohmer: Fidèle à la fidelité"

653 (2010): Noël Herpe and Philippe Fauvel, "L'Arbre, Rohmer, et la Bibliothèque: Entretien inédit avec Eric Rohmer" [Issue 653, February 2010, is a special memorial issue dedicated to Rohmer entitled "Rohmer Forever" which also contains interviews with several of his collaborators.]

Cinématographe interviews

67 (1981): Philippe Carcassonne and Jacques Fieschi, "Entretien avec Eric Rohmer"

73 (1981): Philippe Carcassonne and Jacques Fieschi, "Eric Rohmer: deux extraits d'*Une femme douce*"

122 (1986): Vincent Ostria, "A l'improviste"

Positif interviews

*309 (1986): Gérard Legrand, Hubert Niogret, and François Ramasse, "Entretien avec Eric Rohmer"

*350 (1990): Gérard Legrand and François Thomas, "Entretien avec Eric Rohmer"

*372 (1992): Olivier Curchod, "Entretien avec Eric Rohmer: Coïncidences"

424 (1996): Vincent Amiel and Noël Herpe, "Entretien avec Eric Rohmer: un moment où il ne se passé rien de très important"

452 (1998): Vincent Amiel and Claire Vassé, "Entretien avec Eric Rohmer: les gestes proches du dessin" [available in English translation, "Eric Rohmer: *Conte d'été*" translated by Pierre Hodgson in Walter Donohue and John Boorman, eds., *Projections 9: French Filmmakers on Filmmaking* (Faber and Faber: 1999), 13–21]

518 (2004): Stéphane Goudet, "Entretien avec Eric Rohmer: 'On-dit' ou l'Histoire hors-champ"

523 (2004): Noël Herpe, "Entretien avec Eric Rohmer: on est toujours dans l'image"

*559 (2007): Philippe Fauvel and Noël Herpe, "Entretien avec Eric Rohmer: je suis cinéaste, pas historien"

*590 (2010): Philippe Fauvel and Noël Herpe, "Entretien avec Eric Rohmer: le souvenir de la figuration"

[*Positif* produced a memorial issue containing a Rohmer dossier, 599 January 2011, entitled "Rohmer, l'art du natural" which while it featured no interviews with Rohmer features several interviews with his collaborators.]

Other French-Language Major Interviews

(1967): Philippe Pilard, "Entretien avec Eric Rohmer," *La Revue du cinéma* 210

(1973): J-R Ethier, "Entretien: Eric Rohmer parle de ses contes moraux," *Séquences* 71

(1974): Claude Beylie, "Programme Eric Rohmer," *Ecran* 24

(1976): Guy Braucourt, "Entretien avec Eric Rohmer," *Ecran* 47

(1979): Joël Magny and Dominique Rabourdin, "Entretien avec Eric Rohmer," *Cinéma 79* 242

(1983): Claude Beylie and Philippe Carcassonne, "Inspiration et ordinateur," *Le Cinéma* (Paris: Bordas)

(1984): Alain Carbonnier and Joël Magny, "La critique en question: entretien avec Jean Douchet et Eric Rohmer," *Cinéma 84* 301

*(1985): Claude Beylie and Alain Carbonnier, "Le celluloid et la pierre: entretien avec Eric Rohmer," *L'Avant-scène cinéma* 336

(1986): André Séailles, "Entretien avec Eric Rohmer," *Etudes cinématographiques* 146–48

(1990): Danièle Parra, "Entretien avec Eric Rohmer: retour à la morale," *La Revue du cinéma* 459

(1994): Claude-Marie Trémois, "Le cinéaste, la ville et l'architecte," *Télérama* 2300

(1996): Vincent Remy and François Gorin, "Rohmer: le plus jeune cinéaste français," *Télérama* 2421

(2004): Priska Morrissey, "Entretien avec Eric Rohmer," *Histoires et Cinéastes: rencontre de deux écritures* (Paris: L'Harmattan)

(2004): Noël Herpe and Cyril Neyrat, "Je crois à la litote: entretien avec Eric Rohmer," *Vertigo* 25

(2006): Marie-Noëlle Tranchant, "Le regard du cinéaste: entretien avec Eric Rohmer," *La Nouvelle Revue d'Histoire* 23

*(2007): Priska Morrissey, "Entretien avec Eric Rohmer: La prise de vues a-t-elle une function artistique?" in *Rohmer et les Autres* edited by Noël Herpe (Rennes: Presses Universitaires de Rennes), 185–200

*(2007): Noël Herpe and Cyril Neyrat, "Entretien avec Eric Rohmer: La vidéo prend de l'importance," in *Rohmer et les Autres* edited by Noël Herpe (Rennes: Presses Universitaires de Rennes), 201–4

*(2010): Serge Daney and Louella Intérim, "Faire confiance à un movement naturel des choses, sans trop intervenir," *Libération* 12 January [A shortened version of a 1983 interview included in this collection—included here as this was a memorial edition of the newspaper entitled "Rohmer, au bout du conte," containing many interviews with his collaborators.]

In 1993, after long negotiations, Eric Rohmer granted a televised interview to Jean Douchet. The resulting program, broadcast on ARTE in 1994, was 115 minutes and contains a fascinating and detailed survey of Rohmer's working methods: Eric Rohmer, "Preuves à l'appui," in *Cinéastes de notre temps* directed by André S. Labarthe.

Major English-Language Interviews

*(1971): Rui Nogueira, "Eric Rohmer: Choice and Chance," *Sight and Sound* 40:3

*(1971): Graham Petrie, "Eric Rohmer: An Interview," *Film Quarterly* 24:4

*(1973): Beverly Walker, "Moral Tales: Eric Rohmer Reviewed and Interviewed," *Women and Film* 1:3–4

(1976): Gavin Millar, *Arena: Eric Rohmer* broadcast BBC2 20 October

*(1978): Gilbert Adair, "Rohmer's Perceval," *Sight and Sound* 47:4

*(1982): Fabrice Ziolkowski, "Comedies and Proverbs: An Interview with Eric Rohmer," *Wide Angle* 5:1

*(1982): Robert Hammond and Jean-Pierre Pagliano, "Eric Rohmer on Film Scripts and Film Plans," *Film/Literature Quarterly* 10:4
*(2001): Aurélien Ferenzi, "Interview with Eric Rohmer," *Senses of Cinema* no.16
(2008): Bert Cardullo, "An Auteur for All Seasons: An Interview with Eric Rohmer," *French Forum* 33:3 [This interview is a reproduction of the 1971 interview with Petrie and the 2001 interview with Ferenzi.]

Index

A bout de souffle, 5, 63–64
actors, casting and direction of, viii,
    x, 33–34, 40, 44–46, 48, 52, 53,
    60–61, 65, 67–68, 69, 70, 85, 89,
    91, 97, 104–6, 113, 122, 125–26,
    130, 131–32, 144, 145, 153, 157–58,
    166–68, 175
adaptation, x, 33–34, 41, 42, 51–52, 63,
    171–74
Almendros, Nestor, 20, 26, 33, 40, 47, 56,
    65, 146, 149, 153–59, 166
Antonioni, Michelangelo, 9, 43
architecture, ix, 39, 72–73, 77, 80, 138–39
astrology, 82, 84, 85
audiences, 15–16, 136–37
Autumn Sonata, 78

Balzac, Honoré de, viii, 119–20, 130,
    180–81
Baratier, Diane, 146, 148, 158, 166
Bauchau, Patrick, 20, 37
Bazin, André, ix, 4, 15, 50–51, 104, 130,
    138
Benton, Robert, 56, 65
Bergman, Ingmar, 9, 43, 55–56
Berta, Renato, 146, 156, 157, 158
Big Sky, The, 60
Brialy, Jean-Claude, 19, 22
Bresson, Robert, 53, 60, 131, 148

Cahiers du cinéma. *See* Rohmer, Eric
Carné, Marcel, xi, 52, 54, 78–79, 98, 162
Cassenti, Frank, 44
casting. *See* actors
Cergy-Pontoise. *See* New Towns
Césars, 69–70
Cézanne, Paul, viii, 27, 187
Chabrol, Claude, 4–5, 39, 51, 137, 152, 183
Chaplin, Charlie, 20
Cinéastes de notre temps, 15
cinematography, 146–64
Citizen Kane, 63, 66
Clouzot, Henri, 54
color, ix, 8–10, 34, 56–57, 84, 99–100,
    102, 106, 121, 122, 132–33, 146,
    155–56, 159–62, 184
Countess from Hong Kong, The, 20
Courte tete, 136
Cyrano de Bergerac, 136

Demy, Jacques, 71, 105
Depardon, Robert, 150
Deux ou trois choses que je sais d'elle, 76,
    109
dialogue, x, xi, 17, 19, 22, 40, 43, 46, 61,
    66, 67, 68, 85, 88, 89, 105, 110, 114,
    125–26, 142–43, 169, 171, 180, 184
Dombasle, Arielle, 67, 68, 91, 125, 126,
    129, 131
Doniol-Valcroze, Jacques, 4, 50
Duras, Marguerite, 62, 64

Elisabeth (novel) (Rohmer), 180
Elliott, Grace, x, 140–43
Etchegaray, Françoise, 125, 172, 176

Fabien, Françoise, 28, 38
faith, 29, 83, 117–18, 178
Faust, 15
filming in the street, 52, 56, 87, 93–94, 152
Fountainhead, The, 72
French Cancan, 132

gestures, viii, x, 43–45, 105, 131
Godard, Jean-Luc, xi, 4–5, 39, 64, 68, 71, 76, 108, 116, 131, 148, 152, 153, 183
Greggory, Pascal, 105, 125, 126, 127, 129, 161
Griffith, D. W., xi, 13, 142
Gruault, Jean, 64

Hawks, Howard, 4, 39, 60, 72, 82
Hayer, Nicolas, 151, 152, 153, 158
Hitchcock, Alfred, viii, xi, 4, 13, 39, 116, 117, 148, 177, 186
Hotel du Nord, 79

Ingres, Jean-Auguste-Dominique, 32, 40

Kleist, Heinrich von, x, 63, 173
Kramer versus Kramer, 65

La Chambre verte, 47, 155
La Marseillaise, 142
La Nuit américaine, 64
La Règle du jeu, 79
L'Amant, 136
Land of the Pharaohs, 72
Lang, Fritz, viii, 72, 73, 74, 148, 177
Last Laugh, The, 15
Le Beau Serge, 5, 151

Le Coup du berger, 5
Le Jour se lève, 79
L'Enfant sauvage, 64
Les 400 Coups, 5, 151
Les Corsaires de Bois du Boulogne, 136
Les Cousins, 5
Les Enfants du paradis, 79
Les Enfants Terribles, 108
Les Hussards, 136
Les Mistons, 5
Les Onze Fioretti de St François d'Assise, 83
Les Visiteurs, 136
Les Yeux sans visage, 99
Lola Montès, 78
Luchini, Fabrice, 46, 49, 88, 105, 125, 128, 131

Maintigneux, Sophie, 150, 157
Marne-la-Vallée. *See* New Towns
Melville, Jean-Pierre, 54, 108, 151, 152
Merry Widow, 26
meteorology, ix, x, 53, 78, 82–85, 93, 102, 119, 156, 162–63, 180
Metropolis, 72
Mon Oncle d'Amérique, 64
Murnau, F. W., viii, xi, 13, 15, 39, 72, 82, 177
music, viii, xii, 3, 6, 20, 44, 54–55, 91, 107–9, 116, 121–22, 173, 185
Musset, Alfred de, 51, 58, 59, 79

Napoleon, 142
New Towns, 77, 80, 94, 100, 139, 160
New Wave, vii, 5–6, 41, 43, 52–53, 68, 91, 94, 108, 116, 131, 135–37, 146, 152, 183
Nosferatu, 15
Nougaret, Claudine, 150
Nouvelle Vague. *See* New Wave

Ogier, Pascale, 80, 91
Olivier, Laurence, 47
Orphans of the Storm, 142
Orphée, 151

Paris, as setting in Rohmer's films, 53–55, 56, 73, 75–76, 93, 116–17, 119, 139, 140–41
Paris Nous Appartient, 5
Parking, 105
Pascal, 10, 39, 62, 114, 115
Passenger, The, 43
Petit Theatre, 132–33
Picasso, Pablo, viii, 177, 186–88
Poe, Edgar Allan, 17, 39
Pommereulle, Daniel, 21, 91
Prénom Carmen, 108
Prévert, Jacques, 65–66

Quai des Orfèvres, 54
Questor, Hughes, 105, 106, 109

rain, significance in Rohmer's films. *See* meteorology
religion. *See* faith
Rembrandt, 27, 186, 187
Renoir, Claude, 152
Renoir, Jean, xi, 13, 56, 73, 78, 79, 82, 132, 142, 148
Resnais, Alain, 64, 65, 122
Rivière, Marie, 87, 88, 113, 151, 160
Rivette, Jacques, 4–5, 39, 116, 131, 151, 152, 183
Robbe-Grillet, Alain, 64
Rohmer, Eric: at *Cahiers du cinéma*, 3–4, 50, 54, 84. *See also Elisabeth; Trio en mi bémol*
  Works: *Comédies et Proverbes/Comedies and Proverbs*, xii, 50, 51, 58–59, 62, 68, 70, 73, 78, 79, 98, 101–3, 110, 111, 113–17, 122, 134; *Conte d'Automne/An Autumn Tale*, xii, 168; *Conte de printemps/A Tale of Springtime*, xi, xii, 101–10, 114, 117, 122, 158, 161, 162; *Conte d'été/A Summer's Tale*, 158, 161, 164; *Conte d'hiver/A Winter's Tale*, 111–23, 158, 161, 164, 168; *Contes des quatre saisons/Tales of the Four Seasons*, 101–23; *Contes moraux/Moral Tales*, 6–8, 10, 16–18, 30, 34–35, 38, 41, 42–43, 61, 147, 163, 169; *Die Marquise von O*, 41–45, 49–51, 60–63, 73, 94, 141; *Fermière à Montfaucon*, 150; *La Boulangère de Monceau/The Girl from the Monceau Bakery*, 40, 73, 156; *La Carrière de Suzanne/Suzanne's Career*, 16, 40, 156; *La Collectionneuse/The Collector*, 6, 8, 9, 15, 16, 18–19, 20–21, 25, 26, 30, 32, 34–38, 40, 49, 67, 76, 77, 78, 89, 90, 91, 112, 113, 156, 175, 188; *La Femme de l'Aviateur/The Aviator's Wife*, xi, 50–57, 70, 73, 75, 78, 79, 94, 100, 104, 108, 160, 162, 163; *L'Ami de mon amie/My Girlfriend's Boyfriend*, 100, 101–2, 105, 108, 157, 160; *L'Amour l'après-midi/Love in the Afternoon*, 32, 36, 74, 78, 82, 102, 122, 154, 162, 163; *L'Anglaise et le duc/The Lady and the Duke*, 140–45, 174, 178; *L'Arbre, le Maire et la Médiathèque/The Tree, the Mayor and the Mediatheque*, ix, 124–39, 145, 148, 149, 164; *Le Beau Mariage/A Good Marriage*, 71, 73, 78, 79, 84, 100, 160; *Le Genou de Claire/Claire's Knee*, 8–11, 15, 18, 19, 21, 23–26, 30, 51, 60, 62, 73,

84, 154, 163, 180; *Le Rayon vert/ The Green Ray*, 82, 84, 85, 87–92, 93, 96, 97, 98, 100, 103, 108, 111, 113, 116, 122, 125, 126, 134, 135, 148, 150–51, 160; *Le Signe du Lion/ The Sign of Leo*, 5–6, 15, 26, 40, 73, 74, 75, 84, 85, 94, 98, 99, 110, 122, 151; *Les Amours d'Astrée et de Céladon/The Romance of Astrea and Celadon*, 170–81, 182–84; *Les Nuits de la pleine lune/Full Moon in Paris*, 77–79, 81, 82, 84, 99, 100, 121, 128, 129, 134, 160, 163; *Les Rendezvous de Paris/Rendezvous in Paris*, 158; *Ma Nuit chez Maud/My Night at Maud's*, 8–11, 15, 18, 19, 21, 22, 25, 26, 28–40, 61, 62, 74, 77, 89, 99, 103, 134; *Métamorphose du paysage industriel*, 76; *Pauline à la plage/Pauline at the Beach*, 67–71, 74, 77, 98, 100, 106, 153, 154, 161, 188; *Perceval*, viii, 41–49, 51, 53, 55, 73, 83, 94, 95, 141, 154, 159, 168, 169, 170, 173, 174, 176, 179, 181; *Place de l'Etoile*, 74, 75, 98; *Quatre Aventures de Reinette et Mirabelle/ Four Adventures of Reinette and Mirabelle*, 82–100, 103, 125, 134, 163; *Triple Agent*, 155, 160, 161, 164, 166, 167, 168, 169, 174, 176
Romand, Béatrice, 19, 22, 84, 91
Rossellini, Roberto, xi, 13, 73, 83

Schuftan, Eugene, 152
script-writing, x, xi, 13, 19, 22, 42, 43, 58–66, 134, 143, 170, 173
Shakespeare, William, 42, 58, 102, 111, 117–18, 121, 178
Simenon, Georges, 54

snow, significance in Rohmer's films. *See* meteorology
Spaak, Charles, 65
Stroheim, Eric, 13, 15, 26, 182
Stromboli, 63
Sunrise, 15

Tabu, 15
Tacchella, Jean-Charles, 65
Tartuffe, 15
television, vii, 11–12, 15–16, 39, 40, 52, 57, 69, 76, 83, 111, 125, 127, 128–29, 133, 135, 139, 142, 147, 158, 166, 177, 183
Therese, 83
Tous les matins du monde, 136
Trio en mi bémol (play) (Rohmer), 115
Truffaut, François, 4–5, 39, 47, 50, 64, 75, 136, 137, 152, 154, 183
Turner (painter), 27

Une femme mariée, 109

Valéro, Jean-Louis, 108, 173
Verley, Bernard, 40

water, significance in Rohmer's films, 26
weather. *See* meteorology
Welles, Orson, 48
Wilder, Billy, 82
women, in Rohmer's films, 23, 28–33, 36–39, 45, 150–51

Zouzou, 34, 37
Zucca, Pierre, 170–71, 178

www.ingramcontent.com/pod-product-compliance
Lightning Source LLC
Chambersburg PA
CBHW022009220426
43663CB00007B/1019